INCREASING LEADERSHIP EFFECTIVENESS

INCREASING LEADERSHIP EFFECTIVENESS

CHRIS ARGYRIS

James Bryant Conant Professor of
Education and Organizational Behavior
Harvard University

ROBERT E. KRIEGER PUBLISHING COMPANY
MALABAR, FLORIDA

Original Edition   1976
Reprint Edition   1983

Printed and Published by
ROBERT E. KRIEGER PUBLISHING COMPANY, INC.
KRIEGER DRIVE
MALABAR, FLORIDA 32950

Copyright © 1976 by John Wiley & Sons, Inc.
Reprinted by Arrangement

Printed in the United States of America

Library of Congress Cataloging in Publication Data

Argyris, Chris, 1923-
    Increasing leadership effectiveness.

    Reprint. Originally published: New York : Wiley,
cl976. (Wiley series in behavior)
    Bibliography: p.
    Includes index.
    1. Adult education. 2. Leadership. I. Title.
LC5219.A7 1983   374   83-14874
ISBN 0-89874-666-3

10 9 8 7 6 5 4 3

To

William F. Whyte

SERIES PREFACE

Psychology is one of the lively sciences. Its foci of research and theoretical concentration are diverse among us, and always on the move, sometimes into unexploited areas of scholarship, sometimes back for second thoughts about familiar problems, often into other disciplines for problems and for problem-solving techniques. We are always trying to apply what we have learned, and we have had some great successes at it. The Wiley Series in Behavior reflects this liveliness.

The series can accommodate monographic publication of purely theoretical advances, purely empirical ones, or any mixture in between. It welcomes books that span the interfaces within the behavioral sciences and between the behavioral sciences and their neighboring disciplines. The series is, then, a forum for the discussion of those advanced, technical, and innovative developments in the behavioral sciences that keep its frontiers flexible and expanding.

KENNETH MacCORQUODALE

Minneapolis, Minnesota
December 1974

PREFACE

In this book I have striven to accomplish three interrelated objectives. The first is to make a contribution to the beginnings of a theory of what may be called double loop learning; learning to change underlying values and assumptions. This means that the focus is on problems whose definitions are not clear when one begins to solve them and may change as problem solving advances, and on problems that are highly complex and ill structured, that exist over long periods of time, and are central to the lives of adults.

Adults are charged with the maintenance of society and culture, especially its organizations and institutions. Elsewhere I have tried to show that, because of the ways in which businesses, schools, churches, governmental units, trade unions, orchestra and dramatic organizations, museums, law firms, and hospitals are designed and managed, they are (and will continue) deteriorating (Argyris, 1964, 1970, 1973, 1974). They may have already reached the stage at which they produce valid information for the unimportant problems and invalid information for the important problems. It is no surprise, therefore, to learn that, for the first time in decades, people are doubting and mistrusting the efficacy of organizations (Argyris, 1973). Adults are responsible for this problem, especially those on top.

Hence the second objective of this book is to relate double loop learning to the beginnings of a theory of effective leadership. If we are to face squarely the problems described above, there is a need to develop leaders in all fields of endeavor who know how to discover the difficult questions, how to create viable problem-solving networks to invent solutions to these questions, and how to generate and channel human energy and commitment to produce the solutions. These leaders are people who will know how to create rare events and how to help integrate them in the core of the institutions within which they work.

Human beings develop theories of action to guide their behavior

(Argyris and Schon, 1974). Unbelievable as it may sound, it appears that people program themselves (with the aid—indeed, the coercion—of schools, churches, and other such societal institutions) with theories of action that predispose them, when they interact and problem solve, to cancel each other out; that they will have difficulties with each other; that they will require diplomacy and deception to maintain some semblance of harmony; and, that they will be unaware of the extent to which they contribute to this malaise, yet relatively well aware when others do (with one possible exception—namely, their loved ones. We may marry those people who help us to remain the way we are).

To someone working in this field, it becomes increasingly clear that, in order to bring about truly basic changes in institutions (of all types) and their management that do not wash out under the pressures of everyday life, human beings will have to develop new values, new skills, and new concepts of individual and organizational effectiveness. These new qualities will be difficult to learn, and they run counter to many of the values, skills, and concepts of effectiveness presently held in modern societies. Thus there is not only the educational problem of learning the new, but there is also the requirement to learn how to maintain and enhance the new values, concepts, and skills in a society that finds them hostile to its present makeup. The probabilities of implanting educational processes that threaten the status quo are always low and disheartening.

May I say at the outset that the book is *not* a theory of societal change. It is a book about how to alter individuals' theories of action. Such changes, I hope to show, are necessary for any genuine societal action to occur. There is no known structure, no known law, no known political process that can become a part of human behavior, the living law, and organic political life without people knowing how to behave according to their requirements. In the case that concerns us here, the requirements are even more difficult. We shall see that, even if people know and admire the requirements of the new theory of action that will be proposed, this will not guarantee that they will be able to behave according to these requirements. Motivation and knowledge must be accompanied by competence and skill.

The third objective is to develop a learning environment that helps people to discover their present theories of action and unfreeze them, and that helps them to learn a new theory that can help slow down and ultimately reverse the problems described above. The six individuals who participated in this experiment were all entrepreneurs, at the top of their organizations, with long histories of success. They all manifested what I call the "ineffective" theories of action and had much evidence that they succeeded by using them. In other words, the subjects were selected because they represented people who would resist most of the changes that we wanted them to explore. They were also difficult because, as they put it, they represented people for whom they would not work (Argyris, 1973).

The objective was not only to show that changes occurred in the learning environment; we wanted to show that changes also occurred in the back-home setting under zero to moderate stress. I believe that the data presented illustrate that not only were we able to achieve this, but also were able to go one better. As the book goes into galleys—approximately four years after the start of the experiment—changes are still going on within the individuals and in their organizations, and their scope of impact is being enlarged continually.

Although I believe that we were able to accomplish these three objectives to the degree never done (or at least published) before, the study represents only the beginning. It is more a demonstration of the potential of an approach than the presentation of firm evidence of the power of systematically defined educational processes.

To assert that this experiment contributes to our knowledge of changing human values, effective leadership, and helping others to do the same may seem optimistic, to put it mildly. Each of those topics is a research field in itself. How can we profess to cover them all? First of all, these subjects are not covered completely. There is much more research to be done, and more will be said about that in Chapter 16. However, I do wish to make the following point. The research is based upon what Donald Schon and I call a "theory of action perspective" (Argyris and Schon, 1974). We examine reality from the point of view of the human being as an actor. Changing values, behavior, leadership, learning, and helping others to learn are all part of, and informed by, the actors' theories of action. If theories of action are understood well, they will provide insight into all of these fields. The advantage of learning theories of action is that they are the key to all these activities.

The research also raises questions about the design of professional education. When the requirement was added that people use and produce these concepts in concrete actions in their everyday life, under conditions ranging from zero through moderate stress, we assumed that, once the participants learned and internalized new concepts, they would "naturally" be used and built on by them; thus they could be produced in real life. Implicit in this assumption was another—namely, that there was a continuous relationship between discovery, the formulation of new concepts, and the production of these in real life.

We learned that this was not the case. What people define and accept

as valid discovery and as relevant conceptual learning varies dramatically if they know that the objective educational experience is conceptual learning, rather than if the objective includes the performance of
the concepts to be learned.

If these results are replicated, professional education will, for example, have to reexamine its notion that the design of its curriculi
should leave the matter of performance in real life to practice. This is
especially true for the kind of education described in this book. If people are to be educated to create events that are rare in everyday life, to
expect them to produce what they have learned outside of the learning environment is unrealistic.

It was asserted above that people design and solve problems differently if they know they will end their learning with understanding
than if they know that they will be asked to use their understanding to
make events come about.

The same, I believe, is true for research. The design is different in
order to take the requirements of applicability seriously. Typically, researchers conceive of basic research as including the objectives of discovery and understanding. The applicability of the knowledge generated by the research is left to others, and it is usually considered
developmental research. This project suggests that such a distinction
may be unnecessary and perhaps counterproductive. The knowledge
generated from research whose objectives include discovery and understanding may be different and inadequate compared to knowledge
generated when objectives include the effective performance of what
was learned.

Moreover, the criteria for rigor, accuracy, and precision may also be
different. For example, both perspectives value publicly verifiable statements (i.e., statements that are disconfirmable). Both value the specification mechanisms by which events come about. But the form and
precision of the specification may be quite different. If informing performance becomes a criterion, we may find that precision that permits
one to say that the relationship of X and Y is curvilinear may actually
be too much information to give to an actor. If the actor took the generalization seriously and tried to assess, at any given moment, where he
was on the curve, he would, in all likelihood, become engrossed in
learning and be unable to act within the requirements of the situation.
The production of knowledge to describe the world and the production of knowledge to describe how to alter or change the world may
require different technology and concepts of rigor. Theories of action
may be accurate yet sloppy. It reminds one of Von Neuman's statement
that a characteristic of the human mind was that it could operate effec-

tively with a relatively (to a computer) sloppy calculus, and under conditions of a lot of noise.

STRUCTURE OF THE BOOK

The book is divided into three parts. Part 1 presents an introduction to the theoretical framework that informed the experiment, as well as the setting utilized to introduce the learning environment to eighteen potential subjects.

Part 2 describes the learning seminars that were held over a period of three and a half years (and which continue at the time of publication, which makes it over four years). A primitive model of double loop learning is also presented in Part 2.

In Part 3, the focus is upon methodological issues, such as the validity of the inferences made, the exploration of new methods for research that may be required in this "action-science," and questions for future research.

I would like to thank my colleague, Lee Bolman, who participated throughout the study, wrote Chapter 13, made many helpful comments, and continues to work with the group. Professors Clay Alderfer, Bernard Cullen, Richard Hackman, William Torbert, and Richard Walton read the manuscript and made many valuable suggestions.

Last and first in my gratitude are the six men who joined this venture and made it possible. They represent the kind of experimentation and strength that our society needs desperately in its leaders.

I dedicate the book with a deep sense of appreciation to Professor William F. Whyte, who was a key person in my double loop learning.

CHRIS ARGYRIS

Cambridge, Massachusetts
February 1976

CONTENTS

PART 1   INTRODUCTION

CHAPTER
1   The Theory of Action of the Experiment   3

2   Seminar 1. The Appreciation Seminar   33

PART 2   THE EXPERIMENT

3   Seminar 2. Being an Important Part of
    the Problem   41

4   Seminar 3. Beginning to Discover Their
    Theories-in-use   53

5   Beginning to Invent and to Produce While
    Deepening Discovery   75

6   Invention-Production Related to the Back-
    Home Setting   97

7   Inventing and Producing More Difficult
    Interventions: The Group Becomes More
    of a Resource   115

8   Questioning the Applicability of Model II   126

9   Seminar 4. The Beginnings of a More Integrated
    Learning Cycle: The Case of F   136

10 Discovery-Invention-Production at the Back-
    Home Setting   151

11 Seminar 5. Exploring "Unconscious" Factors   172

12   Organizational Learning (by Lee Bolman)   183

13   Learning Double-Loop Learning   211

14   Conclusions   228

PART 3   METHODOLOGICAL NOTES

15   Methodological Notes   251

INDEX   283

INCREASING LEADERSHIP
EFFECTIVENESS

PART

1

INTRODUCTION

CHAPTER

1

THE THEORY
OF ACTION
OF THE
EXPERIMENT

People may be said to develop theories of action to guide their behavior, to make it more manageable, to make it more consistent, and thereby to maintain their sense of being personally responsible—of being an origin of their behavior. Behavior that is guided by theories, that is consistent, and for which the producers accept responsibility appears to others as rational and responsible. Hence theories of action are, at the basis, for human order (Argyris and Schon, 1974).

It is paradoxical, but I believe true, that the same theories of action designed to achieve order also produce disorder, and since these theories are not very effective in dealing with disorder, they also produce slow, but inevitable, disintegration in the relationships among human beings. Moreover, they also produce group dynamics and organizational problem solving that are counterproductive. Once in existence, the group and organizational factors take on a life of their own, for three reasons. First, they become so complex and so interdependent that they appear beyond the reach of planned change. Second, the people who would have to change them do not have the appropriate theories of action for such change. Third, the people, by and large, are unaware of their responsibility in this problem, and they tend to blame the nonchangeability of organizations upon the organizations themselves. For example, in a recent study of one of our largest and most respected newspapers (a newspaper that clamored daily for change in our societal institutions), its top people insisted that they could not change the newspaper's living system because it was hopelessly massive and complex, as well as brittle (Argyris, 1974).

The objectives of the experiment in adult learning were (1) to help adults become aware of their existing theories of action, (2) to unfreeze them so that (3) they could learn new (but additional) theories of action that would lead to more effective problem solving, and (4) to be able to put the learning into use in the "real" world under conditions ranging from zero to moderate stress.

There are three questions that are dealt with in this chapter. First, what is the nature of existing theories of action? Second, what new and more effective theory of action do we recommend? Third, how do we help people move from the old toward the new theories of action in such a way that the learning does not wash out under pressures and stresses of everyday life?

A prelude to the responses to these three questions is a description of the concept of human theories of action that underlies the perspective that guided the research.

THEORIES OF ACTION: ESPOUSED AND THEORIES-IN-USE [1]

Theories are theories regardless of their origin: there are practical, common-sense theories as well as academic or scientific theories. A theory is not necessarily accepted, good, or true; it is only a set of interconnected propositions that have the same referent—the subject of the theory. Their interconnectedness is reflected in the logic of relationships among propositions: change in propositions at one point in the theory entails changes in propositions elsewhere in it.

Theories are vehicles for explanation, prediction, or control. An explanatory theory explains events by setting forth propositions from which these events may be inferred; a predictive theory sets forth propositions from which inferences about future events may be made; a theory

[1] For this discussion, I draw from Chris Argyris and Donald Schon, *Theory in Practice,* Jossey-Bass, 1974.

of control describes the conditions under which events of a certain kind may be made to occur. In each case, the theory has an "if . . . then . . ." form.

Theories constructed to explain, predict, or control human behavior are in many ways like other kinds of theories. But insofar as they are about human action—that is, about human behavior that is correctable and subject to deliberation—they have special features.

We can observe deliberate behavior and try to account for it as though it were the behavior of fish or tides—for example, "If population densities exceed an upper limit, people become more aggressive toward one another." Here the "if . . . then . . ." relationship holds between publicly observable phenomena. But we can also regard deliberate human behavior as the consequence of theories of action held by humans, in which case we explain or predict a person's behavior by attributing to him a theory of action. For example, we may attribute to a counselor a theory about the way to handle disruptive students: "It is necessary first to speak to them in their own language and to make it clear that you understand them, then to state the limits of what you will tolerate from them, and only then to try to find out what's bothering them." All such theories of action have the same form: in situation S, if you want to achieve consequence C, do A.

Of course, theories of action do not hold when they are put into such simple form. They depend on a set of stated or unstated assumptions. In the previous instance, we would have to add, for example, ". . . *if* you can be sincere in speaking the student's own language, *if* he presents himself as hostile to you in the first instance, *if* he shows signs of overstepping bounds." A full list of assumptions would contain all the conditions under which you would expect the action to produce the desired result. Such a list would be very long; in fact, you could never be sure you had completed it. A full schema for a theory of action, then, would be as follows: in situation S, if you want to achieve consequence C, under assumptions $a_1 . . . a_n$, do A.

From the subjective view, my theory of action is normative for me; that is, it states what I ought to do if I wish to achieve certain results. It is a theory of control. But someone else may explain my behavior by attributing to me a theory of action that accounts for the deliberate behavior he observes. In this sense, theories of action are also explanatory and predictive. We explain or predict a person's deliberate behavior by attributing theories of action to him. A theory of action is a theory of deliberate human behavior, which is for the agent a theory of control but which, when attributed to the agent, also serves to explain or predict his behavior.

THEORIES-IN-USE

When someone is asked how he would behave under certain circumstances, the answer he usually gives is his espoused theory of action for that situation. This is the theory of action to which he gives allegiance, and which, upon request, he communicates to others. However, the theory that actually governs his actions is his theory-in-use, which may be compatible with his espoused theory; furthermore, the individual may or may not be aware of the incompatibility of the two theories.

We cannot learn what someone's theory-in-use is simply by asking him. We must construct his theory-in-use from observations of his behavior. In this sense, constructs of theories-in-use are like scientific hypotheses; the constructs may be inaccurate representations of the behavior they claim to describe.

When you know what to do in a given situation in order to achieve an intended consequence, you know what the theory-in-use for that situation is. You know the nature of the consequence to be attained, you know the action appropriate in the situation to attain it, and you know the assumptions contained in the theory.

Theories-in-use, however their assumptions may differ, all include assumptions about self, others, the situation, and the connections among action, consequence, and situation. In the example of the counselor and the disruptive student, the counselor's theory-in-use may have contained the following assumptions: (1) the counselor can speak the student's language, (2) the student will recognize the sincerity of the counselor as he speaks the student's language and will tend to trust the counselor as a result, (3) the school is a place in which the counselor will be permitted to interact with the student alone and to establish a personal relationship with the student, and (4) the student will be more disposed to alter his behavior if he comes to trust the counselor than if he does not. The counselor's theory-in-use may be said to contain these assumptions, whether or not he can state them, if a change in his beliefs about one or more of them were to lead him to change his view of the actions appropriate in the situation.

If theories of action can be attributed to all people who show deliberate behavior, the scope of the knowledge exhibited in theories of action is immense. Theories-in-use include knowledge about the behavior of physical objects, the making and use of artifacts, the marketplace, organizations, and every other domain of human activity. In other words, the full set of assumptions about human behavior that function in theories-in-use constitutes a psychology of everyday life. All propositions about the structure and operation of society, about the culture, about the design and construction of artifacts, about the physical world—insofar as they function as assumptions in theories-in-use—constitute a sociology, an anthropology, engineering science, and a physics of everyday life. In this sense, everyone is his own psychologist, sociologist, anthropologist, engineer, and physicist.

Clearly, specifying the knowledge contained in our theories-in-use would mean codifying the entire body of informal beliefs relevant to deliberate human behavior.

Levels

Each person has many theories-in-use—one for every kind of situation in which he more or less regularly finds himself. We will call each of these a microtheory, although a person's theories-in-use are not independent atoms of theory. One's microtheories are related to one another through similarities of content and through their logic. As with any complex body of knowledge, a person's theories-in-use may be organized in a variety of ways.

Some theories-in-use have a hierarchical structure, which becomes clear as we consider, for example, how general the counselor we discussed earlier feels his assumptions are. For example, does he feel that by speaking a student's language, the student will trust him more readily, or does he generalize this to mean that all students will trust him more readily if he speaks their language? Or does he generalize even further that anyone will trust him more readily if he speaks their language? How far the counselor generalizes this assumption can be established inductively by observing his behavior in similar situations and noting the range of situations in which he appears to operate on similar assumptions.

To what extent is the assumption part of an organized theory? For example, does the counselor have a theory of the conditions under which trust comes to be established in which this assumption figures as a component? This question too may be tested, roughly, as above.

A person often holds different and incompatible theories-in-use for situations that appear alike to an outside observer. The school counselor, for example, may behave in one way with boys, in another way with girls, and in still another way with members of a group different from his own, although he may behave consistently with each type of student. In this case, he may be said to have a higher-order theory that governs his use of the different subtheories-in-use according to the type of student involved.

Or, the structure of theories-in-use can be determined by their common assumptions. Such an assumption might be, "People will react less defensively when they are less anxious." The resulting structure will not necessarily be hierarchical.

Tacit Knowledge

In what sense do we have or know theories-in-use? What is their status? We can consider this question in terms of existence, inference, and learning.

The problem of existence may be stated as follows. How do we know that a person's theories-in-use exist if we cannot state them? Although we argue that theories-in-use are manifested by behavior, sometimes we say that a theory-in-use exists even though the behavior that ought to manifest it does not appear; we say that a person intends to do A, but something happens to prevent him from doing it. If, then, we say that he has a theory-in-use that he cannot state and according to which, at least in some instances, he does not behave, in what sense does the theory-in-use exist?

There is the related problem of inference. What are the ground rules for inferring theories-in-use from behavior? If the manifesting behavior does not, in some instances, appear, how can we infer the theories-in-use?

There is the problem of learning. How can we change an existing theory-in-use when we cannot state what is to be changed or learned?

These problems are at least as old as Plato's dialogue, the *Meno*. The history of attention to this topic leaves us with three main options.

1. We know only that we can state. If we adopt this view, we lose the distinction between espoused theory and theory-in-use; this view contradicts the general finding that people's behavior is often incompatible with the theories of action they espouse.

2. We know only what is manifested by behavior; theories-in-use are only constructs designed to account for patterns of behavior. This view leaves us unable to account for those situations in which people fail to behave according to their theories-in-use and yet may still properly be said to hold theories-in-use. A person begins an action according to his theory-in-use, but he cannot complete the action: the inhibiting factor may be external—he stumbles or is immobilized by someone else—or it may be internal—he is blocked by some unconscious wish or fear, he is overcome with emotion, he forgets, or he has a stroke. In addition, his behavior may show a conflict of theories-in-use; he may do nothing in

the situation, which might be evidence for the existence of his conflicting theories-in-use.

3.   We know more than we can tell and more than our behavior consistently shows. This is implicit knowledge, or tacit knowledge, as Polanyi (1967) calls it. Tacit knowledge is what we display when we recognize one face from thousands without being able to say how we do so, when we demonstrate a skill for which we cannot state an explicit program, or when we experience the intimation of a discovery we cannot put into words. Polanyi's concept offers a useful perspective on the problems of existence, inference, and learning as they apply to theories-in-use. If we know our theories-in-use tacitly, they exist even when we cannot state them and when we are somehow prevented from behaving according to them. When we formulate our theories-in-use, we are making explicit what we already know tacitly; we can test our explicit knowledge against our tacit knowledge just as the scientist can test his explicit hypothesis against his intimations. When we learn to put an espoused theory of action to use, we reverse the process. Instead of inferring explicit theory from the tacit knowledge our behavior shows, we make explicit theory tacit—that is, we internalize it.

Roles Played by Theories-in-use

Theories-in-use are means for getting what we want. They specify strategies for resolving conflicts, making a living, closing a deal, organizing a neighborhood—indeed, for every kind of intended consequence.

Theories-in-use are also means for maintaining certain kinds of constancy. Certain governing variables interest us (for example, energy expended, anxiety, time spent with others), and we try to keep the values of these variables within the range acceptable to us. Our theories-in-use specify which variables we are interested in (as opposed to the constants in our environment about which we can do nothing) and thereby set boundaries of action. Within these boundaries, theories-in-use provide the programs by which the variables may be managed.

When we say that we pursue a certain end or get what we want, we focus on a single variable and speak of a certain sequence of action concerning that variable exclusively. However, we act within a field of governing variables, all of which are affected by our behavior, all of which we strive to keep within an acceptable range. Instead of actions being related to ends on a one-to-one basis, any given action may affect many variables; all of them are ends in the sense that all behavior is shaped so as to keep all variables within an acceptable range. At any moment, one

variable may be more interesting than others and move to the foreground of our attention, but the other variables affected by the action
cannot be ignored; they may be considered constraints on our efforts to
manipulate foreground variables. That is, whatever we do to manipulate
foreground variables, we cannot allow one of the other variables out of
its acceptable range. In this sense, formulating and selecting actions is a
design problem analogous to the problems of architectural and engineering design, which require the achievement of desired values of a
range of related variables, not just one variable. The actions we take
never have only the intended consequence; in the design of behavior, we
are continually engaged in attempting to mitigate the unintended consequences of our actions on background variables.

Some actions do not affect all governing variables, and some governing variables are not relevant to each action. However, certain governing
variables (for example, level of anxiety, vitality, or self-esteem) seem to
be at stake in virtually every action, constraining the directions that action may take. These variables may suddenly achieve the status of
foreground ends if some action of ours inadvertently takes them out of
their acceptable ranges.

A governing variable ranges within its acceptable limits, only oc-
casionally rising above or falling below them. When one begins to focus
on a new variable, it may initially be above or below these limits. It takes
time to bring the new variable within acceptable limits (consider bringing
someone back to health or establishing a relationship of trust). In setting
oneself an objective in relation to that variable, one sets some requisite
pattern of movement into the acceptable range (the objective function).
Furthermore, both old and new variables require maintenance in order
to keep them within limits; the design problem must not only be solved,
but it must remain solved. Once within acceptable range, the new variable joins the other governing variables that make up a person's field of
constancy—the set of governing variables that must all be kept constant
within their acceptable ranges.

Theories-in-use maintain a person's field of constancy. They specify
the governing variables and their critical relationships to one another—
for example, which variables have priority. They specify the acceptable
ranges for these variables and the objective functions for new governing
variables. They describe the techniques and strategies of design by which
objective functions may be achieved and constancies maintained.

Theories-in-use are the means of maintaining specific constancies, but
they also come to be valued in their own right for the constancy of the
world picture they provide. Since the inherent variability of the behavioral world gives us more information than we can handle, we value a

stable world picture, being predictable, and being able to predict. We work at maintaining the constancy of our theories-in-use.

The two orders of constancy—of governing variables and of the world picture that theories-in-use provide—generate a special conflict. When our theories-in-use prove ineffective in maintaining the constancy of our governing variables, we may find it necessary to change our theories-in-use. But we try to avoid such change because we wish to keep our theories-in-use constant. Forced to choose between getting what we want and maintaining second-order constancy, we may choose not to get what we want.

Theories-in-use as Theories of the Artificial

The stars are indifferent to our opinion of them, and the tides are independent of our theories about them. Human behavior, however, is directly influenced by our actions and therefore by our theories of action. The behavioral world is an artifact of our theories-in-use.

Theories of the behavioral world are, in Simon's (1969) phrase, theories of the artificial. Many of the constants of the behavioral world are accidental—in the sense that they are created by human convention and continued by human choice—rather than inherent in the nature of the universe.

Moreover, each person lives in a behavioral world of his own—a world made up of his own behavior in interaction with the behavior of others. Each person's behavioral world is therefore artificial not only in the sense that it consists of artifacts of human convention but also in the sense that it is shaped and influenced by one's own action and by one's theories of the behavioral world as they influence action. The relationship between theory-in-use and action is special. Here, the action not only applies and tests the theory but also shapes the behavioral world the theory is about. We are familiar with this phenomenon in its pejorative connotations, as in the example of the teacher whose belief in the stupidity of his students results in the students' behaving stupidly. But the usual conclusion of such experiments is the need to avoid self-fulfilling prophecies—as if one could. Every theory-in-use is a self-fulfilling prophecy to some extent.

We construct the reality of our behavioral worlds through the same process by which we construct our theories-in-use. Theory building is reality building, not only because our theories-in-use help to determine what we perceive of the behavioral world, but also because our theories-in-use determine our actions, which in turn help to determine the characteristics of the behavioral world, which in turn feed into our theories-in-use. Consequently, every theory-in-use is a way of doing something to others (to one's behavioral world), which in turn does something to one-self. The second-order constancy that we seek in our theories-in-use is also the constancy we seek in our behavioral world.

Accordingly, one must examine theories-in-use not at one cross-sectional instant in time but in the progressively developing interaction between theory-in-use and behavioral world. One cannot judge theories-in-use without also judging the behavioral world created by the theory. One cannot set about trying to construct a better theory-in-use without also trying to construct the behavioral world that is conducive to the development of that theory-in-use.

Internal Consistency

In a very simple sense, *internal consistency* means the absence of self-contradiction. But in the domain of theory of action, its meaning becomes more complex.

The more important kind of consistency lies not between propositions in the theory ("This man is generous," "This man is stingy") but among the governing variables of the theory that are related to assumptions about self, others, and the behavioral setting. For example, a theory of action might require two propositions—"Keep people calm" and "Encourage participative government"; if participative government can come about only through heated action, the theory is internally inconsistent, although not logically inconsistent. It is not self-contradictory, as saying a horse is and is not white would be. However, efforts to achieve the governing variables would interfere with one another.

Each of these variables has a range that is acceptable; within that range, there are levels of preference. As long as calmness does not rise to the point of inertness, we may prefer to have things as calm as possible. As long as participation does not rise to the point of anarchy, we may prefer to have as much of it as possible.

If two or more such variables are internally incompatible in a particular context, one cannot achieve as high a level of preference for both of them taken together as one can for each of them taken separately. If we call such a relationship *incompatibility*, we can reserve the term *internal consistency* for the special case in which one variable will fall out of its acceptable range if the other is brought into the acceptable range.

Whether governing variables are incompatible or internally inconsistent depends on a number of factors:

1. Other governing variables—for example, variables related to self-protection, courtesy, or protection of others—may limit the means for achieving some variables.

2. The array of actions envisaged in the theory-in-use may be too narrow. Outside of that array, there may be some means of achieving one variable without dropping the other out of its acceptable range.

3. The acceptable range of each variable may be broadened or narrowed to make the two variables more or less incompatible.

4. The assumptions in the theory-in-use may be altered to make the governing variables more or less incompatible. For example, the assumption "People cannot address the problem of self-government without becoming excited" may be absent from theory-in-use but may be valid in the situation; in this case, the agent would find that he cannot reach acceptable levels of both variables, but he would not understand why.

5. The protagonist may act on his world to make it take on characteristics that are either conducive or resistant to the internal consistency of his theory. His behavior may somehow affect people's sense of responsibility in a way that enables participation in self-government without disruption. Or, his behavior may have the opposite effect. Since this behavior is itself a reflection of other aspects of the theory-in-use, theories-in-use may tend to make themselves internally consistent or inconsistent. In the worst case, increasing one's efforts to achieve governing variables decreases one's chance of achieving them; in the best case, increasing one's efforts increases the chance of achieving them.

If two or more governing variables in a theory-in-use are internally inconsistent, then for given settings of ranges, arrays of strategies, assumptions about the situation, constraining variables, and influences of action on the behavioral world, there is no way of falling into the acceptable range for the other.

It is important to notice the relationship between internal consistency and constancy. Theory-in-use may be regarded as a program for action designed to keep the values of certain variables constant within acceptable ranges. It is analogous to a computer program for an industrial process that is designed to keep conditions such as temperature and pressure within acceptable limits of the variables that determine one another. The internal consistency of the theory-in-use conditions the ability of the theory-in-use to achieve the desired constancies; the nature of the desired constancies partly determines the internal consistency of the theory.

Congruence

Congruence means that one's espoused theory matches his theory-in-use—that is, that one's behavior fits his espoused theory of action. A second (and much-used) meaning of congruence is allowing feelings to be expressed in actions: when one feels happy, he acts happy.

These two meanings are complementary and show an integration of one's internal (what one who is aware of my feelings and beliefs would perceive) and external (what an outsider who is aware only of my behavior would perceive) states. Lack of congruence between espoused theory and theory-in-use may precipitate search for a modification of either theory, since we tend to value both espoused theory (image of self) and congruence (integration of doing and believing).

The degree of congruence varies over time. One's ability to be himself (to be what he believes and feels) may depend on the kind of behavioral world he creates. A behavioral world of low self-deception, high availability of feelings, and low threat is conducive to congruence; a behavioral world of low self-esteem and high threat is conducive to self-deception and incongruence. If one helps create situations in which others can be congruent, his own congruence is supported.

There is no particular virtue in congruence alone. An espoused theory that is congruent with an otherwise inadequate theory-in-use is less valuable than an adequate espoused theory that is incongruent with the inadequate theory-in-use, because the incongruence can be discovered and provide a stimulus for change. However, given the importance of congruence to a positive sense of self, it is desirable to hold an espoused theory and theory-in-use that tend to become congruent over the long run.

Effectiveness

A theory-in-use is effective when action according to the theory tends to achieve its governing variables. Accordingly, effectiveness depends on the governing variables held within the theory, the appropriateness of the strategies advanced by the theory, and the accuracy and adequacy of the assumptions of the theory. A strong criterion of effectiveness would require that governing variables stay in the acceptable range once they have been achieved. Some theories-in-use tend to make themselves less effective over time. For example, if an agent tends to become more effective in ways that reduce the effectiveness of others, he may increase the dependence of others on him and make it more and more difficult for himself to be effective. Long-run effectiveness requires the achievement of governing variables in a way that makes their future achievement increasingly likely. This may require behavior that increases the effectiveness of others.

Long-run effectiveness requires single- and double-loop learning. We cannot be effective over the long run unless we can learn new ways of managing existing governing variables when conditions change. In addition, we cannot be effective unless we can learn new governing variables as they become important.

Note that long-run effectiveness does not necessarily mean that action becomes easier. One may respond to increased effectiveness by addressing himself to new governing variables for which he begins by being less effective; progress in effectiveness may be reflected in the sequence of governing variables one tries to achieve.

Testability

Theories of action are theories of control, like the theories involved in engineering, in clinical medicine, or in agricultural technology. They are testable if one can specify the situation, the desired result, and the action through which the result is to be achieved. Testing consists of evaluating whether the action yields its predicted results. If it does, the theory has been confirmed; it if does not, it has been disconfirmed. This tests the effectiveness of the theory.

Special problems regarding testability stem from two related characteristics of theories of action: theories of action are normative (they set norms of behavior), and they are theories of the artificial (they are about a behavioral world that they help to create). There are three basic problems:

1. How can one test theories that prescribe action? How can norms or values be tested?
2. Given that theories-in-use tend to make themselves true in that world, how can they be tested?
3. In a situation of action (particularly in a stressful situation), we are required to display the stance of action—that is, confidence, commitment, decisiveness. But in order to test a theory, one must be tentative, experimental, skeptical. How can we, in the same situations, manifest the stance of action and the experimental stance?

Simple prescriptions ("Don't go near the water!") are not testable because they do not predict results, but if . . . then . . . prescriptions

("If you want to avoid catching a cold, stay away from the water in winter!") are testable. Testing may not be straightforward because assumptions, often hidden, accompany such if . . . then . . . prescriptions. It is assumed here, for example, that you will not expose yourself to other risks of catching cold. Only if we make such assumptions explicit and establish controls for them can we interpret the failure or success of the experiment.

A more challenging problem has to do with the testing of norms or values themselves. Can we test governing variables such as "stay healthy"? In one sense, the answer to this question must be no, because governing variables are not if . . . then . . . propositions and make no predictions. But if one looks at the entire range of variables—the entire field of constancy involved in a theory-in-use—it is meaningful to ask whether, over time, these values will become more or less internally consistent, more or less congruent with the governing variables of espoused theory, and more or less effectively realized. For example, a set of governing variables that includes "stay healthy," "disregard advice," and "seek out dangerous excitement" may turn out to become increasingly incompatible. In this sense, one may test the internal consistency, congruence, and possibility of achievement of governing variables. But one may do so only in the context of a theory-in-use in interaction with its behavioral world over time.

The second basic problem of testing theories of action is their self-fulfilling nature. Here are two examples. A teacher believes his students are stupid. He communicates his expectations so that the children behave stupidly. He may then "test" his theory that the children will give stupid answers to his questions by asking them questions and eliciting stupid answers. The longer he interacts with the children, the more his theory will be confirmed. A second example involves a manager who believes his subordinates are passive, dependent, and require authoritarian guidance. He punishes independence by expecting and rewarding dependence, with the result that his subordinates do behave passively and dependently toward him. He may test his theory by posing challenges for them and eliciting dependent responses. In both cases, the assumptions turn out to be true; both theories-in-use are self-fulfilling prophecies because the protagonist cannot discover that his assumptions are mistaken or that his theory as a whole is ineffective. The so-called testing brings the behavioral world more nearly into line with the theory, confirming for all concerned the stupidity of the students and the dependence of the subordinates. We call such a theory *self-sealing*.

An outsider may find that the teacher's and the manager's theories-in-use are incompatible with the outsider's perception of the situation. But the outsider operates on a theory-in-use of his own that is different from that of the protagonist. The protagonist himself cannot discover that his theory-in-use is mistaken unless he can envisage an alternative theory and act on it.

The protagonist may find that, over the long run, his theory becomes less consistent, less congruent, and less effective. This depends on the stability of the conditions under which he operates, the other values that make up his field on constancy, and other factors. As time goes on, the protagonist is less able to get information from others (students or subordinates) that might disconfirm his theory-in-use. Others become less willing to confront, to display conflict, to reveal feelings. In this sense, the protagonist's self-sealing theory becomes progressively less testable over time.

Consider those affected by the protagonist's theory-in-use. The students, for example, may deceive their teacher about their real feelings and beliefs and yet remain open to others who reveal that the teacher's assumptions are inaccurate; after all, the students live in many behavioral worlds, not only in the world of the school. But perhaps the students have no behavioral world free of these assumptions. If so, others could not discover real feelings and beliefs different from those which confirm the teacher's theory. Deception of others would have been converted to self-deception. In the behavioral worlds created by such theories-in-use, there would be no way to discover that the teacher's theory is self-sealing. For this discovery to occur, outside events would have to cause the theory-in-use to fail, or someone with a different behavioral world long enough to recover their awareness of feelings and beliefs different from those expected by the teacher.

Let us turn to a brief description of the model that accounted for much of the behavior that we studied (Argyris and Schon, 1974).

MODEL I: THEORY-IN-USE

Picture human beings who have programmed themselves to behave in ways that are consistent with four governing values or *variables* (Table 1). These variables are (1) achieve the purpose as the actors define it, (2) win, do not lose, (3) suppress negative feelings, and (4) emphasize rationality. Human behavior, in any situation, represents the most satisfactory solution people can find that is consistent with their governing variables.

It was also found, through our research, that human beings create certain *behavioral strategies* that are congruent with their governing values or

Table 1

THEORY-IN-USE

1 Governing Variables for Action	2 Action Strategies for Actor and Toward Environment	3 Consequences on Behavioral World	4 Consequences on Learning	5 Effectiveness
Achieve the purposes as I perceive them	Design and manage environment so that actor is in control over factors relevant to me.	Actor seen as defensive	Self-sealing	
Maximize winning and minimize losing	Own and control task	Defensive interpersonal and group relationships	Single-loop learning	Decreased effectiveness
Minimize eliciting negative feelings	Unilaterally protect self	Defensive norms	Little testing of theories publicly	
Be rational and minimize emotionality	Unilaterally protect others from being hurt	Low freedom of choice, internal commitment, and risk taking		

variables. The primary behavioral strategies are to control unilaterally the relevant environment, the tasks, and to protect themselves and others unilaterally. The underlying behavioral strategy is control over others. As we shall see, people vary tremendously in the way they control others, but few people do not behave in ways that control others and the environment.

One of the most powerful ways to control others is to control the meaning of valid information. The basic act of creating a concept whose meaning is given by us to others and whose validity is defined by us for others is a powerful control. It is probably the most powerful control we have over our children. We give them the meanings that we believe their lives should have.

The behavioral strategies have *consequences for the actor, for others, and for the environment.* Briefly, these strategies tend to produce defensiveness and closedness in people because unilateral control does not tend to produce valid feedback. Moreover, unilaterally controlling behavior may be seen by others as signs of the actors' defensiveness. Groups composed of individuals programmed according to Model I also tend to create defensive group dynamics, reduce the production of valid information, and reduce free choice.

It was also hypothesized that the consequences mentioned above will tend to *generate a particular kind and quality of learning* that will go on within the actor and between the actor and the environment. There will be relatively little public testing of ideas (especially those which may be important and threatening). Consequently, the actors will tend to seek little feedback that genuinely confronts their actions. The others will tend to play it safe (they are not going to violate their governing values and upset others—especially if they have power). One result is that many of the hypotheses or hunches that the actors generate will tend to become self-sealing or self-fulfilling. Moreover, whatever learning the actors develop will tend to be within the confines of what is acceptable. This is called single-loop learning because, like a thermostat, the individuals learn only about those subjects within the confines of their theories. They will find out how well they are hitting their goal (maintaining a particular temperature). However, few people will confront the validity of the goal, or the values implicit in the situation, just as a thermostat never questions its temperature setting. (Such confrontation would be double-loop learning.)

Under the conditions given above, problem solving about technical or interpersonal issues will be ineffective. Effective problem solving occurs to the extent that individuals (1) are aware of the major variables relevant to their problems, (2) solve their problems in such a way that they remain solved (at least until the external variables are changed), and (3) accomplish the first two without reducing the present level of problem-solving effectiveness (Argyris, 1970).

People programmed with Model I theories of action produce Model I group and organizational dynamics that include quasiresolution of conflict, uncertainty avoidance, mistrust, conformity, saving face, intergroup rivalry, invalid information for important problems and valid information for unimportant ones, misperception, miscommunication, and parochial interests. These, in turn, produce ineffective problem solving and decision making. Under such conditions, top administrators become frustrated and upset with results and react by striving to increase control, by increasing secrecy about their own tactics and strategies, and by demanding loyalty of subordinates that borders on complete agreement with their views (Argyris, 1964, 1970, 1973).

In addition to these defensive interpersonal group and intergroup dynamics, the pyramidal structures, and management information systems (including budgets) will also compound the consequences described above (Argyris, 1964, 1965) and create a stable state, indeed, one that is ultra stable (Schon, 1972).

DOUBLE-LOOP LEARNING AND MODEL II

One possible model that would lead to consequences that are the opposite of those of Model I is a model that is identified as Model II (Argyris and Schon, 1974). The governing variables or values of Model II are *not* the opposites of those of Model I. The governing variables are valid information, free and informed choice, and internal commitment. The behavior required to satisfy these values is not opposite to that of Model I. For example, Model I emphasizes that the individuals be as articulate as they can be about their purposes, goals, etc., and simultaneously control the others and the environment in order to assure that their purposes are achieved. Model II does not reject the skill or competence to be articulate and precise about one's purposes. It does reject the unilateral control that usually accompanies advocacy, because the typical purpose of advocacy is to win. Model II couples articulateness and advocacy with an invitation to others to confront one's views, to alter them, in order to produce the position that is based on the most complete valid information possible and to which people involved can become internally committed. This means that the actor (in Model II) is skilled at inviting double-loop learning.

Every significant Model II action is evaluated in terms of the degree to

Table 2

MODEL II

1 Governing Variables for Action	2 Action Strategies for Actor and Toward Environment	3 Consequences on Behavioral World	4 Consequences on Learning	5 Effectiveness
Valid information	Design situations or encounters in which participants can be origins and experience high personal causation	Actor experienced as minimally defensive	Disconfirmable processes	
Free and informed choice	Task is controlled jointly	Minimally defensive interpersonal relations and group dynamics	Double-loop learning	Increased effectiveness
Internal commitment to the choice and constant monitoring of the implementation	Protection of self is a joint enterprise and oriented toward growth	Learning-oriented norms	Frequent public testing of theories	
	Bilateral protection of others	High freedom of choice, internal commitment, and risk taking		

which it helps the individuals involved generate valid and useful information (including relevant feelings), solve the problem in such a way that it remains solved, and do so without reducing the present level of problem solving effectiveness.

The behavioral strategies of Model II involve sharing power with anyone who has competence and who is relevant in deciding or implementing the action. The definition of the task, the control over the environment, is now shared with the relevant actors. Saving one's own or others' face is resisted because it is seen as a defensive nonlearning activity. If face-saving actions must be taken, they are planned jointly with the people involved. This is not true, however, for individuals who can be shown to be vulnerable to such candid and joint solutions to face saving yet who need to be protected from others and, since it is done unilaterally, from themselves.

Under the conditions described previously, individuals will not compete to make decisions for others, to "one-up" others, to outshine others for the purpose of self-gratification. Individuals, in a Model II world, seek to find the people most competent to make the decision. They seek to build viable decision-making networks in which the major function of the group is to maximize the contributions of each member; thus, when a synthesis is developed, the widest possible exploration of views has occurred.

Finally, under Model II conditions, if new concepts are created, the meaning given to them by the creator and the inference processes used to develop them are open to scrutiny by those who are expected to use them. Evaluations and attributions are minimized. However, when they are used, they are coupled with the directly observable data, which leads to the formation of the evaluation or attribution. Also, the creator feels responsible for the presentation of evaluations and attributions in ways that encourage open and constructive confrontation.

If the governing values and behavioral strategies just outlined are used, the degree of defensiveness in individuals, within groups, between and among groups, will decrease. Free choice will increase, as will feelings of internal commitment and essentiality.

The consequences for learning should be an emphasis in double-loop learning, in which the basic assumptions behind ideas or present views are confronted, in which hypotheses are tested publicly, and in which the processes are disconfirmable, not self-sealing.

The end result should be increased decision-making or policy-making effectiveness, increased effectiveness in the monitoring of decisions and policies, an increase in the probabilities that errors and failures will be communicated openly and that actors will learn from the feedback.

One of the major objectives of this research is to learn how to help individuals become competent in creating Model II theories-in-use. In stating this objective, we do not mean to suggest that Model I theories-in-use should not be used. On the contrary, we would recommend Model I theories-in-use for unimportant problem solving, decision making, and implementation. In addition, Model I may be more effective than Model II under extreme crisis conditions. Perhaps one reason that top executives of public and private organizations create crises is in order to maintain the legitimacy of their Model I theories-in-use, which they use to administer and manage others.

As was stated above, Model II is not the opposite of Model I. However, individuals programmed with Model I theories-in-use are limited in the types of learnable behavior that are opposite to Model I. (They may go from high control to low control such as withdrawal, or they may create conditions of oscillating Model I.)

Neither of these conditions was acceptable in this research. The goal was to help people to learn how to extricate themselves from this Model I trap and move toward Model II. Such learning would require that individuals reflect on what informs their present behavior and question it genuinely. But this means that people perform double-loop learning, which, we have suggested, is not within the repertoire of individuals programmed with Model I theories-in-use.

A PRELIMINARY FRAMEWORK FOR TRANSITION
FROM MODEL I TO MODEL II

The path toward Model II is therefore not only difficult, it is also not self-evident or produceable by the students. They would require a model of transition, of how to move from Model I to Model II.

When the experiment began, we had several models of transition that informed our activities. The first was a model that suggested that transition activities could be described as (1) identifying and surfacing dilemmas in the students' theories-in-use; (2) the students exploring new alternatives; (3) the students publicly testing these alternatives; and (4) practicing, perfecting, and internalizing the alternatives that they preferred (Argyris and Schon, 1974).

We now realize that this model assumed (1) that people were ready to learn and (2) that people would not knowingly impede their own learning. The latter assumption seemed acceptable, since it was a model that was defined to be valid after people were motivated to learn Model II. What we did not recognize adequately was the number and complexity of the impediments that people created, not because they wanted to do so, but because they were programmed to do so. Model I theories-in-use are not very helpful in learning Model II. First, we shall see the depth to which the participants were programmed for single-loop learning. There were many times at which the only kind of reflection they seemed to do was that which would help them develop a more effective Model I theory-in-use.

Second, we shall see how pervasive and counterproductive were the group dynamics created by the subjects. Even though they wanted to move toward Model II, they tended, during the early phases, to "help" each other through unilateral evaluations, attributions, competitive put-downs, and conformity-producing remarks. These group dynamics helped to create a culture that fed back to make it difficult for the students to learn from each other. To compound the problem, it took several sessions before the participants realized that their "help" was not helpful. As we shall see, it took a confrontation with tape recordings to get the participants to question the glowing reports they made about their learning.

Third, we did not predict correctly, and still do not understand adequately, the central role of, and the necessity for, practice. The learning of Model II competences requires repeated trials. The iterative learning comes through practice, but practice is not helpful unless the complex learnings are decomposed into manageable tasks that eventually may be recomposed.

The reader will sense that people seemed to be repeating themselves. The sense of repetition occurred for several reasons. First, it took many trials to learn a new skill (how many trials does it take to swing a golf club or tennis racket correctly?). Second, each participant developed his own practice schedule, and the participants took turns in practicing in front of others. Third, we did not know, and still do not understand adequately, how to decompose the tasks effectively. If we had known more about decomposition, we might have been able to design the learning environment so that the participants tackled relatively similar problems at the same time, thereby helping each other and reducing the repetition.

Fourth, we did not realize how frequently the validity, plausability, and practicality of Model II had to be questioned by the participants *after* they "learned" it and "accepted" it. The two words are placed in quotation marks to indicate that they have meanings of various depth. For example, the reader will see that early in the experience there was a confrontation about the practicality of Model II that lasted nearly six hours. At the end of the intense discussion, the participants reported that they were convinced and were now prepared to move forward. In moving forward, they discovered new problems, and again the practicality of Model II was questioned.

But all the difficulties that we did not predict were not predicted by the participants. Thus when they accepted Model II as a theory-in-use, they had no idea that learning to use it would raise new issues (e.g., their fear of experimenting). In order to overcome these new issues, they had to go through additional painful learning. Every time this type of choice became evident, they asked themselves the question, "Is this trip necessary?" In order to answer that question, they had to reexamine the practicality of Model II.

Fifth, we did not predict an important impediment regarding the participants' ability to learn. Learning may be described as a complex process or cycle including four phases: discovery-invention-production-generalization (Argyris and Schon, 1974). We assumed that adults knew what it meant to discover problems, to invent solutions, to produce the solutions, and to generalize from their experiences. The participants assured us that these activities were "old hat" to them. They had been performing them, not only in their home life, but especially in their organizational life. Indeed, this was a central characteristic of being an entrepreneur.

What we learned was that the participants knew how to discover-invent-produce-generalize about Model I phenomena. They could not discover-invent-produce-generalize about Model II phenomena. Moreover, they were unaware that they could not do so; every bit of their behavior helped to reinforce their unawareness—they became unaware that they were unaware.

THE TRANSITION PROCESSES DURING THIS EXPERIMENT

This book is organized around the major themes or phases that the group members created and experienced while attempting to move from Model I toward Model II. These themes or phases were not known clearly and completely before the experiment began. They evolved as the writer was trying to make sense out of listening to the tape recordings of each session.

A case could be made that these phases are generalizable beyond this experiment because the ways in which they are consistent with the theory known ahead of time and the interventions planned by the faculty before and during the sessions can be shown. We try to make this case in the book, but we do not assert it with finality. More research is needed in order to make such an assertion.

The phases are outlined as follows to help the reader anticipate what is coming and hopefully to make better sense of the book. It should be pointed out that the phases are identified with the session in which they first became prominent. Thus they may have begun earlier—future research is required to tell us precisely when and under what conditions. We do know that many of the themes or phases, having become prominent, continued to play major roles. We make explicit which phases lasted beyond their first session and how long they lasted, as the description of the experiment progresses.

Some of the prominent negative and positive feelings are included with each phase. We mean by negative feelings those which are commonly accepted as uncomfortable and distasteful. Negative feelings can be very important, even necessary, if progress in learning is to occur. Therefore, the faculty did not attempt to inhibit the existence or the suppression of such feelings. Positive feelings are those commonly considered to have positive affect. Positive feelings can facilitate learning, but they can also inhibit it if they surface out of phase with the development of the learning processes.

Displays such as Table 3 help in organizing complex issues. However, their disadvantage is that they may present a picture that is false in the sense that the themes and phases were not as clearcut as depicted. Moreover, there were cases of phases simultaneously supporting and inhibiting each other, as well as phases feeding back to do the same. We attempt to identify some of these interactive qualities as they become relevant to the description. However, we should admit to the reader that we do not understand them well enough to provide a useful model of their actions. Again, more research is needed.

There is one major phase that was not included in the table because it became prominent in a session held after the manuscript was written. I would describe this phase as the recognition of the importance of skills, of guideposts, of heuristics that might help the participants in their on-line actions of designing and producing Model II behavior. Along with this came the recognition of the importance of practice.

We had very little to offer the presidents along these lines beyond that which is included in the book. I left the experience with the feeling that much more effective progress can be made if more skill-practice sessions could be developed and more heuristics and guideposts generated. Again, this is another major goal of future research.

The Role of the Faculty

After reading the list of issues that we did not predict accurately, one might wonder about the role of the faculty. How did they cope with these surprises?

Although the phases might have been new, the behavior within each phase and the feelings that accompanied the phases were not new to the faculty. Lee Bolman and I had extensive experience in dealing with diagnoses, confrontations, punishment, competitiveness, bewilderment, frustration, and failure in other learning environments. Thus we were able to cope with them as they arose. What was new was the development of a systematic map of the transition which made explicit how the phases might progress given our interventions. The map has been used subsequently to make other experiments move more effectively and efficiently.

In other words, the faculty were relatively competent in dealing with whatever phase of feelings arose. They did not know, at the outset, under what conditions these phases and feelings would arise. But this was one of the purposes of the experiment: to generate the maps that could be used to understand the learning processes and to design future learning environments. Incidentally, the participants knew that they were participants in a genuine experiment. Their willingness to join was generated, we believe, from their belief that the faculty could cope with future contingencies and that they, as participants, could quit any time that they wanted.

Some readers may wonder about the role played by any charisma and reputation of the faculty. No doubt, these factors had some effect, but not as much as some might suspect. Again, more research is needed. The writer, for example, was known and respected by the participants. But, as we shall see, 50% of the participants quit after the first session.

Dr. Lee Bolman, who was a coeducator, is younger and was less well-known than the writer. He had the task of earning his reputation under difficult conditions. That Bolman succeeded is attested to by the fact that he was invited to help the presidents in their back-home organizational settings, and that sessions have since been scheduled that the writer did not attend (and the members knew ahead of time that he would not). The point here is that reputations may be helpful to get people to the first session. After that, the faculty have to earn their respect. This is how it should be.

The role of the faculty included:

1.   Development of technology that would help the participants to become aware of that which they are unaware and of that which

Table 3

PROMINENT PHASES OF, AND FEELINGS DURING THE TRANSITION

Chapter	Session	Phase	Prominent Feelings	
			Negative	Positive
2	1	Awareness of the problem; establishing that it is worth pursuing	Bewilderment, sense of incompetence	Inquiry into own inconsistencies
3	2	Developing first-hand experience that they are programmed to generate ineffective problem-solving and group dynamics	Frustration, tension, bewilderment, competitiveness increasing	Inquiry into own inconsistencies
4	3	Diagnosing their theories-in-use, learning Models I and II, and to discover, invent, produce, generalize Model II solutions fail; members begin to sense the difficulty in producing Model II; their awareness that they cannot discover invent, produce, generalize Model II	Frustration, tension, bewilderment, competitiveness increasing and being magnified; anger and attack increasing; shame	Feeling of all equally incompetent and in the same boat
5	3	Confronting the faculty with the applicability of Model II as well as with their productions of Model II solutions; surfacing their fears about their subordinates' acceptance of Model II; diagnosing their own competitiveness	Feelings listed above begin to level off	Sense of success, confidence, and competence beginning to develop
6	3	Inventing and producing experiments designed to introduce Model II behavior in the back-home setting	Feelings above continue to decrease	Feelings above plus sense of collaboration increasing

4	Discovering dilemmas of power as a result of back home experimenting; increased interest in inquiry and personal causation	Same as above	Feelings of confidence in others and in the group increasing; also, above feelings increase
7	Inventing solutions and producing solutions to difficult back-home problems previously deemed unsolvable with Model II behavioral strategies	Same as above	Same as above
8	Inquiry into dilemmas of power deepened; increased awareness of credibility problems with subordinates with whom they have played deception and open secret games for years	Same as above, but feelings of frustrations and tensions rising related to back-home challenges	Same as above
9	Surfacing deception and open secrets held within the learning environment; helping members get a more accurate view of their impact in the group; refocus on competitive; members, in turn, begin to reduce their deception in the group and in the back-home setting	Same as above except negative feelings related to back-home problems being reduced	Same as above
10	Members experiment in the back-home setting with Model II theories-in-use; the degree of success varies, but all members surface failures and try to learn from them	Same as above	Same as above
11	Members begin to deal with deeper self-sealing processes and double binds	Same as above	Same as above

prevents them from becoming aware of their unawareness. The major technology was the use of paper and pencil instruments, on-line questioning, role playing, the examination of tape recordings, and the development by each participant of a map of his theory-in-use (all to be described below).

2.   The ability to connect the information generated about the participants' behavior within the learning environment to their behavior in their back-home organizational setting. The faculty took every opportunity to connect, for example, the impact of unilateral attributions or win-lose dynamics generated within the learning environment by a given president with the tape recordings and observations of his behavior in his organization.

3.   The faculty worked hard not to become seduced into accepting as a legitimate role for the participants the reciprocal of Model I, which is a passive and dependent role. It was easy for the presidents to expect the faculty to take charge of their learning, and in more than one case, they attempted to place the responsibility for the design and the production of the learning setting in the hands of the faculty.

The faculty reduced the probability of the success of this passivity by two types of strategies. One, they confronted attempts to place them in charge by showing the participants how counterproductive that would be. Second, they developed strategies to help the executives become responsible for their learning that had a respectable probability of succeeding. For example, they discussed concepts by continuously illustrating them with directly observable data (i.e., tape recordings). They made their inference processes as public as possible. They also invited confrontation of their views and their behavior. They modeled the possibility that advocacy could be combined with inquiry and that inquiry was not necessarily a sign of weakness.

4.   The faculty were able to care for and value the participants when they (the presidents) did not care for themselves. The faculty rarely felt pessimistic about the potential of the participants for learning. Part of this predisposition may be attributed to the faculty's underlying concern and respect for people. But the more the faculty examined their sense of care and optimism, the more another factor loomed as being a very important cause of these feelings. The other factor was the increasing awareness, by the faculty, of the complexity of the learning being undertaken and the primitiveness of the knowledge about creating the requisite learning environments. Given the Model one-ness of the participants, of their environment, of their world, and of the lack of knowledge as to how to design effective Model II worlds, it is not unfair to say that we were asking these participants to become revolutionaries.

5. The faculty had to be able to produce Model II behavior spontaneously under zero to moderate stress, especially to illustrate the problems that the participants insisted had to be accomplished with a Model II theory-in-use. The faculty therefore had to model the ability to advocate, combined with inquiry, to take risks, to make statements that were disconfirmable, to test their ideas publicly, to own up to their feelings, and to be aware and accepting of when they were not behaving according to Model II.

There is a basic paradox involved in a learning environment designed to help people move from Model I toward Model II. The participants experience it as follows:

I know that there is something that I do not know, but I don't know what it is.

I am frightened (or feeling uncomfortable) to know that there is something that I don't know that I should know.

So I pretend to know it, but since I don't know what I am supposed to know, I have to pretend that I know everything. That is nervewracking.

I can focus on whether I feel wanted, loved, and accepted in the group and upon whom I want, love, and accept in the group. This is a cop-out to untying the knot just defined (Argyris and Schon, 1974).

Another way to begin to deal with the paradox was for the faculty members to state early in the seminar (or confirm) that they *did* know something and that the something was Model II; that Model II was learnable and teachable, and that the choice of learning and internalizing Model II was up to each individual. If, as had always been the case to date, most of the members' behaviors tended to approximate Model I, the members also learned that the reason they did not know Model II was *not* necessarily because of some personal imcompetence or incapacity, but because our society did not tend to teach Model II as a theory-in-use. This could have the impact of reducing the individuals' guilt about not knowing Model II and thus free them to make the fact more public, thereby increasing the probability for public testing of hypotheses and reduction of self-sealing processes.

The faculty therefore admitted and owned up to the paradox. They (1) made explicit the model toward which they were prepared to help the individuals move, (2) invited genuine confrontation of the model, (3) invited genuine shared planning in the development of the learning episodes that would lead toward forward movement, and (4) encouraged the freedom to reject or stop the learning process as long as the rejection was requested and accomplished openly so that again, all individuals could choose.

6.   As one reads the protocols enclosed, one can see that the faculty made some, but not many, mistakes. What was the frequency and role of error making during the sessions?

No count was made of faculty errors for several reasons. Least important was that the faculty, especially during the early stages, had to work hard to get in a word edge-wise. Consequently, they were kept busy helping the participants learn from their errors.

More importantly, the faculty were relatively skilled in Model II theories-in-use. Consequently, many of their interventions were produced in ways that invited public testing, confrontation, and inquiry. Under these conditions, everyone learned from a mistake. Hence, error developed a positive function.

The point is that, under Model II conditions, error making does not have the negative impact it may have under Model I conditions. Error making would have a negative impact under Model II conditions if the same errors were repeated, because that would indicate that the individuals were not learning.

CHAPTER

$$\boxed{2}$$

SEMINAR 1:
THE
APPRECIATION
SEMINAR

Most human beings have not participated in a learning seminar that is designed to teach double-loop learning as well as Model II theories-in-use. The objective of the first seminar was therefore to give potential participants some experience in such learning environments so that they could make a more informed choice. The seminar could not provide an introduction to the entire range of experiences. It could, however, provide the potential participants with experience in utilizing their own behavior as a basis for learning, in becoming aware of discrepancies between their espoused theories and their theories-in-use, in testing ideas publicly, in giving and receiving information from fellow participants, and in the range of subjects that might be explored.

Since no choice, especially one of this nature, could be completely informed, it was very important that the potential participants realize the depth of the commitment the faculty had to creating growth-producing environments, to discouraging growth-inhibiting or harming environments, to encouraging the participants to reevaluate their choice to participate continually and openly and to leave with minimal coercive pressure from anyone.

In selecting potential subjects, several criteria were utilized. First, the subjects had to be adults. Second, they should hold positions of significant power in some organization. Third, they ought to be as ornery or as difficult as one could possibly find; that is, participants were sought who would be extremely hardnosed about entering double-loop learning environments and equally suspicious about the applicability of Model II.

One source that came to mind was the Young Presidents Organization. Many of its members are young, aggressive entrepreneurs who have built or rebuilt the organizations that they head. Also, YPO members have a history of keen interest in learning and an equally strong reputation in rejecting learning experiences if they are not helpful.

Once a year YPO has their University for Presidents. The University is usually located in a resort area and is held for one week. There are many different courses scheduled during the week, and the presidents choose whatever mixture of learning experiences they desire.

A brief and somewhat abstract description of our course was included in the preliminary catalogue of one of these Universities. The announcement included the comment that the course was experimental and that it would require at least two hours every day during the entire week. Although this time requirement was unusually long, there were over three hundred applicants. In order to reduce the number of potential participants, the class was scheduled to be held from 7:30 to 9:30 a.m. every morning. This reduced the list by one hundred. Through various selection mechanisms designed and managed by YPO officials, fifteen presidents were selected. Three "crashed" the seminars, and the first class therefore began with eighteen participants.

The selection process raises questions about the generalizability of the findings. These questions will be discussed, in detail, in Chapter 14 in which we explore several issues about generalizability. At this time, two points may be made. Although the motivation to enter the seminar was uniformly high, the subjects' motivation to produce data about their own behavior and to learn varied widely with the individual and with the degree of difficulty and threat of the learning episodes. Thus initial high motivation did not guarantee continued high motivation. This was as it should be. If the individual taking this difficult and potentially threatening course were continually enthused, either he was not being reached, or he was being reached but was suppressing his negative feelings. The expression of negative feelings, if they existed, was an important learning in this seminar. Consequently, the suppression of such feelings would be counterproductive.

The second point is related to the values I held about conducting research. I am not interested, as an educator or researcher, in producing knowledge about how to coerce people into learning experiences they prefer to reject. Such knowledge would violate Model II theory-in-use. The findings, therefore, are limited to conditions of continual relative free choice to participate. These are conditions that I hope become associated with more social experimentation. As I have shown elsewhere, strict adherence to traditional methods for designing experiments may lead to the production of knowledge about manipulating and controlling people—and such findings support a Model I world (Argyris, 1975).

The first phase of the seminar began with each president describing some key aspect of his leadership style. Although I asked the presidents to focus especially upon an aspect of their style that they felt good about, most found it difficult to do so. They suggested that it should remain to others to say how good they were as leaders. They preferred to focus on problems that they faced. The focus upon the negative aspects, as we shall see, was not necessarily based on modesty or courtesy. The presidents had strong views about their strengths. However, many have been attacked (by their peers, subordinates, and members of their families) about these strengths. The presidents are caught, as we shall see, in a dilemma. On the one hand, their authoritarian, controlling leadership qualities lead to high performance. On the other hand, the subordinates they prefer to keep (the wives they love, the children they admire) reject these leadership qualities.

Certain themes began to appear, primarily at the espoused level. The next step was to try to get to the theory-in-use. Therefore, the presidents were asked to select an issue and describe it with a concrete case. The more frequently the presidents described the problems with concrete behavior, the richer the material became as a basis for learning, that is, the more it produced discrepancies between espoused theory and theory-in-use. These were not difficult to identify. For example, A described himself as being open and participative in dealing with B. Yet when he described what he said and did, many of the presidents felt that he was closed and unilaterally controlling of B. As has been the case in all the research conducted so far (Argyris and Schon, 1974), any given individual tended to be unaware of the discrepancy between his espoused theory and theory-in-use, while his peers were able to identify these incongruities easily and immediately.

The presidents did not hold back in their feedback, and this produced a new level of discrepancies to be identified and from which to learn. For example, C may have just told A that he had behaved in a closed and controlling manner in his encounter with B. A, who did not see his behavior in this way, denied the attributions. C responded by becoming more insistent and controlling and simultaneously more closed to being influenced. A would then accuse C of being uninfluenceable. C, in turn, would deny the attribution, and the remaining members would jump in in a competitive, win-lose manner that escalated the attributions, evaluations, and the resulting uninfluenciability of the discussion. The participants were soon generating more heat than light. This, in turn, raised the level of frustration, escalated the competitiveness, and produced statements by the presidents that were also counterproductive. "OK, we've had enough of this," or "We're not getting anywhere," or "Most of you are missing the point," or "If we would all read this more carefully, it would become clear that. . . ," were illustrative of the dialogue.

I was able to select specimens of the competitive, win-lose behavior and show how they caused less effective problem solving among the presidents. I was also able to make predictions that, if they behaved back home the way they behaved in this seminar, their leadership styles would probably produce relatively high degrees of conformity, fear of risk taking, and single-loop learning.

The responses were immediate, and they contained the beginnings of the identification of inconsistencies that people with power experience. For example:

1.   The presidents insisted that they did not behave this way at home. They were more competitive in the learning setting because they felt freer with their peers. Yet the examples they gave of their back-home behavior suggested that they behaved the same way in their firms. Moreover, why should executives who say they feel freer reduce each others' freedom?

2.   Their subordinates were strong and were not intimidated by such behavior. Yet the presidents spoke of back-home meetings that took hours because people talked too much and generated more heat than light, or they didn't talk enough and we (presidents) have to pull the ideas out of them as best as we can.

As dilemmas such as these became more numerous, the members began to confront the inconsistencies rather than sweep them under the rug. For example, several presidents were close friends of a more competitive member. They challenged the latter's descriptions of his back-home behavior by citing illustrations of his behaving competitively and creating win-lose dynamics.

These dilemmas provided the energy and the commitment for the presidents to examine more carefully their leadership behavior. The results are published elsewhere (Argyris, 1973). In the language of this report, the YPO presidents described themselves as Model I squared—a few insisted "cubed."

The men became so involved that they asked if a special session could be held to include their wives. The session was scheduled subject to the condition that the wives would be free to decline to attend. The men assured the faculty member that they would be careful not to coerce their wives into attending. Two sessions were held, and in both cases all wives but one said that they had attended because they had been coerced. "Are you kidding?" asked one wife with mixed feelings of amazement and anger, "I'm here because he wants me to be here!" Some of the men protested. They had struggled hard, they insisted, to make it a free choice for their wives. Some of the wives countered with actual quotations attributed to their husbands. Others began to role play how they received the invitations. The evidence was overwhelming. The wives had been coerced.[1]

At the end of the week, the presidents requested another seminar. The writer agreed to design a seminar that would be based on two major learnings to date. The first was that there was a consistent discrepancy between the way the presidents described their leadership behavior and how their leadership behavior was seen by their peers when they gave actual examples. Also, there was the discrepancy between what the presidents said and how they actually behaved in the seminar (toward each other and toward their wives).

If they agreed that these were key findings, it made sense to take them into account in designing the next learning seminar. The presidents agreed. The presidents were then asked to tape record some sessions of the meetings they chaired with their top executive group (in their respective back-home settings). They were asked to tape record a session that they considered typical and one that they judged to be extraordinary (on any dimension) but not to identify them for the faculty. The faculty would listen to all the tapes and abstract from them vignettes totaling not more than ten pages for each president. These cases would be used as the basis for discussions during the second seminar.

Nine presidents agreed to continue their learning on this basis. The reduction did not trouble the faculty. It helped to assure that those attending were willing to pay the increased "cost" for learning. Also, generating these requirements helped to increase the probability that the presidents would think carefully about their commitment.

---

[1] The fact that the wives had permitted the coercion, and the dependency that this implied, was raised by one wife, but it was not discussed.

PART

2

THE EXPERIMENT

CHAPTER

$$3$$

SEMINAR 2: BEING AN IMPORTANT PART OF THE PROBLEM

During the previous session we began to see that the presidents wanted to learn about their behavior. However, they did not appear to know how to discover nor did they know how to help each other discover. An example of the former was that the presidents did not know what to look for in their behavior nor how to invite feedback about their behavior. An example of the latter was that the moment someone identified a discrepancy, the presidents would give each other abstract, attributive, evaluative feedback that escalated into defensiveness and competitiveness. This, in turn, created win-lose, nonadditive group dynamics that led, at best, to single-loop learning.

The difficulty faced by the faculty therefore was that the members were programmed with theories-in-use that apparently would make reflection and double-loop inquiry impossible. Yet these were the qualities most needed. How does one get participants to consider reflecting, especially on the dilemmas for learning that they create for themselves?

The basis for many of these dilemmas was that the executives held theories-in-use that were power oriented. They sought to advocate their positions clearly *and* to control others unilaterally. Advocacy coupled with unilateral control over others was as natural as apple pie and as necessary for effectiveness as apples for the pie. There was little or no reflection on these assumptions because they were self-evident. Indeed, they were axioms.

The faculty encouraged reflection on these assumptions. Their unassailability became the cause of many dilemmas. The faculty modeled how to reflect on assumptions by asking the participants to reflect on one of their (faculty's) key dilemmas in the seminar. The dilemma was one related to the use of power. On the one hand, the faculty believed that they had a new model of behavior (Model II) that the participants should learn. The faculty also believed that they knew how to help the participants move toward Model II. Finally, the faculty had evidence that, by themselves, the presidents would not move toward Model II.

On the other hand, the faculty adhered to a Model II process of learning. This meant that the presidents should be in control of their learning and should be fully informed about the next steps before these steps were taken. The faculty also knew that an informed choice about the steps could not be made without taking the steps.

One way to deal with the dilemma was to surface it—to remind everyone of his right, indeed obligation, to choose his degree of involvement, and to ask for discussion. The faculty began the seminar with this action. The response was one of bewilderment. Most participants said that they did not experience a dilemma. The faculty were the leaders, and they were the students. It was the faculty members' responsibility to design and manage the course. It was the faculty's obligation to advocate and to control. If they did not agree or like what the faculty members did, they would take over.

This response was, as pointed out in Chapter I, predictable from those who hold a Model I theory-in-use. The response was, in effect, an oscillating Model I. The faculty should advocate and control to achieve their purposes. If the presidents did not approve of what was going on, they would take over.

It was too early in the learning to process or explore the inconsistencies in these responses as well as the built-in inhibitors to genuine double-loop learning. Such an exploration would make little sense to individuals who had yet to identify adequately the incongruities between their theory-in-use and their espoused theories.

The first step was therefore to help the members diagnose for themselves the degree to which they manifested these incongruities. Since the participants were saying, in effect, that they expected the faculty to take control, the faculty was free, as part of their use of this power, to take the initiative and, simultaneously, to encourage confrontation of their designs and strategies for learning. Thus the faculty could say:

We hear the message that we should begin with our design, and we will. One part of the design is to encourage you to confront it whenever you wish to do so.

This did not resolve the dilemma; it simply served to identify it. The task was to keep it in mind. As we shall see, the participants hesitated to identify and surface dilemmas. Once they did so, they felt compelled to resolve them immediately. Such haste inhibited learning and increased the defensiveness of the participants, because the dilemmas would not go away easily.

Encouraging confrontation also would help to assure the participants that the faculty meant it when they had said that the choice to remain in the learning environment (or to alter the learning environment) should be continually reexamined.

THE CASES

The presidents were asked to tape record several sessions of some key deliberations in their back-home settings. Most chose meetings with their immediate subordinates. The focus on the back-home setting was deliberate. The objective was to begin as early as possible to relate the learning within the seminar to back-home problems. The assumption was that such integration would make learning more meaningful, and it would facilitate the transfer of learning.

The request for tape recordings was based on several ideas. First was the notion that one could not learn about one's theory-in-use by collecting espoused-level data. Second was the notion that the best way to reduce dependence on the faculty was to provide everyone with the same relatively directly observable data. Hence, whenever a faculty member or a participant made an inference about someone's behavior, everyone had access to the same data. Third, the way to encourage people to think and act on the basis of directly observable data is to begin doing so with the first assignment. Finally, the tape recording of such meetings would act as a cue to the subordinates that their superior was in a learning situation—one that required him to look at his behavior. This might help the subordinates test the credibility of their superior's motivation to learn, as well as to set the foundation for their own learning.

The faculty listened to the tape recordings and had transcribed from each tape about five to ten pages of verbatum material. These cases were then reproduced and given to all the participants (with identifications such as names eliminated) when they arrived at the seminar. They were given time to read the cases during the first evening. As we shall see, all the men had reason to reread and reread the cases.

A word about the nature of directly observable data belongs here. All data in real life are inferred and therefore no datum is, strictly speaking, directly observable. The key is the degree to which the data are presented with categories whose meanings can only be known and validated by the creator of the data. For example, if the participant said, "I dealt with him carefully and cautiously," the meaning of carefully and cautiously is known only to the participant. If the participant can then produce a tape recording of what he said, this would reduce the others' dependence upon the participant for drawing their own inferences of what happened. They may now agree with him or say, in effect, "If I were on the receiving end, I would not feel dealt with carefully and cautiously for these and these reasons."

However, a tape recording misses much behavior, especially that which is nonverbal. Consequently, video tapes may be helpful. We have not used video tapes for several reasons. First, the verbal behavior provides so much information for learning that all the seminar time was easily consumed discussing this behavior. Second, as these issues were discussed the participant started to use nonverbal cues in the learning seminar. They were then picked up by others and became part of the data that were examined.

Finally, video tapes may overload the information circuit. They may provide too much information. Indeed, it may well be that they are most useful in the early stages as quick exercises in unfreezing and at the later stages as a basis for further learning. However, once people become more sophisticated in diagnosis and action, they begin to make requirements of the film that, in order to fulfill, may escalate the costs.

Initially, the faculty and the presidents were concerned about whether the cases would sample the important and the key inconsistencies in the participant's behavior. We have, as a result of listening to numerous tapes, found that it is relatively easy to obtain a valid sample of important inconsistencies, because human behavior, in noncontrived settings, is redundant and overdetermined. Presidents (and subordinates) express themselves in many different ways, yet they seem to have a finite set of theories-in-use that they repeat in almost an infinite variety of combinations. This finding appears to be congruent with the idea that human beings are finite information systems. It is doubtful that they could store, retrieve, and use a very large number of basically different behavioral strategies.

THE SEMINAR ACTIVITIES

The seminar began with one of the participants volunteering to have his case discussed. He was asked to define the kind of help he was seeking. The group was then asked to accept the following task:

President A has given you the case as a specimen of his behavior. He has hired you as consultants to help him become more effective in the areas he has just identified. You are now in his office, and you may begin in any way that you believe is most helpful to A.

The participants began with a one-to-one relationship with the president. Each attempted to help the president in accordance with his theory-in-use. Not surprisingly, the discussions soon became competitive, win-lose, evaluative, and, at times, punishing of each other. The faculty attempted to ask the group members to examine the way in which they were giving "help" to each other. For example, they observed that A had just told B that he (B), in effect, controlled and punished his subordinates and did so in a controlling, punishing manner. Or, that E told D that he missed what his subordinates were "really" trying to tell him. Yet E had misunderstood D.

The faculty were attempting to get the presidents to explore the negative consequences of, and the inconsistencies related to, their behavior. The participants listened to the faculty's interventions approvingly and with patience. Indeed, they would report that they valued "being told off" in no uncertain terms because so few people did it to them back home. They would then return to their competitiveness, unilateral attributions and evaluations, and win-lose dynamics, apparently unaware that they had not been told off nor that they were not relating the faculty "help" to their behavior.

Examples of the Participants' Behavior

A transcript was analyzed of a session that had occurred about midpoint during the seminar. A had asked for help as to how to manage the executive committee meetings more effectively. Excerpts have been taken from the transcript to illustrate the Model I character of the discussion.

Dialogue of the Discussion "to help" Mr. A	Probable Impact on Mr. A
G: The reason that it (the meeting) is so bad is because you think they're all stupid.	Attribution statement made with no directly observable data.
G: (Sure you are setting prices). On page 37, it is almost like you've zeroed in on him.	Attributive.
A: No, that's not what happened.	No attempt to help A discuss his views or his feelings.
G: Why do you think morale is so lousy?	
A: If I had to pick one reason, it is the impression that I have given by drastically switching my management style.	
D: How does your change (in leadership style) effect the profits? You haven't spoken of money yet.	Focus on profits when A said that his problem was with Mr. ____.

LATER

A: I took the action because . . . (states reason).	
G: (an employee in A's firm) doesn't agree with you. Hell, look, on page 33 he says . . .	Coercing A to see reality the way G sees it.
A: Well C is a guy I can only describe as a kind of guy you'd be worried about in your company.	

LATER

B: How are you going to hold this guy? What are you going to say to him?	
A: Well, I've said to him that his job is crucial for our company.	Responses are not in directly observable data.
E: Do you believe that?	
A: Yes.	There is a climate of lawyering, as if A is on a witness stand.
E: Why not tell him so?	

A: Because in truth, I've reduced
his responsibility in the company. I feel guilty about that.

F: How old is he?   Most questions are about A's employee and not about A's behavior.

D: Are you sure you want him
around?

LATER

A: Here he is at a meeting of vital
interest to him and he said one
thing.

D: Well, do you think you might   Making   untestable   attributions
have scared him? Maybe he is   about people other than the presi-
terribly insecure?   dent.

B: Let's turn this question around. Asking questions that are rhetorical.
Have you *really* thought about B doubts that A has thought about
whether you're going to hire a   hiring a new V.P.
new V.P. next year? Have you
really   consciously   thought
about that?

LATER

H: Do you think you stimulate   Asking loaded questions.
ideas?

A: Not for this guy.

H: Maybe your problem is that   Making untestable diagnoses.
you've created a straw man
there.

LATER

G: Why can't you sit down with the Tells A what to do with none of the
guy and tell him that he is a   advice presented in the form of di-
damned good manufacturing   rectly observable data. Advice is gen-
man, but the way things are   eral.
going, he may have to leave the
company.

A: I have done that.

G: You have? (Said disbelievingly.)

Again, the impression of A being on the witness stand.

A: Yes, three times.

G: What happened?

A: I don't think I reached him.

G: What did he say?

A: He listens.

B: No reaction?

A: No, no reaction. (Later, under questioning, of C, A said that the individual had told A that A had been destructive. He said to A, "You've destroyed me.")

LATER

C: (to A) What are you asking of us about the case?

A: Well, I'm not sure. I don't know.

A had not thought through what kind of help he wanted from the group.

LATER

I: If I were your V.P. I would *really* be confused. I would think that the only thing that is consistent about my boss is that he is inconsistent.

Negative evaluation of A's behavior with no directly observable data. A may have felt punished.

LATER

I: (to A) I've learned in my company never to change targets midstream.

Competitive and evaluative comments.

F: I don't agree. If it made sense to lower the target, I would.

I: Well I wouldn't lower it. I'd tell them to do better.

F: That's not realistic. All you are teaching me is that you are a taskmaker.

LATER

L: What has this (subject) got to do with pricing?

F: I don't think it has anything, but I think it's A's way of showing his anger.
                                    Attribution—no data.

L: OK.

F: I think that when A takes punitive action he's just trying to emphasize his sincerity and belief in what he's saying! (exclamation point, the author's).
                                      Attributions with no attempt to connect to directly observable data.

D: Could A have been responding to the anger of his subordinates?

LATER

D: (Feels hurt by something F said about him.) I don't think you meant that intentionally and consciously—maybe unconsciously—but we all have slips like that. It didn't bother me particularly. It would have bothered me if you had said it happens frequently.
                                      Attribution.

                                      Denial of feelings.

F: I didn't say it happened frequently.

D: I know you didn't. But you said I'm driving this guy into the corner and it had to happen (D's subordinate told him he was full of shit.)

F: No, I didn't say that . . .

D: Has it ever happened to you?

F: Not that I can remember. But I don't want to say it never has happened to me.

D: OK, We have a guy saying on tape that I'm full of shit. Have

you ever driven a person to the
point where he felt you (F) were
full of shit but didn't say it
openly?

F: Yes (laughter).

G: Once yesterday and once today.

. . .

LAUGHTER

How may the reader judge how representative these excerpts from a
transcript are? I should like to postpone answering this question until
Chapter 14. For the moment, let us focus on some of the episodes developed by Bolman that illustrate the quantitative analysis made from the
tape recordings of the entire session.

EPISODE 1.   B began criticizing A's handling of a particular subordinate
("It seems to me that you entered the meeting knowing this man wasn't
committed. Then you proceeded to push him even further in this direction.") G began asking President A whether he had ever explained all the
facts to the subordinate so that he would understand the company's
decision. A responded, "Sure, we spent a lot of time on that." The discussion continued with B telling A that he had pushed the subordinate
into a corner, and C continually asking A whether he had really
explored the facts of the matter. Several participants tried to offer feedback to A, but much of it was punitive ("You're hammering the nails in
this guy's coffin") or attributive ("I think that subconsciously you called
the meeting in order to get him"). A showed signs of feeling misunderstood and of feeling wounded.

EPISODE 2.   D said he agreed with E that E had mishandled a situation
involving a dispute with one of E's subordinates, but added the following:

D: We may not think so for the same reasons. Why do you think you
    blew it?

E: Well, first of all, I got angry.

D: I mean, why do you think you got angry?

E said he got angry because this was another of several situations in
which this particular individual had overreacted on minor matters. Fac-

ulty member C asked D to share his own diagnosis of the situation, and D indicated that he felt the subordinate was very much like M [1]; neither of them liked to be in a situation in which they were vulnerable.

M acknowledged the feedback but showed a persistent tendency to respond to feedback by going into accounts of the way he did things at his firm. President H pushed M on the issue of subordinate vulnerability, discussing how he would feel in such a situation. G added, "He might even tell you you're full of shit." M had said in the initial session that he would fire anyone who used that phrase, and this was not the first time that C reminded him of the statement. M bristled and said he was concerned with civility, not content. D asked M whether he wanted to change his behavior. M said that he might to some extent, but a complete change in personality would not be sincere, and he had never been the type to "walk on eggshells."

EPISODE 3.   For a time the discussion centered around the difficulty several members had in believing that F really wanted to change anything about his behavior, and the discussion periodically returned to F's ambivalence.

E: (to F) You like to put things together from disparate elements which are not necessarily in good relation, and then put them in order and then move into another situation where you bring together elements like that. That is a challenge to you, which is my definition of what an entrepreneur is.

F: Except I want to make sure that they keep reading my Mao Tse-Tung book, and keep my picture on the wall in each of these things.

D: You mentioned yesterday that you had to be a dictator in order to produce profits. One thing you didn't mention is that it's fun to be a dictator . . . You mentioned the discomfort you feel that caused you to attend this seminar. Is the discomfort with your style, or that the company will outgrow your style?

F: Well, I suppose I feel the company would outgrow my style. I do enjoy being a dictator—I enjoy every minute of it. But I also realize that perhaps a dictatorial kind of management is not going to work. I have to be able to make some adjustments to my style.

D: Suppose we say to you, F, we're consultants, you respect us. Your present style will work, you can take your company to a billion in sales, you don't need to change.

---

[1] M dropped out after this meeting.

F: Then would I change? I would want to change because I still want to make life easier for myself—this personal inner conflict that I have at having to give these things up. I get very unhappy with myself at that point. I've very difficult for other people to live with. I don't like myself as a dictator.

The discussions, in conclusion, produced win-lose dynamics, highly evaluative, sometimes punishing feedback, untested attributions, self-sealing statements, frequent attempts by one member to control another or the group, little additiveness to the discussions, and little learning that could be a basis for change. These consequences are congruent with those predicted in Model I.

Toward the end of the seminar, the participants were asked to evaluate it. They responded favorably to each other's "openness" and "candor." When the faculty pressed for what they had learned during the two days, they all admitted that they had not learned much that was new. They liked the session because they now realized that others had similar problems. There was a sense of comfort in learning that others one respected had similar problems.

The faculty then played back a few minutes from a tape of the session, and the participants' reactions ranged from surprise to shock at competitiveness, misunderstanding, punishing, unilateral controlling, etc. The faculty felt that this session provided evidence that they were probably programmed with Model I theories-in-use, that they created the consequences predicted by Model I in the seminar, and they hypothesized that the same consequences were being created back at home with, and again another hypothesis, greater impact because subordinates would probably not feel as free to compete and fight back as the presidents did with each other.

The presidents so far have shown their capacity to produce a Model I world for learning. Such a world would eventually develop many of the problems that they, as presidents, identified in their respective companies. Consequently, if this Model I behavior continued, the learning environments would not produce learnings that went beyond this insight.

The seminar closed with the presidents requesting another, longer seminar in which they could examine more consciously, deliberately, and systematically their theories-in-use.

CHAPTER

4

SEMINAR 3:
BEGINNING TO
DISCOVER THEIR
THEORIES-IN-USE

A five-day seminar was held about eight months after the second seminar.[1] In planning the session, the faculty kept several points in mind. First, the participants had experienced two sessions in which they learned how ineffective they were in helping themselves and each other diagnose their theories-in-use. The participants reported, at the end of the previous session, that they were ready to move forward. They asked for material about Model I and Model II to organize their learning.

The faculty felt, therefore, that the appreciation phase had been achieved. The time had arrived for the members to learn Models I and II, to develop their own model of their theory-in-use, to have it confirmed or disconfirmed by the others in the seminar, and to develop some back-home experiments based on the learning during the seminar.

---

[1] Two members had to drop out, and one died of a heart attack. The remaining six continued throughout the entire experiment.

The faculty also knew that, since the participants were programmed with Model I, it was not likely that they would be able to reflect competently to discover their Model-oneness (to do so would be to manifest double-loop learning). Therefore, some instrument was needed that would help them to produce a map of their theories-in-use.

Why a map? The purpose of the map was to help organize some of the blooming, buzzing confusion that was produced during the seminar. If the map was an effective one, it would help the participants make sense out of where they have been, where they are now, and where they might go next. Moreover, a map is an excellent device with which to store economically and retrieve efficiently enormous amounts of information. Both of these capacities would be especially required when the participants attempted to conduct experiments in their back-home settings.

What kinds of instruments would be required? The instruments used should produce directly observable data so that the data base for learning was as concrete as possible. Also, the data produced should be clearly relatable by the individuals to their respective theories-in-use. The instruments and learning activities should also maximize the individual's personal causality and responsibility in the learning situation. The individual should not be able to place the responsibility for the inconsistencies and incongruities "in" others in the case, in the faculty, or in the instrument.

Since we knew that the participants tended to be blind to the incongruities and inconsistencies, it was important that the instruments and the learning activities designed by the faculty make the blindness explicit. To make explicit systematic blindness in individuals who are not aware requires, at a minimum, an instrument that does not activate whatever defenses human beings must have that prevent them from being aware of their blindness. Nor should the effective use of the instrument require an attribution that all the people who use it are blind. To do so would be to give individuals a coercive instrument which, even if it worked, could make them anxious as they became aware of their blindness, thereby activating other appropriate defenses to reduce the anxiety. In other words, the instruments used should not permit the participants to attribute their inventions and productions to the instrument. The instrument should act as a learning facilitator and not as a creator of behavior normally not manifested by the participants.

Finally, the instrument should be as economical of individuals' time and energy as possible. Thus the instrument that was used could be completed in less than one hour and with the use of no more than four typewritten double-spaced pages. However, it was so designed that it was open ended enough for the participants to fill in as much as they considered relevant and necessary for their learning objectives.

Another task of the faculty was that of becoming monitors of the interpersonal and group dynamics. We now knew, from the last two sessions, that, left to their own theories-in-use, the presidents would unknowingly inhibit double-loop learning. It would be the faculty's task to surface these behavioral bottlenecks. It would also be the task of the faculty to seek and reward any rare occurrences of attempts at double-loop learning by the members so that the feelings of frustration and failure did not become overwhelming. The faculty could also help the presidents by being accepting of the frustration and failure as natural and expected. This should lead the presidents to feel that the frustrations and failures are legitimate, to reduce their level of aspiration concerning how fast they will learn, and to increase their willingness to learn from failure. The faculty also modeled episodes of effective action by behaving effectively, thereby showing the presidents how it could be done. All these roles could facilitate learning *and* dependence. It would be necessary to reduce the latter (while increasing the former). The development of legitimate dependence is another important faculty skill and a quality of the learning process. These are discussed in detail as they arise during the progress of learning.

Finally, the design of the instrument and the learning activities should focus heavily on discovery, but discovery with the intention of invention-production-generalization within the learning environment and the back-home setting. Discovery for the sake of discovery is a significantly different learning process than discovery for the intention to invent, reproduce, and generalize. The former is exhilarating but, by itself, could become counterproductive because it could produce individuals who feared the challenge of invention and production. Thus every time the members were asked to discover something, they knew it was with the intention to invent and to produce.

Learning to learn that is limited to a seminar environment may also be exhilarating. Again, such learning could produce theories of action that are minimally transferable. The objective of the entire program is, as has been stated before, to enhance effectiveness in the noncontrived world. Model II learning limited to seminars will not help individuals, nor can it become a basis for organizational and societal change.

THE FIRST INSTRUMENT

The participants were asked to generate, before they arrived, a case of an important and challenging intervention that they had made (or expected to make). The case should include (1) a brief description of the purpose(s) of their intervention, (2) a brief description of the participants, the setting, and any other situational conditions, and (3) their behavioral strategy to achieve their purposes (see Table 1).

The participants were also asked to write, in scenario form, what actually happened (or what they thought would happen). They were requested to divide several pages in two columns. In the right hand column, they should write whatever they said and others said. In the left hand column, they should write anything that they were thinking and feeling while the conversation was going on. Finally, they were asked to read their case and infer the underlying assumptions about effective intervention and action.

All the cases were received several weeks before the seminar. This gave the faculty an opportunity to make a diagnosis of the participants' positions on a path from Model I toward Model II. All the cases depicted Model I theories-in-use (indeed, a few were, as the members had said, Model I cubed).

Table 1

AN EXERCISE FOR UNDERSTANDING YOUR OWN BEHAVIOR

Please write about a challenging intervention or interaction with one or more individuals. This case should represent a situation or episode.
1. one you have already experienced
2. one you expect to experience in the near future
If you have difficulty with either of these conditions, please try a case that you have yet to experience but are concerned about how effective you would be.

Please begin the description with a paragraph or so about the purpose of your intervention, the setting, the people involved, etc.

Next, please write a few paragraphs regarding your strategy. What were your objectives, how did you intend to achieve them, and why did you select those goals and strategies?

Next, please write a few pages, in scenario form, about what actually occurred or what you expect may occur. Please do it in the following format:

On this side of the page, please write what was going on in your mind while you were talking or when the client was talking (whether the talking was real or imagined).	On this side of the page, please write what you said (or expect to say) and what the client(s) said or what you expect them to say. Continue writing the "play" until you believe your major points (purpose or concerns) are illustrated. (The scenario should be at least two pages.)

Finally, as you reread your case, what underlying assumptions do you think that you held about effective action?

The seminar began with a brief review of the previous seminar. Then there was a presentation of Model I. The theory of instruction operating here was to use Model I as a basis for analyzing the cases. This is how the faculty began to give a structure and a thrust to the learning processes. They did not, as was true in the previous seminar, encourage the individuals to "freewheel."

Why not encourage the participants to develop their own model? First, it would take too much time. If it took the authors two years to develop such a model, it might take at least as long for the presidents to do the same. Second, these presidents, when they began, were not at all skilled in being reflective and learning from action. These two reasons would add up to, at best, a series of seminars in discovery and not in invention, production, and generalization.

Beginning to learn Model II is somewhat like going to the moon. The rocket ship must have an initial thrust that overcomes the earth's gravity. Participants need an initial thrust to help them overcome the human gravity caused by everyone's being programmed with Model I theories-in-use and the culture and its institutions being designed in accordance with these theories-in-use. One way to give them the thrust is somehow to tell, persuade, show, and lecture them toward Model II. But even if they learned, it would be through a Model I compliance process. When they would try to move from the espoused learning to the theory-in-use, they would be unable to do so. Indeed, they would also realize that the theory of instruction used by the faculty was to espouse Model II and to behave Model I.

Another way to help with the initial take-off is to decrease the dependence the participants had upon each other for all their learning. In a T group, for example, in which such dependence is a basic source of cohesiveness, the members focus early on such questions as (1) who am I in this group, (2) how am I perceived, (3) how can I become fully accepted so that I can learn? In order to answer these questions, the individuals must take action to show who they are and then inquire to learn about their acceptability. Such inquiry places an early emphasis on interpersonal closeness. To continue the analogy of the rocket flight, if we were to take on this solution, people would spend time building up their cohesiveness before the blast-off. In our case, increased knowledge about theories-in-use, etc., are the destination. Cohesiveness may inhibit as well as facilitate such learning. Also, if we could design a trip in which everyone did not have to get along maximally to learn, we would increase the pay-off possibilities.

But, the reader may recall, defining concepts is a Model I act. Is not a lecture on Model I a Model I act? The answer is yes. This is congruent with the paradox, described at the outset, that is embedded in all such learning experiences. The challenge is for the faculty to be aware of the Model-oneness of their behavior, to help the participants be aware, and to realize that this necessarily Model I initial step can be altered toward Model II by a process of internalization of Model II. How is Model II internalized? A tentative model of the process was described in Chapter I. The more detailed answer·is the subject matter of this book.

Finally, dependence on faculty by individuals who are programmed with Model I inhibits learning minimally when the dependence is seen as legitimate and temporary. Hence, a lecture by the faculty that provides the conceptual underpinnings of the course can help the individuals make a more informed decision if they wish to continue, and if so, a further decision about the degree to which they believe the faculty are competent to help them. If they decide the faculty can help them, the participants' willingness to become temporarily dependent will lead to moving away from dependence as they learn the new skills and competences.

We now turn to a description of the cases that the presidents brought to the seminar.

EXAMPLES OF CASE STUDIES

The case studies submitted by G and E are included to give the reader an indication of the quality of the information provided by the case studies. G's case represents a typical Model I approach. E's case represents a president further along toward Model II, but, as we shall see, still influenced by Model I governing variables.

President G

G wrote that the objectives of the meeting that he chaired were as follows:

1. To create awareness among key executives of the profit squeeze and loss of market share problems—and initiate actions to solve the problem, for example,

   a. increased volume (emphasis on new customers and new markets)
   b. better pricing (pass on raw material cost increases)
   c. control costs

2. To get commitment from key executives to achievement of corporate objectives.

   a. 20% earnings per share growth in fiscal 1973/4.

   b. Increase by 1%/year our share of the X market while maintaining at least 20% R.O.A.U.

   c. Get similar market share of Y market while maintaining at least 20% R.O.A.U.

   d. Expand into other items that are within our basic concept of do-it-yourself apparel, accessories, and decorative items for the home.

   e. Develop the management depth to support our corporate objectives.

      1. Implement an effective new organizational structure.

      2. Management by objectives program.

         a. The Big Three Program.

         b. Tie in objectives with executive bonuses.

         c. Quarterly review of progress toward achievement of objectives.

      3. Compensation system.

      4. More effective reporting and review procedures.

Below are reproduced two portions of G's case of what happened in the meeting.

If we were only doing what we are supposed to be doing all along we wouldn't be in this problem.	G: All right, gentlemen, these are the facts. Our profits are off 50% from last year, and we are losing market share. Our problem is: how can we come on like gangbusters the last six months of our fiscal year so that we end up with our 20% earnings, and how can we gain market share in our two key product lines of hand knitting and stitchery kits?
That's a real cop-out. You get everybody's sales figures every three days,	A: I didn't realize that our profit situation was so bad. I knew that

and even though we only present a quarterly profit report, it has no secrets and everybody sees each other all the time and this is the type of information you should be exchanging.

Let's concentrate on the problem.

The other guy always has a lower price.

This is such a great management tool I can't understand why everyone in the company doesn't use it.

my division was way off, but I thought the other divisions were doing very well.

G: What should we do for the remainder of the fiscal year so that we can make this year a success?

B: We don't have the low-priced product that our competition has.

G: Our raw material price is higher than our competitor because we have stuck to a higher quality product where everybody makes more money. To what extent do the quality advantages offset the lower price of our competition?

C: The low-price stuff is increasing its market share. We can no longer ignore it. We have to meet it with a similar price and a similar lower quality.

G: We have been unsuccessful on implementing the management by objectives program, and one reason has been given that it is too complicated. Therefore, I have come up with this Big Three approach to answer that objection and to simplify it so that we can develop a sensible program. Furthermore, our procedure manual provides for executive bonus to development and achievement of objectives, but this has never been implemented, and this new format of the Top Management Committee rating objectives ahead of time will then tie them in with executive bonus, as we do find that people tend to put their efforts where they are really being measured. Thirdly, our Procedure Manual calls for quarterly review of achievement toward objectives, but we have never had objectives developed well enough to review them. Now we will review these Big Three quarterly.

A: Sounds great with me.

Sounds like the usual "Yes, boss," and then they go back to running their old ways.

G: The problem is we have always said it is good, but we have never carried it out. We had a task force on this specific subject, and the chairman of the task force came up with a proposal he himself didn't even use in his own division, so what makes us believe that we are going to use this?

Unless you set a deadline nothing will happen, but maybe if I force it going then perhaps it will be an effective procedure and then more than lip service will be given to it.

G: Commitment of the top levels is important, and an example to our subordinates is important; therefore, I have given you my Big Three, and I want you to give your Big Three to me as well as to your key executives. Let's set a deadline as to when your Big Three will be presented to me.

B: Right now, we passed our deadline on the presentation of the Long Range Plan, and we are making all these management changes that you will have to let us know which you want first. We can't do everything.

Another cop-out. Why can't you do everything? It's like the baseball player saying, "I can't be both a fielder and hitter, so tell me what I am supposed to do."

G: It's the age-old problem of the urgent and the important. Somehow we have to get both done. Long-range planning, management changes, managerial techniques are all essential to successful performance of our company. Perhaps if we were doing these things better in the past we wouldn't be having our problems today.

President E

President E wrote the following about his case:

1. Our parent corporation is constructing a multifamily housing development that will house in excess of 1000 people. Twenty percent of the units will house low-income families with their rent subsidized. The remaining inhabitants will pay rents ranging from 65 to 100% of the general market rents.

The neighborhood is transitional, both racially and economically. Our primary corporate goal is to create a stable and harmonious racially balanced community. We hope to establish a pattern of 25% black renters, and we are determined to limit blacks to 40%, this being the maximum percentage considered possible short of an "upset," at which time the resident whites would flee and potential new white tenants would avoid the project.

Our second corporate objective is to achieve true economic integration, a task we consider more difficult than racial integration.

Our third objective is to bring substantial social services to the project in an effort to assist the disadvantaged residents in the improvement of their lives.

Finally, we conceived, financed, designed, constructed, own, and now will manage the project. All of this was done and is being done in the hope that we could be instrumental in creating a better life for the 1000 residents of the project. If we failed to do this, we would have failed in the project regardless of the amount of tax shelters, design awards, or profits we might realize in the process. Management is most critical to this question.

2. The overall management function within our organization is directed by a vice-president with limited practical experience. Since we are a relatively new organization and since this is to be our first major management responsibility, the party, R, assigned to this role, has, over the last 12 months, devoted no more than 20% of his time to management, although it is understood that it would become a full-time function as the several planned projects are completed, probably in late 1975.

The resident manager for the subject project, hired in late 1972 and trained for 6 months, recently resigned unexpectedly for health reasons.

Since the first residents will begin to move in during August, R is quickly moving to interview and hire a new resident manager.

3. I wanted to persuade R to assume the project manager's role for the next 12 to 18 months or more. I wanted to persuade rather than request or order because of the importance that I attached to the early leasing function. If R were to perform with efficiency but without enthusiasm, warmth, and imagination, the entire project could be damaged. My reasons for wanting R to perform directly rather than hire another are more complex.

I have come to suspect that R is fascinated with theories of property management and sees it in terms of building maintenance, deliquency, ratios, accounting, and housekeeping. More and more, there have been clues that he considers people (tenants) as a necessary nuisance, a threat to efficiency. I have given attention to this concern in the past by arranging management discussions of corporate objectives as regards management—particularly the need to make it people oriented. R enters freely into these discussions and is skilled at expressing our objectives with apparent sincerity. Still, at a level close to intuition, I am concerned. For this precise reason, I want R to dirty his hands with the act of management, and I want to judge his performance by actions rather than words.

4. My strategy was to arrange a direct meeting with R. This subject was to be a briefing of me on the resident manager problem with particular reference to the emergency nature of the problem because of almost immediate occupancy. I hoped to avoid manipulation and yet have R volunteer to take over the project's active management with enthusiasm.

President E's scenario went as follows:

	E: R, I'm going to be out of the office most of the time until September 1, 1973. Would you please tell me of your problems and plans for the next 6 weeks?
Good—he is concerned and may be more open than sometimes.	R: I'm really covered up. Since X resigned, I've been processing rental applications in addition to my regular duties, and I'm not sure I'm doing justice to either. I've got to find a resident manager right away.
Do I have any time?	E: Do you have any interesting applicants?

Good!

This is sincere concern—both for the person and for the situation.

Projects are known to me but status is new—he is doing too much, and this may account for some of my questions.

R: I'm not sure—one possible, but I'm not close to a decision.

E: Can I help any—do you want to talk about your schedule, your situations? I don't want you to be overextended.

R: (Now spends about 5 minutes describing his current work load in terms of projects.)

E: R, this is too much. What can we cut out—how do you see the priorities?

R: I must find a resident manager. That would ease my work load, and I could handle things then.

E: But the projects themselves —ignoring for a moment any particular part of a problem —what is your most important project now?

R: Lane Park (subject project) is as important as everything else put all together.

E: If you weren't so pressed for time, would you enjoy this period of actually setting up a new housing project for 1000 people?

R: I'm not sure (thoughtfully).

E: Let's look behind the current problem for a moment. How about your basic direction to specialize in property management? How do you feel after a year spent getting ready for a whole new direction?

R: I feel OK about it. I think this is the right place for me in the Company. I have no regrets.

I hadn't sensed this sense of resignation before, and it concerned me.

E: What happened to the excitement of a year ago? Have we just spent too much time getting ready?

R seemed to be groping, thinking—I liked his willingness to show doubt.

R: I don't know. I don't think so. Somehow I just feel off balance all the time.

E: Is it possible that the new situation is forcing you to rely too much on theory, not enough on experience?

I felt like the intensity was threatening—I wanted a recess for him. Things were moving well, but now I wanted him to take over.

R: I hadn't thought of it that way.

E: R, I've got a luncheon date, as you know, and I'd better start. Could we continue later today? Say 4? OK.

(We meet again, about 4 hours later.)

R: (Very serious) Talking this morning really stirred me up. I think I said things that might make you lose confidence in me. I *do* want to be in property management. Can we talk about it some more?

Here I was afraid of saying too much.

E: By all means.

R needed or at least wanted help, but I was determined not to speak.

R: (Pause that almost forced me to speak.) I'm afraid that I'll let the Company down. I know how important this is to you . . . (another pause), and yet I just can't get everything done—at least not right now.

I found myself moving here without having made a decision to—it was contrary to my rather vague plan, but it felt right.

E: We talked about priorities this morning, and I'd like to suggest that you pick out the most important area of your activity—throw yourself into it and let me reassign the rest of your duties. Would you consider that?

R: I can't justify what ought to be done. I should just be running Lane Park myself, but we can't afford my salary in the manager's slot.

E: That's right as an on-going expense, but that isn't a problem during the rent-up and organizational period of the next 18 months—you'd be a bargain for us. But how about your own rewards? Would that give you the sense of satisfaction that everyone needs?

R: (almost embarrassed laughter) If you aren't worried about the money, I'm not worried about that.

E: Let's do it . . .

R: OK.

(This was followed by about 20 minutes of animated planning. R was really energized and has been for the 10 days since then.) President E followed his scenario with the following comments:

I'm pleased. R is proud of himself for having the courage to volunteer for what appears to be a lesser job, but one that is critical. I think both R and I will know in 6 months if he should be heading up our management function.

THE PRESENTATION OF MODELS I AND II

The next step was to present Model I. A lengthy and spirited discussion ensued. The participants identified their behavior within the model. They began to illustrate the concepts with their behavior. The more the discussion developed a sense of consensus about the validity and relevance of the model, the more the members asked for an alternative model. It was as if they were saying, "The model does represent our life. Do you have anything to put in its place? If not, you are placing us in a very uncomfortable position."

The faculty then presented Model II. Before making the presentation, the faculty cautioned that understanding Model II might be more difficult than understanding Model I. It would be more difficult for them to fill in the concepts with samples from their own or others' behavior. Consequently, Model II would probably be understood, if at all, at a much higher level of abstraction than was the case for Model I. Model II could be evaluated initially as "motherhood" or as "fine but romantic, and impossible to implement in real life." The faculty requested that, no matter how positively or negatively the individuals reacted, they should make the evaluations explicit (especially the negative ones); thus the faculty could be confronted, as well as the participants' evaluations tested publicly.

There were several purposes for this request. The first was to encourage confrontation of Model II. Questioning the effectiveness of Model II, especially with concrete examples, was an excellent way to begin to reduce the level of abstraction. The questioning of the model may also provide one of the first opportunities for the participants to invent and produce behavior about confronting others (faculty) effectively and publicly. The substance of the facultys' reaction, as well as the way in which they reacted, would also be important. The first may help to clarify the model. The second should begin to provide a living model of how the faculty were able to strive to approximate the requirements of Model II while they were under stress. Such an exercise could also provide a model for the participants of how the faculty advocate and encourage confrontation, a central characteristic of Model II.

After some discussion about Model II, one of the participants suggested that the discussion be continued by referring more explicitly to the cases they had written. All agreed, and E volunteered to examine his case in terms of Model I and Model II.

This Discussion of E's Case

The discussion of E's case began with F saying, "It strikes me as the best example of Model II." E agreed and added, "Although there are a couple of things that I would do differently, if I were doing it over again, I'm basically satisfied with the way I handled the case."

C asked E to give examples of his behavior which led him to infer that it was congruent with Model II.

E's response included the following points:

1. I entered the interview with a feeling that R was preoccupied with technique—but I wasn't sure, and I decided I would get more input from him.
2. His response (to my question) made me realize that R felt overworked.
3. At that point, I changed the direction in which the meeting was going from my standpoint.
4. I was determined

   a. to work on the problem of his workload
   b. to work on his feelings of viability within the corporate structure
   c. (later) to explore his taking the job that I had in mind

Before turning to the discussion, it is instructive to note what E associated with Model II. First, there was an orientation of being employee centered. E appeared to be very sensitive to the impact that he believed he was having on R. Second, he did not test his attribution about R's being overworked with R. Third, he invented and produced a new strategy ("I changed the direction of the meeting") unilaterally. E decided unilaterally to help R on his workload and viability problems. One might characterize E's theory-in-use as being guided by principles of client-centered approach to diagnosis and a Model I unilateral and covert approach to the invention and production of action strategies.

G saw and identified some of these characteristics and, in a didactic manner, added several attributions about E's impact on R. One of those was an attribution that E tested his views about R privately. Yet G's assertions about E were also tested privately (and incompletely, since no one had data from R) and were communicated as tested attributions.
He said:

1. E held assumptions about R with no directly observable data.
2. E held the assumptions privately.
3. E unilaterally protected R from the pressure that R was describing.
4. E put words into R's mouth. For example, E said to R, "After a year spent on the job, you wouldn't want to go to a whole new direction."
5. E may have made R feel guilty. For example, "You don't have the old spark there."

E said he could not agree with G. B and F felt that R had to respond the way he did because of E's questions.

C asked the group to focus, for a moment, on the here and now behavior of the way they were dealing with E. The purpose was to help the group members become aware that they could be developing Model I dynamics that would not be productive of learning. C also gave concrete examples to illustrate his points.

C commented that E might be having trouble in learning from the feedback because B and F were not including directly observable data. Nor were they describing concretely other alternatives to illustrate their suggestions, such as that E should minimize eliciting certain answers from R.

After making such an assertion, C attempted to model several examples of redesigns of E's discussion with R. Thus the faculty member began with the learning phase of discovery, but attempted to invent and produce behavior that illustrated the points he was making at the espoused level. There were several purposes to such an intervention:

1. The participants would not be helped to focus on theory-in-use level learning unless the faculty combined the espoused level of learning (which the participants were becoming good at) with theory-in-use level of learning.
2. The participants were offered concrete productions to illustrate that the theory can be used to design new behavior.
3. The participants were offered an opportunity to experience their own reactions to the new behaviors as well as the reactions of others.
4. The participants would learn, by observing the behavior of the faculty, that helpful learning interventions are those that include discovery, invention, production, and generalization. This need not be accomplished in one intervention (as it appears below), but it could come over several episodes. The learning would be that they should remember the responsibility they have to generalize about their interventions.

For example:

E said to R	*E could have said to R*
What happened to the excitement of a year ago?	How would you describe your feelings now compared to a year ago?

E's phraseology included a message that E believed R's excitement had diminished. That was an inference that required testing. The phraseology permitted an answer from R that included "no change" in excitement. If R did not feel anything had happened to his sense of excitement, he may also feel that E had reached conclusions that were not valid.

R said to E	*E responded to R*
I must find a resident manager that would ease my work load. I could handle things then.	What is your important project now?

E could have responded to R

How would you expect to use a resident manager?

and/or
How would that ease up your work load?

Such a response may bring out R's strategy for resolving his work pressure. E could than help R obtain the resources that he needed, or he could question the basic strategy.

A pointed out that E stated that one of his objectives was, "I hope to avoid manipulation and yet have R volunteer to take over the project's active management with enthusiasm." A felt that the objective was unilaterally defined, coercive, and to compound the problem, E wanted R to accept the new role with enthusiasm.

Several presidents confirmed A's position, but added that this was a central problem for all of them. How can a president advocate a position without being manipulative?

C replied to the question by providing an example:

E said to R	*E could have said to R*
This (workload) is too much. What can we cut out? How do you see the priorities?	How would you evaluate the list of your load activities?

E's response could have the impact on R of E's taking the responsibility for judging the work load; that E would take the initiative to lighten R's work load; that R could depend on E to say that the work load was too much. The suggested response would ask for R to evaluate the degree of pressure, for E to confirm it (since he agreed with R), and for E to ask R what actions he wanted to take. The thrust would be to permit R to be responsible for diagnosing and changing his workload.

Two presidents suggested that the responses seemed to them as "splitting hairs" and "too sophisticated for me." C responded that he understood how they felt that way and wondered how R would react and how others in this seminar reacted. Two responded that they did not find the responses as "splitting hairs," but they doubted that they could produce them on their own. L pointed out that if R had said "I've got a priority problem," the question "How do you see the priorities?" would be helpful. If R had made no comment about priorities (which was the case), the question, "How do you see the priorities?" may tell R that the president felt that R had priority problems.

D wondered whether E was not being somewhat dishonest in his question, since he came to the meeting with the objective of getting R to take the job of resident manager, and with enthusiasm.

E said that he still felt the meeting went well:

"I really feel that the way this meeting came out was what I had hoped for from the beginning, but for a different reason. I went into the meeting with a design which I abandoned during the meeting!"

L pointed out that he had analyzed E's case. E's behavior was very high on helping R expand his choices, but very low on making E's feelings and views accessible to R. E strove to help R to expand the diagnoses, to consider new options, to design new choices. All this seemed to L to be very helpful. However, E rarely told R about his views about R's insensitivity to people, his wishes for R to take on the new job, E's turnabout in the middle of the meetings, etc..

E responded that he doubted that he had to share his feelings, strategies, and beliefs, because in a one-to-one situation the other person would know. C recalled that E had said, in a previous meeting, that he divorced his first wife because of constant miscommunication—misunderstandings—yet that was a one-to-one situation. Also, E brought a case to the group during the previous seminar that indicated that he had communication problems with several executives within his firm.

L provided several examples in which E was learning about R, during the meeting, and consequently was changing his views of R and of the possible actions. "The primary characteristics of the learning about R is occurring in E's head; it is nonpublic and unilateral. R could leave the meeting without knowing that E had a hypothesis that R was insensitive to people." Had such an hypothesis been tested publicly, R may have had an opportunity to question E about how he developed such a view, the possible meaning this had about their relationship, the concern that R might have that E is constantly making private evaluations of R and not checking with R.

Such questions may help the E and R relationship. They may also help E to obtain new insight into his leadership style. He would begin to see that he presented a picture of a conflicted leadership style. He wanted to be open, risk taking, etc., but he was closed with feelings, evaluations, and diagnoses, thereby not risking them with the relevant people. He asked people questions about their feelings and views, yet rarely expressed his own.

E agreed with the diagnosis and said that he was beginning to see his behavior in a new light. However, he continued that he would be glad to express his feelings *if* people would only ask. B asked what E did to invite questions, especially since he was the president. A commented that, if he understood Model II, the best way to invite such comments was to be candid and ask for feedback.

L then switched the focus to the here and now. He noted that he had told E that he had seen his actions as partly conforming to Model I and partly conforming to Model II. The latter confirmed partially what E had said and what he hoped others would say. L continued:

L: I heard a lot of responses from you on my view that disconfirmed your views. But I heard no comment on the fact that I confirmed much of your behavior. I said to myself, E did not give positive evaluations. He did not share those he had about R with R, nor have you given any to me, if you have any. Perhaps R feels the way I do, a little deprived.

A: That's true. Why did none of us pick that up?

B: It is not our tendency to compliment people on a good job.

F: It is a conscious struggle for me. Sometimes I feel as though it is manipulative.

G: Yes, but lately, I've gotten feedback that it makes sense. I give compliments only when I mean them, and it is coming through that way. It is working.

E said that he felt the consensus of the group that was most of his behavior was manipulative and that he appeared to be what C called internally conflicted. "Is that a correct reading?"

Yes, was the unamimous response.

E: Well, I have a lot of thinking to do. It (the case) is not as good as I first thought.

The session ended with an important learning for everyone. The group had begun by judging E's case as an example of Model II behavior. As a result of their discussions, they, including E, concluded that the behavior did not approximate Model II as much as they had thought. They began to realize that even the most advanced members had something to learn. As a result, several men reported that their difficulties became more legitimate. "If E has this trouble and can admit it, why shouldn't I?"

LEARNING TO DATE [1]

Before we continue the description of the third seminar, let us identify some of the learnings that the participants appeared to acquire from participating in the seminars to date.

[1] All of these conclusions have been found to exist in other learning environments designed for double-loop learning (Argyris and Schon, 1974).

1.   Human behavior, in general, and their behavior, in particular, is informed by theories of action. It is ironic that people rarely focus on understanding the factors that explain their behavior. People are apparently illiterate about their theories-in-use, yet are not aware of their illiteracy or its dangers.

2.   There tends to be a systematic blindness to inconsistencies within espoused theories and theories-in-use. There tends to be a systematic incongruity between espoused theories and theories-in-use.

3.   For the most part, each participant has been blind to his own incongruities. Others, however, were not blind to these difficulties. However, being programmed with Model I theories-in-use, they did not consider it helpful to inform others of their apparent blindness.

4.   The inconsistancies, incongruities, and blindness, coupled with the socially approved norm not to comment on them, are a major cause of miscommunication and misunderstanding. They are also a cause of ineffective group dynamics (within the learning environment) and intergroup and organizational dynamics (in their back-home organizations).

5.   To alter their behavior to be congruent with Model II will require changes in their governing variables, in their capacity to invent new forms of behavioral strategies, in their capacity to produce these forms in a noncontrived setting in such a way that they advocate or communicate what they intend *and* simultaneously encourage inquiry, public testing, and confrontation. Gimmicks and tricks will not be appropriate material to learn.

6.   People in general, and they in particular, hold many different espoused theories. Espoused theories vary among individuals and with the situation in which the same individuals may be imbedded.

This rich complexity of views seems to be lost when people produce their theories-in-use. The theories-in-use people hold do not seem to vary with individuals and with the same individual under different circumstances. The same may be said for (the equivalent of) the theories-in-use manifested by groups, intergroups, and organizations.

Individuals appear to create worlds in which uniqueness and difference are primarily at the espoused level. Sameness and conformity reign at the level of theory-in-use. Whenever the participants have designed, on their own, a contribution to the learning environment, they have produced the sameness and conformity described above.

7.   The participants have the capacity to facilitate and to inhibit learning. They are relatively effective at facilitating single-loop learning. They are highly ineffective at facilitating double-loop learning.

The fact that these participants have succeeded in creating and managing complex enterprises may have helped to hide from them the degree and extent to which they are central causal factors in the problems that confront them in everyday life.

8.   At this point, if the participants are left to learn from each other, the process, at best, would be inefficient (in human costs) and, at worst, detrimental (in that they would tend to·reinforce the very factors that should be unfrozen). The desire to behave according to Model II is necessary but not sufficient to learning Model II.

It cannot be overemphasized that the participants are, at this stage, "dangerous" to each other's learning even though their motivations are clean and their commitment is genuine.

9.   To be able to see that they are "carriers" of the very illnesses that they decry is an important step forward. This leads to a dilemma. During the early phases, increased awareness of one's own incompetence produces an increased sense of failure if one strives to invent and produce new behavior too early.

All of the participants held an unrealistically high level of aspiration about how fast they could learn. This acted to coerce them to premature inventions and productions which, in turn, produced more failure. During the early phase, it is important to develop a realistic level of aspiration. One way to begin to accomplish this is to connect a genuine sense of success with the development of an increased awareness of one's incompetence and one's holding of theories-in-use that produced many of the very problems that were decried and condemned.

10.   To move from Model I toward Model II, it is necessary to design a life that will become full of·dilemmas and paradoxes. It is important not to use Model I modes of dealing with these issues (deny the dilemmas and/or select one aspect of the paradox in order to dissolve it). A strong leader is one who can live with and learn from the dilemmas or paradoxes.

One way to learn these new skills is to watch the faculty deal with them and to practice them while dealing with problems of the seminar. For example, how do the faculty deal with the paradox that they believe in Model II yet consciously design learning environments that, at the outset, are congruent with Model I? Another example is how the faculty cope with the dilemma of advocating their views strongly yet encouraging inquiry.

As we shall now see, it was not easy, and the faculty were not always as effective as they aspired to be.

CHAPTER

$$\boxed{5}$$

BEGINNING TO INVENT AND TO PRODUCE WHILE DEEPENING DISCOVERY

The previous phase was concerned primarily with discovery of one's own theory-in-use and the meaning of Model II theories-in-use. The phase ended with the participants' realization that E's case did not represent a Model II theory-in-use. This realization also implied another: that the members could not identify a Model II theory-in-use. If they could not identify one, they could not invent one. If they could not invent one, two alternatives were possible. First, they could ask the faculty to invent one. Second, in order to win and not lose, they could deny the applicability of Model II. The second alternative seemed premature, because it might raise a question about the credibility of the participants' commitment to learning Model II, and more important, the participants were eager to see examples of Model II. They could always attack Model II after the faculty made their presentations.

We knew therefore that in the next phase the faculty would be asked to invent and produce Model II solutions. The strategy planned was twofold: first, to ask the participants to try to invent Model II solutions with the hope that their processes of invention could be slowed down and opened up for inquiry. This should lead to an examination of the barriers toward effective double-loop invention and production. Second, if this was not agreed on by the participants, the faculty were prepared to invent and produce samples of Model II behavior. The participants chose the first strategy. Before we describe what happened, let us identify the barriers against double-loop invention and production of Model II theories-in-use that might be surfaced.

BARRIERS TO EFFECTIVE DOUBLE-LOOP INVENTION AND PRODUCTION

The first barrier was the obvious one that participants programmed with Model I theories-in-use could not invent or produce Model II responses. The most they were capable of was the invention of behavioral strategies that were opposite those of Model I, or oscillating Model I.

The second barrier was the presidents' unawareness that they could not invent or produce that which they wished to invent or produce. They believed that if they learned and genuinely accepted a new concept, they could produce it. To realize that there is a gap between espousing an invention and inventing it would upset the presidents because it would create a barrier to progress of which they had been unaware. The tension would be compounded by the fact that the gap implied that they could not be masters of their own fate.

This realization would be especially disconcerting because the presidents knew that they had been quite successful at inventing and producing. Indeed, they produced complex organizations that many financial experts said could not be done. They were entrepreneurs who had started their own businesses against very difficult odds. Those who had inherited their organizations had changed them dramatically, again under difficult conditions because the organizations had been accustomed to "the old man." During their lifetimes, they had rarely faced the possibility that they could not achieve something to which they aspired. Finally, they perceived the source of their success to be themselves. It was their high degree of commitment, energy, hard work, competitiveness, compulsiveness, singlepurposedness, etc., that had led them to succeed (Argyris, 1973).

However, in the learning environment, things were beginning to be different. They were beginning to realize that they could be their own and each others' worst enemies. Everything they did (during the early stages) seemed to be incorrect and not helpful. In this environment, they began to represent the odds they had to beat. The presidents were creating a double bind for themselves. If they did not participate actively, they would not learn. If they did participate actively, they also would not learn.

To compound the problem, these presidents were not accustomed to double binds, especially ones that they created. Nor were they accustomed to surfacing a double bind. As in the case of dilemma, the admission of such feelings was seen as a weakness. Nor could they turn to the faculty for advice because that too would suggest a weakness.

One predictable reaction that leads to the third barrier would be that the presidents would begin to see Model II as unreal, romantic, impractical, or not much different from Model I. Such a reaction would create a new dilemma, because it was tantamount to questioning the faculty, which, in turn, ran the risk of raising interpersonal feelings, a consequence that violated Model I.

Again, the reaction could become a pivotal point in the learning process. For the first time the presidents would behave in ways that could produce emotional reactions on the part of the faculty. If such feelings did occur and if they were handled competently by the faculty, the participants would have the first living evidence that Model II could be useful.

It is important therefore that the faculty not interpret the attacks on Model II as valid personal attacks. The attacks were the most likely ways the presidents had to defend themselves. This admonition was easier to write or read than to follow. For example, one evening the writer became angry and punished E for behavior that he felt was unfair. As we shall see, the incident was discussed openly, and everyone learned.

By the way, whenever faculty became defensive, the participants invariably expressed astonishment. It is as if they said, "We did not expect *you* to become defensive." I have always wondered about the dynamics of the participants seeing the faculty as unflappable or rarely defensive. Several reasons come to mind. First, the faculty are less frequently defensive partly because they have been through these experiences before, and partly because the focus is primarily upon the participants. Another reason is that, if they can conceive of the faculty as strong and minimally upsettable, they can attack the faculty without fear that such attacks would upset them and cause them to violate their Model I governing variables. Finally, the participants may need to conceive of the faculty as steady as the Rock of Gibraltar or they would not entrust themselves to them in such a difficult learning environment.

Implicit in this reason is that strength is correlated with never becoming defensive. Strength could be correlated with the ability to learn from being defensive. But the latter scenario implies an ability to be accepting of one's defensiveness, an ability that these executives did not have. Or, if they did have it, their subordinates, who saw them in the same light that they (executives) saw the faculty, would not permit them to use such abilities.

The Leverage for Overcoming the Barriers

The forces for learning in this situation may be discovered by asking the question: why cannot the actors invent and produce Model II behavioral strategies if they wish to do so?

In the cases brought to the seminar (see pages 58–66) G and E included comments on the left-hand side of the page of feelings and views that they were experiencing but they chose not to express. For example, G reported such feelings as (1) "If (my vice presidents) were only doing what (they) are supposed to be doing . . . we wouldn't be in this problem." (2) "That's a real cop-out. You should know the profit picture by this time." (3) "Why blame the other guy?"

G questioned the competence and alertness of his management team. He believed that, unless he was "on top" of things, the company would not do well. The subordinates, in turn, complained that G supervised too closely and did not trust them. If we compare these statements with what G said, it is clear that G chose to hide his assumptions about the basic problems in the firm.

Why did G hide the assumptions? Model I predicts that the actors will hide information that may be threatening to others and to self. The preference is to suppress information that may produce emotionality and to express such problems in more "rational" and "task-oriented" ways. This is what G did. He focused on the budget figures and not on the mistrust (which, as the sessions continued, became the major problem, as evidenced by similar spotty performance by the vice presidents on other problems such as production, marketing, and purchasing). The vice presidents, programmed with Model I, did not confront the president with their feelings that he mistrusted them; they too were hiding important information.

Another aspect of this problem is related to the attributions G made about the members of his top management team. Model I programs actors to make these attributions covertly, to test them privately, and to act on them as if the test were not subject to distortion. An individual programmed with Model I would experience no problem in doing what G did. Indeed, it would be seen as "civilized" behavior.

A third cause for the actors not expressing their basic assumptions (if they would threaten others) is that they would feel vulnerable. If G surfaced his sense of mistrust, the vice presidents might feel that their superior went too far. They would expect that such issues would be discussed privately. If he violated this expectation, they could unite against the superior because he had publicly violated the governing variable of Model I. If they did not choose these reactions, but did not choose to fight back, G would be in difficulty because he was not skilled in coping with interpersonal conflict openly.

A fourth factor is that G would have to ask himself such questions as: Why do I tend to see my team as less committed and alert than I think they should be? Do I hire the wrong people? Do I coerce them to behave this way? Are my goals for them unrealistic? And, what is it about me that prevents me from asking these questions of the individuals who are affected by my hidden assumptions?

If we look at the four causes just enumerated, we find that G *is* able to conceive of his basic assumptions. G *is* worried about being unfair and upsetting others. G's subordinates *are* concerned about being unfair with him. Both sides *know* that they are not discussing the basic problem. It is an open secret, namely, a tacit collusion that both sides would not talk about the basic issue, would act as if they are talking about the basic issue, and would not surface the fact that they are playing the game.

These factors that inhibit effectiveness can also be the basis for change. The key is for the actors to come to see them as reasons for change and not for the maintenance of barriers. For example, if G felt that he should test publicly the basic assumptions with his team or if they felt the same about testing their basic assumptions, progress would begin. Thus we see that people create worlds in which they cannot invent and produce what they wish to invent and produce, yet they have the information necessary to do so and they are blind to this fact.

CONFRONTING THE FACULTY

The participants asked the faculty to show how they would behave in the case of E (which was the case they felt was close to Model II). The faculty agreed. C began by asking E certain questions that were designed to discover what E had been thinking before he interacted with R. C then attempted to identify explicitly the purposes and strategy that E had developed. Once this was made explicit, E was asked to confirm or disconfirm it. E confirmed it. C then inferred two dilemmas that were embedded in the purposes and strategies. E again confirmed these dilemmas.

C then stopped to ask whether given this new information, someone wished to try to role play a more Model II scenario for the case. Part of the reason C did not move toward doing this himself was the many cues some of the participants gave that they wanted to try out a new scenario based on the added knowledge.

Let us turn to the transcription to see what happened.

C (faculty member) asked if he could control the learning environment for a few minutes and, through questioning, see if a Model II approach to E's case could be designed. "Let's do everything in slow motion, so to speak, to think out loud every step of the way."

Agreed.

C: E, what was your goal in the case with R?

E: I wanted to persuade R to volunteer with enthusiasm. A reluctant volunteer would not work in that situation.

A: Why wouldn't a reluctant volunteer work?

E: I could have easily gotten him to volunteer by just hinting that is what I wanted him to do. He would have done it to please me. Enthusiasm was necessary to sustain him through a very difficult role.

C then thought out loud with the group:

1. E wants to influence R to take the job enthusiastically.
2. E wants to accomplish this without telling R that he wants an enthusiastic response from him.
3. Knowing what he wants R to do and keeping it secret are Model I behavioral strategies.
4. Yet E says he does not want to do it according to Model I, right?

E: Correct. If this job is to be done effectively, it requires internal commitment. I want him to be unconflicted about his choice. I want him to feel (if he takes the job) he really wants to do it.

C: As I see it, E is facing two dilemmas:

1. E wants R in the job, yet he cannot persuade or cajole him into the job because that would lead to an external commitment.
2. E wants R to be enthusiastic, but to say this openly could reduce the enthusiasm.

E: Correct.

C: OK. E has shown us in his case the strategy he used. Does anyone have another strategy that would be more congruent with Model II?

D said he had one. He began by saying that E should tell R exactly what was on his mind. C asked D to produce this in the form of directly observable data. D then role played the situation as if he were E talking to R.

D: (role playing E) R, we have a situation here that I'd like to discuss with you. You're probably familiar with some aspects of it, possibly not all the aspects. This project that we have is critical to our future.

C: Just go a little slower (writing on the board). One is, "I'd like to discuss project." Go ahead, keep going. "Project is critical."

D: Project is critical, and it's apparent to both of us that we've got a serious problem in terms of renting the space, which requires unusual ability on the part of the responsible individual, in terms of not only that it's a major project; there are racial considerations that are required. This requires an innovative approach, because we're not experienced in the firm at this kind of project, and the area is unique. Our time is extremely limited. We're having difficulty. It's your responsibility to find a manager, and you haven't been able to find a manager yet, which I'm not at all critical of. This is our situation now.

C: OK, fine (writing on the blackboard).

D: (continuing to role play E to R) In thinking this through from my point of view, it seems to me that one of the alternatives that we should consider is for you to handle the leasing role here, as I feel that there are significant advantages to your doing this. One, you're a member of the organization. You communicate well; you understand our objectives here probably much better than a manager we would hire to do this. Secondly, you're extremely competent; we work well together, and I have confidence, and other members of the organization have confidence, in you. I am not concerned about the cost. We would pay a lot less for a manager. The job is so important, and requires so much that's new and experimental in terms of what we're doing, that in terms of paying your salary instead of a lower amount for a manager, it doesn't concern me. It's certainly worthwhile.

C: Could I stop you, because I'm feeling overloaded with information.

D: Right.

A: If I were R, I would think that's a Model I approach.

C: Let's comment in terms of directly observable data.

A: OK, what I (as R) heard was, the very thing that E said that he didn't want to do, which is, "I've been asked to take this job, and I've been given the reasons: true, valid reasons, why I would need to take this job. And now, I will feel the very thing I heard E say he didn't want this guy to feel, which is, 'If I say no to this, I'm gonna let E down, and I don't want to do that'."

C: Let's get a range of reactions to this, OK? Anybody else have any other reactions?

G: I felt that was really a Model I behavior. Do you want to know why?

C: Well, let's keep trying to give D the directly observable data from which you made that . . .

G: Well, he was selling him. It wasn't a free choice.

A: I would say, the place where D got off on Model I was at the very top, when he used the word, this is a "critical" situation.

C: Critical project?

A: Yes, a critical project. That punched my button and said, we're back in Model I. OK. I react that D is saying to me, D is steering me, and the funnel is narrowing. I clearly hear him, by innuendo, saying, "Hey, I want you to take this job." I don't feel that I can get out of this. I feel I'm getting funneled into this. Ask me, how would I say that . . .

C: I'm having a little difficulty. What might be a way of getting at that?

B tried it, and he also used a "funnel" strategy only his was through questioning. He asked R questions, the answers to which B knew; he knew that R knew, and B expected the questioning would make R's choice for the job self-evident.

C: I must say that I feel now that I'm being led down the path where if I say, "It's either equal or more important," you'll say, "Well, R, why don't you then take it over?"

F: Jeez, C, I cannot conceive of a much better Model II thing than the way E handled it. He's saying, "We talked about priorities this morning, and I'd like to suggest that you pick out the most important areas of your activity, throw yourself into them and let me reassign the rest of your duties. What would you consider then?" So he's saying to the guy, "You tell me what your priorities are," and then the guy says, "I can't justify what should be done, I should just be running my part myself; we can't afford my salary in the manager's slot." So boy, he's set the priorities as "my part is the most important."

C: I'm considering how can we get into the point that he (R) takes all that initiative . . .

E: That would be hard for some facts that aren't clear. This guy draws $24,000 a year, and the budget that HUD gave us for that project is $12,000; and even with two or three thousand dollars, or four, I can see that we could stretch it, but I think it would be very hard to get anyone to say, "I'm worth $24,000 because that's what I'm being paid, and I'll do this for x months."

C: Well, OK. If you have that assumption, then you're saying to me that there is no way that he could make that choice by himself.

E: I thought he made the choice if I would take the financial constraints off.

C: I guess I'm asking, is there a way in which we could be both more open about what we want, and creating as much of an opportunity for him to take more responsibility.

B: Yeah, I'll give it a try. I think the last point there (pointing to the blackboard) and I can't quite read the words . . .

C: "Internal commitment to the job," and it should be, "fulfilling of his own needs."

B: Right. I guess at this point, if I felt that this was really an important thing, I think I would try to start talking about that.

C: And what would you say?

B responded in directly observable terms. The group concluded that this attempt also was coercive of R.

To review what has occurred so far, E believed his scenario was more Model II than I. All members but F disagreed. The faculty member then attempted to surface from E what he was trying to do. The objective was to see how consistent E's aims were and how congruent they were with Model II. For example, E's major purpose was to generate internal commitment "into" R for the new job. But internal commitment cannot be generated by an external person. E not only wanted to control the task, but he also wanted to define R's feelings about the task. These were Model I strategies.

D then attempted an invention that he produced in directly observable data. It too was rejected by the group. After a critique of D's strategy, B tried it and he too failed. The presidents were becoming tense and frustrated. They were experiencing the new and threatening feeling that they could not invent and produce that which they wanted to, even after a series of critiques. As these feelings became stronger, the faculty member felt that he was in a situation in which he had to produce (to show it was possible) and that the participants (who were quite competitive) would probably take a pessimistic view of his productions.

C started by pointing out that one consistent theme in all the productions had been the exclusion of the basic assumptions held by the actor about R (the equivalent to the material on the left-hand side of the page). C also asked the group to recall what E had said about how he had designed, in his mind, what he wanted to come out of the encounter.

C: Well, if I understood E, he wanted R to be resident manager. Because the job was stressful, he wanted a resident manager who was as unconflicted as possible toward the company, and a person who saw this job as central to his career. But E was also concerned that he would not get that if he required R to be there. E is in a bind. Right?

A and E: Right.

Then, said C, one approach would be to say to R: "I'm in a bind, and I'd like to talk to you about it. On the one hand, I would like you to be resident manager of so and so, for these and these reasons. But I'm also aware that if you're in any way coerced into this, we have the following consequences."

C stopped and the first reactions to an example of a Model II approach began to develop. All the speakers felt that C's approach was coercive and Model I. Several felt that the original strategy by E was less Model I. The strongest confrontation came from E, whose case C had evaluated as incongruent with Model II.

E: Can I be R? And you just said that to me? I'd say, "Well, gee, E, if you'd like to have me do that, I'll drop everything and start tomorrow."

C: (continuing role playing with E) What you're saying to me is, the way to resolve my dilemma is for you to accept an order for me.

E: Sure, I think that's clean Model I, right straight down the line.

G: I think—I'm going back to where F was a few minutes ago—that E's approach was better than that.

E: That's what I think.

C: Well, let's go one at a time. What's Model I about it? (C open to confrontation and asking for directly observable data.)

E: Because you clearly conveyed to me that that's what you'd like to have happen.

C: Right.

E: And I'm going to be a good, loyal part of this organization, and I'm going to say, if that's what you'd like, C, I'm going to do it.

C: And what was my reaction to that? (C strives again to get more directly observable data about how E experienced C's behavior.)

E: Then I think you'd desperately try to find out whether I was really being loyal or whether I was . . .

C: No, I wasn't feeling desperate. I said, "I don't want that." You're not resolving my . . . (C disagreed and attempted to respond with directly observable data as to why he disagreed with E.)

E: OK. You didn't say that. Let's go on then.

C: I said, "That isn't resolving my conflict. What you're telling me is (speaking again to E who had just played R) that I leveled with you about my dilemma, and your response is to salute me. I don't feel that's the way to resolve my dilemma. That puts me in a situation where I am coercing you, something that I do not want to do."

E: (continues role playing R) OK. I know that you're sincere in saying these things. But I don't think as an organization we have any other alternatives. I'm here. I don't understand the project. I think the project is terribly important, and with this information I should do it.

C: Are you saying to me that, as far as you can tell, my approach leaves you no other alternative but for you to salute?

Later

C: And if you also feel it's difficult to be open with R because he might salute you, and you don't want a salute, then that's the valid information I would mention to R.

E: And you'd come right out and say that?

C: Sure.

E: (E pauses for a moment and continues with a new confrontation.) I have another piece of information. I want you to take this job, and I think you're the guy to do it. But on the other hand, I don't want to coerce you. . .

C: That isn't what I said . . . (cut off)

F: That isn't what he said. He said, "I'd like to take this job," but as I understand the process, what he's saying is, there are valid reasons for his taking the job. He wants to say that outright, because he feels that way. If the guy says right away, "I salute," then he challenges the guy. He's on a very firm ground there, I can understand that, because he's saying, "Hey, did I coerce you? Because if I did, that wasn't the name of the game."

E continued to press C in ways that the latter felt were distorting his position. C felt condemned for behavior that he did not manifest. Finally, C reacted angrily.

C: Look, E, R isn't a little baby. I don't have to hold his hand, and to tell him by some nice, nondirective questioning (speaking disparagingly of E's approach) what's valid information. R is a big boy. R will tell you, if you (E) are willing to be a big boy and to say what you mean, and to make it clear that you are not going to let him seduce you through saluting. I see E as almost telling me that R is so weak that the only way I'll get valid information from him is to hide my sincere feelings and by rather skillful nondirected questioning, discover his views.

L intervened to confront his co-worker with the unsurfaced meanings in the statement above. In doing so, he not only helped C but he also provided an opportunity for the group to see how the faculty strove to confront each other and to learn from their errors.

L: C, can I ask, when you start using phrases like, "Big boy, little boy," what are your feelings?

C: I'm saying, you know, I can see the enormous control and the lack of respect he has for R and other subordinates. What E is saying to me is that all subordinates are weak and subservient.

L: I'm attributing a feeling of annoyance for something at E.

C: Anger.

L: Anger at E, but I didn't hear that expressed, and that's what I'm trying to
    . . . for E to have this guy set priorities. Are you saying that by E asking him
    to set priorities, that's kind of babying him, which in a way is manipulative?
    Also, that E should test publicly if R is that "weak"?

C: Yes, I would strive to provide a role model, and to see if the other person
    will follow that role model. My role model toward R was to be open and gen-
    uine. E's role model was to have R salute. The moment he did that, I
    wouldn't accept it.

F: I hear you saying that in our case, and I'm not singling out E to be the only
    one, we lay out a thing, and it becomes a kind of purloined pact. You're say-
    ing that we should be candid and lay out the alternatives as we see them, and
    let the guy confront them. The resulting discussion should produce alterna-
    tives to which he is internally committed. I mean, I can't conceive of having
    to sit there straining over, "Gee, did that word manipulate the guy or didn't
    it?" I'm much more comfortable with what you did, because it's truly open.
    If the guy salutes, I can say, "Hey, wait a minute, are you saluting because
    it's me?" And if he doesn't salute, I can say, "Look, I was giving you my open
    thoughts; let's talk this thing through."

C: If I were feeling (toward R) the hostility that I felt toward E (playing R) then
    I'd also feel free to say, "Now I'm feeling a sense of anger. I'm open. I talk
    about the conflict and the paradox, and the only thing I get is the very be-
    havior that I fear." So I let him know, as a subordinate, how I feel about this.
    Now you might go and say to me, "Hey, but uh. . ."

F: I really am ambivalent, because as a subordinate, a subordinate would say,
    "I know what you're driving at, but you want me to arrive at it by a different
    route." The more I think about it, the more that I feel it makes a lot of sense.

E: I hear what you're saying, but I don't know how that helps the solution. If
    we live in a Model I world, and people are going to respond to us in a Model
    I way. . .

F: Part of what I heard C do was that he said, "Look, here's where I am, I have
    a dilemma." And this is one of the things that I want to keep reinforcing.
    The first thing he said was that "I have a problem."

A then said to the group that the discussion had provided him with several here-and-now learnings. One was that the faculty can become
defensive. Second, it made sense to surface each other's defenses and attempt to work them through. Third, he concluded that no one had to be
or could be perfect. The key was to be able to learn.

F agreed and noted that he had felt somewhat surprised that the faculty member had become so defensive. "I then realized that I was not
perceiving him as human, a person with limits and tolerances. Then, and
this is what hit me, how often I get upset back home because my people
expect me to be perfect."

A paused to review the previous episode. After C discussed openly the causes of his anger toward E, F intervened to repeat back to C what he (F) understood to be his position. After having it confirmed, F pointed out the positive aspects of C's invention. A agreed with F, and F publicly stated that C's suggestions began to make sense. Others began to provide further reasons for the usefulness of what C had said. E then wondered out loud, that, even if they accepted the usefulness of this approach, would those outside this seminar be equally receptive? This is a crucial question, because the presidents will some day face this issue if they attempt to use their learning in the back-home setting. The answer is that Model I people will resist Model II behavioral strategies exactly as E and others had done in the seminar. The objective is *not* to design interventions that will reduce all resistance (which is not possible) but to encourage the expression of the resistance because it provides the basis for eventual internalization of the new ideas. Individuals cannot become internally committed to new ideas unless they have an opportunity to work through their disagreements.

This was true for the presidents. They too needed to work through these issues at their own pace. As we see below, E and F began to accept the new view and to act as interpreters of Model II to B. In doing so, they may have acted to reinforce or increase their internal commitment to the applicability of Model II.

B: You're not ringing true to me. Let me say why you're not ringing true. Just as you may be coercing a guy, no guy's going to volunteer that much unless he's a first-class idiot; no guy who thinks things through at all as any kind of a manager, when he puts it that much on the line, "C, I hear you, and I want the job."

C: There are two mistrusts being expressed now. Don't trust R, never trust R, and never trust C. Don't believe C about this business of being in a double bind, he's really doing this as a gimmick; it's a smooth, suave technique to get R; and I'm saying, under those conditions if your fundamental approach is that no party can be trusted, then I think you're right; then that's the issue we ought to work on.

E: That's the Model I world that we live in. The Model II world is, if I were to say to C, "C, I understand you have a dilemma and you'd like me to take this job, but I'd really like to talk through what the implications of this job are." I'm still not trustful in a Model I world, and I ain't about to say, "Hey, buster, you got the job filled" unless I genuinely want that job. I'm going to do a lot of searching, which gives C the opportunity to say, "Look, I don't want you to take this, just to solve my dilemma. I only want this if you see clearly that it's the kind of thing you want to do."

C: And I think I would add, in addition to that, "R, I'm open with you that I'm

enthusiastic about this possibility, so I need your help to keep track of something. If you sense at any time that I'm in effect trying to nail you into it, let
me know. Because I genuinely don't want it under those conditions."

F: You come back and review it at any time. You say, "OK, I'm really enthusiastic about this, but if it really isn't challenging, as you just suggested, I can
come back and we can talk about it." Then I feel very comfortable about
having accepted that assignment. There's a provisional acceptance. Only it
turns out to be as exciting as we both think it might be.

B: OK, but the guy that I heard E describe, with the loyalty that I think this
guy feels toward E, as I heard E describe it, I wonder whether he can feel
the way F just described.

C: What is the loyalty that you heard?

B: That E said, "That if I ask him to take this job, there's no question he
would." The basis of E's dilemma is, "I just don't know to coerce him, I want
him to come up and volunteer. How can I get him to volunteer? Because the
moment I let him know that I'd like for him to take the job he'll take it."

C: All right, let's look at that. What I hear you saying is, E's relationship with R
is such that E cannot be honest with his feelings at the outset. Perhaps E has
created such loyalty. Now, if that's true, and if I were E, I would begin with
that as an issue.

For example, "One of the fears that I have is the kind of loyalty I have
helped to generate in this company; it's a loyalty in which people salute if
they, in fact, deeply believe I want it. I think I have done that, if what you're
saying is true. I don't want to do that anymore. I realize saying that doesn't
change me overnight, but it's a genuine attempt to tell you that I want to
start changing and I'd like to start doing it in this interaction, here and
now."

The presidents began to see the validity of the approach that C and L
represented. They also began to realize that the approach would not be
easy to implement. The hour was late, and they asked if they could continue the discussion in the morning. We all agreed to stop.

CONFRONTING EACH OTHER

The second discussion surfaced some genuine fears the presidents had
about how their subordinates would react if they were to behave according to Model II. These fears included that the subordinates (1) would
not believe the presidents, (2) would resist taking initiative, (3) would
tend to seek what they thought the presidents wanted and do it. Such
fears also implied that they saw the subordinates as people who could
not be trusted to be candid (if the presidents were candid and asked for
others to be the same).

The episode began, during the next morning, when the discussion returned to E's case. Some still felt that, since E's style was asking R questions, he was being nondirective. Wasn't being nondirective congruent with Model II?

The faculty responded that asking questions is not necessarily a sign of Model II behavior. Model II encouraged advocacy with inquiry. The problem with E was that he had attempted to mute what he was advocating. It was not congruent with Model II for the president to withhold his feelings and views. This meant that the model the president was using was that the person who had power must hide some of his goals and purposes for fear the subordinates would be forced to agree with them. Under these conditions, the president was telling R that an organizational problem existed (R's new job), but that the president had no personal problem (which was not true, since he did not feel free to tell the subordinate his views because he feared the subordinate might "simply salute"). Thus the president was modeling a theory-in-use that informed others that (1) he must withhold information, (2) he must keep the fact secret, and (3) he must act as if he were not withholding information. Assume that subordinates learned that this was their president's theory-in-use. This may lead to their trying to figure out what information the president might be withholding before they committed themselves. Such behavior may be seen by the president as the subordinate trying "to feel him out" (which would be true). This inference may also be seen by the president as evidence that subordinates were seeking to salute him (which was now a self-fulfilling prophecy).

To compound the problem, the subordinate may internalize the president's model when he is in a relationship in which he had power over others (e.g., with his subordinates). Also, the subordinates of the president may spend time trying to generate intelligence about the state of mind of the president by talking with others within the organization. Thus valuable time could be spent in trying to generate information that the president, if he used a different model, could give to the subordinate easily and quickly. Finally, the people the subordinate was questioning regarding the president may sense this to be the case and may wonder why they were selected, which places them in a (temporary) power relationship which, in turn, could lead them to withhold certain data.

The analysis made sense to the presidents, including E. However, he had this difficulty:

E: My strategy is to ask for their feelings, so that they're free to ask me mine. I just don't see how that ties their hands. If I am concerned about their feelings and their positions, I would think that would help them to be concerned about mine.

The group helped E to see that his strategy would not tie the hands of his subordinates *if* he were candid about his strategy. If he asked subordinates only questions about their views, and if (as he said was the case) he felt that subordinates would not confront him, why should asking them about their views and feelings be seen by them as an invitation to examine the president's views and feelings?

C suggested that if E expressed his views about not controlling R's response, this would be something to say and to work through with R.

C: For example: "I have some views (on the subject) but hesitate to give them because I believe that they may inhibit you (R). I realize that is an untested attribution about you and I would like to test it out. I would like to cite some examples in our relationship which has led me to build up this attribution of you. (He then gives examples with directly observable data.)

F: Hey, that sounds like a Model II opener.

G: Yes, you are saying what you believe, trying to give the evidence, and asking for it to be tested.

B doubted that this would work. He role played what he described as a disbelieving subordinate and added, "You know, we have plenty of those sons-of-bitches."

B: I can see a subordinate saying, "Look boss, I'm not that kind of a guy who will salute you. I will give you an independent point of view, not because you may want to hear it, but because that is the kind of guy I am."

C agreed that this was a legitimate possibility. His response would be designed from the following thoughts:

1. I think that subordinate(s) will salute me.
2. S assures me that this is not the case.
3. I have now a new and prior problem. Am I distorting the motivation of my subordinates? I should test it out. I will give him directly observable data, the incidents that led me to my attributions and obtain his response.

F then said that he was beginning to understand, and with the understanding came the conclusion that it would take a long time for him to be effective in terms of Model II. He also began to see that it might be easier to experiment with the new behavior with some vice-presidents than with others.

G agreed and also said that he was beginning to try to specify the situations in which he would be able to try out Model II types of behavior. He realized that Model II behavior was especially useful when valid information, informed choice, and internal commitment were paramount in the decision-making process. He simply felt that he would not try this out in all decisions.

The group began to develop a contingency theory for transition, delineating the people and conditions under which they felt freest to experiment and to learn. They also raised the point that one way to speed the transition was to increase the number of people who could become resources for their learning. This meant that the subordinates would soon have to be invited into the learning process. As we shall see, such action has been taken.

CONFRONTING F ABOUT HIS BEHAVIOR IN THE SEMINAR

The first two episodes consisted primarily of the participants confronting the faculty about the usefulness of Model II. Because the issues were discussed openly and because this, in turn, led the presidents to reduce their resistance, the presidents also experienced a here-and-now sample of how an adherence to Model II behavioral strategies can work under difficult confrontations.

Such a discussion raised the ante of openness and increased the sense of trust among all the participants and the faculty. One result of "attacking" and beginning to work through feelings about power people (in this case the faculty) was that the participants began to explore the relevance of their learning to each other. In our terms, the participants were beginning to generalize their learning to other settings, namely, to each other. This reaction is found frequently. As we shall see, whenever the presidents' back-home interventions were confronted by their subordinates, it was inevitably followed by the subordinates' confronting themselves about the same issues.

The events that appeared to bring on the third episode were embedded in the first two. As they looked back on the first two, the presidents were impressed with how competitive they were toward the faculty and that the faculty were also capable of becoming competitive. This led them to discuss their competitiveness toward each other.

In the first sessions the presidents recalled that they talked about their competitiveness with a sense of pride and bravado.

Boy, did we give it to you today.
Of course I compete with F; I've competed with that lovable bastard for years.
I hate to lose; I hate to look lousy; to be at the end of the line—any line.

Now the presidents began to dig deeper for other meanings that competitiveness had in their lives. In one such discussion, E began to describe how he dealt competitively with others (outside the seminar).

E: Knowing F, I would say that he consciously strives to excite others with his own ideas. He describes his ideas with apparent expectation of approval.

F: I would not have used the same words. I have a habit of trying to excite other people with my own ideas; that's clear. And OK, I do it with apparent expectation of approval. I want people to sit around me and say, "OK, F, I agree with you." But I think I'm open to confrontation. I want to hear their views; it is just that I have a well-developed selling technique, but I am open to my ideas being disconfirmed.

A: I don't know if I can buy that.

C: Are you saying that he is closed to disconfirmation?

A: Yes. I buy that F excites with ideas; he describes with apparent expectation of approval, I buy that. But I don't buy the idea that he is open to confrontation. (Then gave several examples to illustrate his view.)

F: OK. I can see your point. The second example really hit home. I guess one thing now is that I would like to change my behavior so that it is clear to the other person that I am open to disconfirmation. (Several group members nod approvingly.) I've got to learn to pick up the signals when I am selling. I want to encourage others to challenge me. I guess the only way I can do that is let them know that I want it and I may not show it.

L gave several examples of another related quality of competitiveness. He illustrated that F had expressed enthusiasm for a concept (during the previous seminar). During this conference, he expressed a different concept that showed that he had changed his beliefs. He expressed the new concept with enthusiasm and with little invitation for disconfirmation.

L: And what I am inferring is that F does learn, but he learns privately. There is a lot of thinking that goes on in F but it is private.

F agreed and gave several examples during this seminar in which he experimented with listening more and asking questions that might help the other person to explore his ideas. Several members confirmed that they recalled that behavior. One of the recipients admitted that he was surprised by F's question and was sure that F was doing it "to set me up. I remember feeling—what a cagey guy—now what the hell is he up to?"

F laughed and commented that this illustrated how he could be misunderstood. C reminded him that the group members had a long history with F selling and not listening. C suggested that this incident illustrated why it may be important for people who were experimenting with new behavior to say that they were experimenting. If F (or anyone else) stated that he was experimenting, that may lead others to give feedback. All the members agreed. A then laughed and said:

> You know I agree with your suggestion C, but I wonder how long it will be before we do it. I know my inclination is to look good. I practice my behavior privately then I want to hit them with it and watch their faces!

E agreed but said that such an attitude meant that they would be trying out new behavior with the same old values, namely, *win*—don't lose, and with the same old behavioral strategies, namely, control others. This produced an interesting discussion of the feelings that some members had about announcing that they were experimenting with new behavior and asking for feedback. Somehow that rubbed them the wrong way. "I'd feel stupid to ask for help." One reason for feeling uncomfortable was that they knew that others were not aware of such ideas as Model I and Model II. Again the issue was raised about the education of their colleagues.

A second reason described by the group members was that they had viewed asking for help as a sign of weakness. Some of their subordinates did so. The second possibility worried them more than the first because the subordinates would probably not be candid about their feelings.

L then commented that he felt that F was very selective of who he tried to learn from. L noted, for example, that F frequently asked questions of C but not of others. B agreed and asked, "Does that turn off other people who F doesn't think are experts?" (Several nodded affirmatively.)

A: F, let me add another fact. I think you are very bright; probably one of the brightest guys in our group. Because of your brightness, you make it difficult for me to confront you.

Several members agreed immediately. C asked A and others to consider a reformulation of their views. "F, given my reaction to very bright people, I am unable to confront you," or "I have difficulty in confronting people who I see as bright and articulate." These statements make the problem a joint one. F may have changes to make, but why should it be in his brightness? Also, what changes might A, B, G, and others consider so that they are not so intimidated by brightness?

A: OK. That's a good point. How can I blame *my* inability to confront him on his intelligence?

G: When we do this we also push F's button because he values his brightness.

B: This doesn't mean that F might not change his competitiveness.

C commented that intelligence and brightness are human assets. It is the way F uses them *and* the way others feel about these qualities that are alterable. F might explore how to use the intelligence in a less controlling manner. A, B, and G might explore what was it about intelligence that they found intimidating.

A agreed, laughed, and noted, "It is this goddamned competitiveness again! I know I want to see anyone who is bright toppled a bit. But when it happens sometimes I am surprised and feel let down."

F: All this is very helpful to me. I realize that those people who may have superior intelligence have to be careful how they use it. Other people are very sensitive.

C: I have the same problem in this group. When I became angry at E the other night, several of you were surprised *and* pleased.

A: Yes, that is true. When I just said surprised and let down, I was thinking of you the other night. Your getting defensive is so rare that it is easy to remember.

B: There is always the tendency to topple the leader up there, the golden leader up there, the guy who can't make mistakes.

C: Yes, I feel that sometimes in this group and in other groups.

A: Yes, but there is another side to this. I felt good when you (C) became defensive. I felt good that even you can make errors. Then I realized how foolish it was that I needed your failure to increase my self-confidence.

A's comment led the group members to explore new dimensions related to competitiveness. For example, when they returned to their organizations were they not the "golden leaders"? Did they feel that others were out to topple them? If so, were these issues discussable? "If not," added someone, "maybe it is because we have a bunch of yes men."

One member said:

> *If we think either that others were out to topple us or that if they were not, then we had not much respect for them.*

"Agreed," said another, "and to make things worse, this low respect might be a factor that made it necessary for us to come into a meeting with 'impeccable logic,' or 'with all the answers' and all these other qualities of ours that we have discussed."

> *I can see that we have a long way to go.*
> *Yes, but the road is becoming a little clearer.*

ADDITIONAL LEARNINGS

The reader has seen the many multilevel learning processes that occurred. These processes are connected in ways that are still unclear to us. Much research must be done to make more explicit how one level of learning can create another.

But, as we have seen, progress is not only forward movement in that new problems are discovered. Progress also occurs when individuals return to old problems either to reexamine them for new meanings, to design new inventions, or to attempt new productions. Progress therefore is not linear. It appears to involve many iterations that create loops whose movements are forward and backward.

Thus the learnings about inconsistencies within espoused theories and theories-in-use, as well as the incongruities between the espoused theory and theory-in-use, continued to occur in this new phase in which the emphasis on invention and production increased. The conclusion that genuine learning requires the alteration of basic values (governing variables) as well as alterations of behavioral strategies was also illustrated repeatedly. Rather than repeat the learning identified previously (pp. 47–48), I should like to add the following additional ones:

11. The participants have difficulty in inventing and producing what they wish to invent and produce.

12. The invention and production of Model II behavior is not simply a matter of practice. It is a matter of changing one's espoused theory and theories-in-use.

13. The time perspective of the participants has become longer. Group members are now beginning to see five years and more as the time period required for themselves. A few have wondered if it makes sense to think of a time period because they will be learning for the rest of their lives.

14. The participants find that they have a capacity to produce meanings about which they are unaware as well as to produce meanings that are precisely those they deliberately set out not to produce.

15. The participants tend to keep private the thought processes that occur while they are inventing and producing. Any inferences, attributions, or evaluations that they may make during these processes, they either do not test or test privately. Both these strategies greatly increase the probabilities that they produce self-sealing activities.

16. Others receive the meanings that the actor produces (whether he intends them or not) and produce their own meanings. Others therefore attribute meanings to the actor of which the actor may be unaware.

17. The participants are accustomed to designing responses quickly

and without much consciously deliberate thought. One characteristic of an adult is the ability to collapse the discovery, invention, and production phases into one. This acquired skill that has been a basis for confidence in one's self is an inhibiting factor for new double-loop learning. First, it creates an unrealistic level of aspiration. The participants feel a sense of failure when they are unable to produce responses quickly and effectively. Second, it inhibits the participants from deliberately slowing down the design processes and making more explicit what goes on during the discovery, invention, and production phases.

18.   As they become increasingly aware of the scope of the change required to become effective along Model II lines, the participants begin to wonder if those in a Model I world will accept the implications of Model II. They tend, in other words, to place part of the cause of their resistance to Model II on how others would resist it.

19.   Resisting Model II openly can be an effective basis on which to overcome resistance. The faculty encouraged confrontation of their own views and attempted to respond concretely to the criticisms made by the participants. They saw all the criticism (with one exception in C's case) as legitimate, and believed that the criticisms should be worked through openly because some day the presidents would face similar criticisms from their subordinates.

20.   The participants learned that Model II was not equivalent to nondirective approach. Model II requires high advocacy with high inquiry. To label Model II as nondirective or "passive" is a distortion that may be invented in order to reject Model II.

The purpose for rejecting Model II, as we shall see, is deeper than what is involved in the rejection of a model. A more important purpose for rejecting Model II is related to a discovery, not yet made, that learning Model II requires the participants to surface questions and fears they thought they would not have.

CHAPTER

$$\boxed{6}$$

INVENTION-PRODUCTION RELATED TO THE BACK-HOME SETTING

The final phase of seminar 3 was to help the participants construct maps of their respective theories-in-use and to generate a few realistic experiments to be carried out in the back-home setting.

Such maps are conceptual representations of theories of action. Consequently, one way to accomplish this task was to ask each participant to develop his own theory-in-use. Each president used the maps of Model I and Model II as a basis for developing his theories-in-use. The participants were asked to identify their governing variables, their behavioral strategies, and the consequences of these on others, on learning, and on their effectiveness. They were also asked to illustrate every entry with concrete examples.

The participants were told that they would have an opportunity to present their models to the entire group for confirmation or disconfirmation. Also, the group could help them in designing their back-home experiments.

The participants took the exercise very seriously. They were concerned about whether they could do a good job by themselves. Had they developed enough expertise to develop a valid model? The faculty suggested that each president might list some of the questions that bothered him in trying to develop his model. The faculty members would try to answer the questions and would, of course, be available for individual consultation. As the hesitation continued, one of the presidents broke the log jam by asking if the cause of the discomfort might not be the old issue of competitiveness. They did not want to look bad in front of each other and the faculty. Four agreed that this was a factor; two did not. However, the comment did seem to create the impetus for all to agree to try out the exercise.

The presidents became very involved in developing the models of their theories-in-use. They could be seen working in their rooms; some reported taking walks to think more clearly; some met with faculty and fellow presidents to raise questions; and all, interestingly enough, found time to ask each other how well they were doing. (Competitiveness is difficult to alter.)

Perhaps the most important indication of how seriously the exercise was taken was the long and thoughtful group discussions held on each model. No discussion was finished within the two-hour allotted time. Many of the men continued the discussions "after hours" and between sessions.

Because of space limitations, all the theories-in-use cannot be included. Three have been selected. One is E's theory-in-use. E, the reader may recall, had presented a case that many felt had illustrated Model II behavior. B represented a relatively high degree of mistrust of the applicability of Model II. F was an individual who focused on intellectual analysis, who believed genuinely that he did have Model II experiences with a few of his top people, but whose beliefs were doubted by the other members.

E'S THEORY-IN-USE

A. *Governing variables*
   1. People are more important than things.
   2. Company is treated as a proprietorship and used as a conscious vehicle to pursue social objectives.
   3. Hide feelings that may give others equal control and influence.
   4. Very high levels of aspiration for individual and organizational effectiveness.
B. *Behavioral strategies*
   1. I develop high control over the high risk decisions, most of which happen to be mine.

2. I withhold telling others how risky decisions may be (for I fear they might not consider them).
3. I retain control over corporate policies.
4. I screen all my strategies unilaterally for the impact upon people. (I describe or hide strategies depending upon what I believe their impact may be on others. I also hide this fact.)
5. I conceal personal feelings except when asked. I can become open at the initiation of others (not by myself).
6. I seek information from others by asking nondirective questions (because I do not trust answers given to me by direct questions).
7. I monitor the behavior of others continually and excessively.
8. Flexible in positions that do not threaten the governing variables.

C. *Consequences on self and environment*
1. Associates are used primarily as information producers. They are rarely used as providers of feedback to me.
2. Associates become dependents.
    a. Every key issue is thought of and controlled by me.
    b. They seek cues to feel out my positions.
    c. They continually check to reaffirm my strategies (everybody seems to be monitoring).
3. Associates hesitate and resist probing important areas that they believe I am concealing.
4. Dissent on major risky issues, by subordinates, is difficult.
5. I am seen as uncompromising about my personal goals (which are listed here as the governing variables).
6. I am blind to people's rights when they interfere in reaching corporate objectives.

D. *Consequences on learning*
1. Associates give very little help to me on risky issues.
2. Little double-loop learning.
3. High on self-sealing.
4. There is public testing of others' job satisfaction. Low public testing of self and others' personal feelings as well as basic company policies (the latter are closely tied to my personal feelings).
5. Nondirective questions become covertly directive.

B'S THEORY-IN-USE

A. *Governing variables*
1. Win, don't lose.
2. Maximize the intellectual aspects and minimize emotional
3. Maximize positive feelings and evaluations. Hide negative feelings and evaluations.
4. Define my goals and achieve them as I define them.

B. *Behavioral strategies*

1. Avoid confrontations on business and interpersonal issues if they could surface negative feelings.
2. When others resist my views, manipulate them more to get them to agree with me.
3. My behavior vacillates from dominance to withdrawal. (I dominate when I want to control and withdraw when there is little need for me to control or where feelings are becoming strong.)
4. Sell people my views and include in the selling saying dishonest things (if I think that this will win them over).
5. I am a perfectionist. I set very high standards.
6. I withhold ideas and feelings (until I think they will be accepted).
7. I reject people that I do not value (but I do it diplomatically; i.e., I suppress negative feelings and lie about rejection).
8. Continually categorize people and ideas.
9. "Selling" conclusions without directly observable data.
10. High attribution and evaluation.

C. *Consequences on self and others*

1. Others withdraw from taking initiative.
2. Others see me as defensive and manipulating, but they hide these views.
3. Others become cautious and try to psyche me out before they act.
4. Mutual mistrust (because we talk about candidness but neither of us is candid).
5. Dependence on me for the major decisions.
6. Low internal commitment to the major decisions (since they are my decisions).
7. Distorted communication.
8. Rivalry and intergroup conflict.
9. Does not invite feedback which could level peaks and valleys of enthusiasm.
10. Indiscriminately receptive but covertly discriminating.
11. Anger toward others.
12. Withdrawal by others.
13. The development of an "inner" and "outer" group.

D. *Consequences on learning*

1. Defensive processes are self-sealing.
2. Others withhold valid information when they don't believe that I want to hear it. (They also keep this fact secret.)
3. Public testing of only those issues that I consider important.
4. Private testing of issues that involve emotional components.

F'S THEORY-IN-USE

A. *Governing variables*

1. Achieve purposes as I perceive them.
2. Value innovation highly.
3. Value professionalism very highly.
4. High on intellectual issues; low on emotional issues.
5. Win—never lose.

B. *Behavioral strategies*

1. High competitiveness to win (keep selling, be enthusiastic, listen to others in order to win them over and change their minds).
2. Structure all situations in a way that positions myself to win.
3. I design the environment and manage it.
4. Share ideas as a way of achieving interpersonal consequences.
5. Controls through teaching.
6. High level of aspiration for effective problem solving.

C. *Consequences on self and others*

1. Has willingness to share other people's problems. OK when I am controlling others or when others need me.
2. Discomfort with confirmation of my own innovation.
3. Low invitation to others to describe their enthusiasm.
4. Excites others with own ideas—describes them with the apparent expectation of approval; is open to confirmation and not open to disconfirmation.
5. Others do not know what and when to believe.
6. Difficult for others to know when I have been reached.
7. Dependency on me for key issue.
8. High double-loop learning on technical issues (constrained by those technical issues that are threatening to me).
9. No double-loop learning on self and interpersonal issues.

Space does not permit us to include the discussions of each theory-in-use. We would see, for example, that E began to explore why he was in conflict about being open with his feelings. Why did he feel that raising questions about other people's feelings would help them to raise questions about his feelings, especially when he gave no such clues? Also, if he believed that people were more important than things, why did he maintain high control over the key goals of the organization? If he trusted people as much as he espoused, why did he retain such high control over company policy?

B began to realize that he appeared to others as frightened to discuss issues that could surface interpersonal and intergroup conflict, yet B's organization was full of highly competitive individuals, with a substantial degree of departmental competition and mistrust. What impact was this having upon his subordinates? For example, could not a department hide its difficulties because being candid could lead to emotionality? Or, could not a department that believed it was losing on an issue polarize the situation and create intergroup conflict? They could predict that B would have to handle the issue and do so privately and in a way that might be a compromise; therefore they might not lose as much.

B also became aware that he was beginning to be perceived as the member who most mistrusted the applicability of Model II. However, B also felt that he valued Model II and showed, through his behavior, that he was one of the members who was capable of learning Model II very quickly. How could one mistrust a model that he could learn quickly and value highly?

One possible answer was that Model II recommended that feelings be expressed, that difficult issues be confronted, and that interpersonal and intergroup conflict be worked through (not swept under the rug). Yet these were some of the conditions that made B uncomfortable. One way to deal with this was to believe that the subordinates would mistrust his attempts at Model II behavior, that they would see such behavior as a new and more subtle manipulation, a consequence that was concerning him. In other words, B began to see that as long as he mistrusted Model II or perceived that others would see it unfavorably, it made little sense to use it, even though he had the skills to learn quickly. (B, one should add, took steps to begin to confront interpersonal and intergroup issues more effectively.) Also, B's mistrust of the applicability was very functional for the group. He was able to express doubts that the other presidents had but were hesitant to express. Moreover, B was able to role play these doubts effectively. Consequently, he provided excellent material with which to explore important issues.

None of these theories-in-use represent final statements. The presidents are continually enlarging them and modifying them. They represent a map of some very difficult terrain, a map that the presidents report unanimously that they find very helpful in thinking about their impact upon others and in designing new behavior.

The last phase of seminar 3 was for each member to develop specific back-home plans and to present them to the entire group for discussion. These plans represented each president's view of the experimenting that he wished to explore in his organization. Two of these discussions are presented below.

B'S BACK-HOME PLAN

B had now become more aware of the extent to which he controlled the key decisions within his firm. One of his specific plans was to try to reduce the degree of unilateral control that he exhibited over crucial meetings. Before B came to the conference he had scheduled and defined the agenda for an important meeting to be held on his return. Now he wanted to throw away the agenda and develop one with the help of the top group (with whom the meeting was to be held).

B: How do I do this? What do I say to them when I begin the meeting? Should I even begin the meeting? If I don't, won't they wonder?

C suggested that B be candid and say to the group that he learned something about the way he managed meetings during this week. He could say, continued C, that the normal pattern was for him to control the meeting. Perhaps they had other alternatives that they wished to suggest. Maybe, questioned A, he could just start off with some new alternative without saying that it is something new. "But won't they sense it?" asked someone. "Of course they will—that's the point. Why then make a big deal of it?"

These questions are typical of the dilemma faced by people who are interested in trying to experiment with Model II behavior in a Model I world. On one hand, they want to try out new behavior and expand their learning. On the other hand, such experiments on their part are rare, and the people in the back-home environment could become confused by or mistrustful of the new behavior.

If the presidents were to behave consistently with Model II, the first step would be to surface the dilemma with the people about whom they were feeling the dilemma. Also, they would have to say that they realized that discussing dilemmas was a novel approach and could be misunderstood. Finally, they would have to include the fact that (1) they were concerned because they are not fully competent to do this well, (2) therefore they needed feedback especially when they do not seem to be behaving according to their espoused theory, and (3) they realized that such requests might not be believed or not found credible.

None of these alternatives was compatible with concepts of "strong leadership" held by the presidents and their subordinates. Thus the presidents were trying new behavior that did not fit the values of their subordinates and that was still questioned by the presidents. Surfacing dilemmas is based on the assumption that learning is as important as advocacy, that advocacy is most effective when there is confrontation and learning, that effective advocacy generates the most enduring internal commitment to decisions made.

D: I think B has to say something more than that he is going to try something different. He has to explain why the different approach and ask for their reactions.

F: Some will disbelieve, they will be careful.

E: Fine, all this will take a while.. It is not necessarily bad that they will be careful.

B: In order to be comfortable with this, I have to learn to be above the table and honest. I don't think that I can walk into that meeting without making some reference to this conference. I won't be honest and I would start off on the wrong foot.

L: How did G's suggestion of being candid strike you?

B: Fine, I can be honest about this. The problem I now have is that I think the group will be on their guard and thinking, "What is he up to now; what's going on; maybe I'll let someone else talk."

A: Are you saying that they might see it as a new form of manipulation?

B: Yes.

E then pointed out that all the presidents will have these fears and doubts when they go back home. "I don't know how whatever I do (when I go back home) could be met with more skepticism than C was met with the first night here."

The group members realized that, since they had been in continuous session for five days and they were still skeptical about the applicability of Model II, there was no reason to expect the subordinates not to be skeptical. In fact, suggested E, we should encourage these feelings on the part of whoever is doubtful *and* encourage their expressing them. That is how they and we will learn. "Remember," added another president, "C and L encouraged us to express our doubts about Model II. It resulted in the reduction of our doubts."

E: I don't know why we should go home and expect instant success. It is a Model I world out there, and it is going to be a long time, in spite of our best efforts.

A: Yes, and some of our best efforts aren't yet so good.

E: Correct, we have much to learn.

B then asked if he could try role playing how he might behave back home. "I'd like to try this again and you can really shoot me down." Note his request for a Model I evaluation, as if he were preparing himself for a loss. Note also that, unlike previous meetings, B naturally tried out new behavior instead of simply espousing what he might do. This was a major change that occurred almost imperceptibly among all the members. They were no longer satisfied with general statements. This contrasts with the first meeting, at which they resisted describing their ideas with directly observable data.

B then said, as if talking to the executive group at home:

B: You received the agenda that I sent out several weeks ago. I have had an opportunity to think about it quite a bit and frankly, I am not comfortable with it. This has resulted from some experiences that I had while I was gone last week. The reason that I don't like it is that it is pretty cut and dried and does not give you full opportunity to get your views and feelings on the table. Therefore, I would like to have us talk about it and maybe develop a different agenda. I would be perfectly comfortable if you developed it and I was just a participant. If you want me to assume more leadership, that's fine too.

Two members responded that they felt good about the first part but not the material that came after the "therefore." They found that material restricted them more than it helped them to unfreeze. Two others agreed, but two others did not agree. They did not find the second part restrictive. A commented, "I was ready to talk until the 'therefore,' then I wondered what the hell you wanted me to say." "So," responded B, "I could have stopped at that point." Several agreed. E commented when B said, "If you want me to take the leadership" that he felt some subordinates might see that as an invitation to let B run the meeting.

B then said that he had one further question before his time was up. He wondered to what degree he should withhold some of his concerns. "For instance, I'd question seriously that anyone will talk about power issues, yet they are critical."

E: Well, why not raise them yourself?
C: Yes, Model II does not mean that one should be nondirective. Say what you believe but do so in ways that invite confrontation. The invitation may not be believed for a while because of the history you have developed within your company.

"But," asked B, "what if someone agrees that it is a power issue and adds 'Yes, boss, as long as I control it, we'll do a better job'?"

"Then," responded C, "his statement can also be tested and confronted. How does he know this? What directly observable data can he suggest to illustrate his views? How do others react to these examples?"

G'S BACK-HOME PLANS

G began his discussion by mentioning that, about a year ago, he hired a key executive who he had hoped to groom for the presidency of the company. Unfortunately, his performance was so bad that they had to fire him several months ago. Younger people were promoted from within, and they were doing a very good job. During a meeting, one of the younger executives asked G if he had thought of hiring an executive vice-president who would report to him. G responded that he thought it was a good idea and promised to take the initiative in exploring candidates. Several weeks later the younger executives told G that they now had doubts about their suggestion.

G: I have two problems; first, when I return I must sit down with the fellows and find out why they had second thoughts. I've been thinking how I would do this and believe that I would tell them that I have a dilemma. On the one hand, we need a new man to be an executive vice-president. If we bring such a man in from the outside it could be seen by you and others as a vote of no confidence. So, I would stop there and see what happens.

Second is the new man whom we may hire. He could become the new chief operating officer. I thought that we would go through all the usual search procedures. When we have come down to the final one or two candidates I would like to sit down with each one and say, 'Here is the kind of guy I am' and see their reaction. I want to find out if he feels he can work with someone like me.

C: What might you say about yourself?

G: I tend to be a guy who wants to do it all by myself. I tend not to listen. I tend to be insensitive to feelings, etc.

C: Are you saying that these qualities are unchangeable?

G: No, not at all. But I have to level with the guy. I want to change my behavior, but it is not going to be easy. *And* I will need some guys who are going to level with me.

B wondered if the candidate really wanted the job, he might not lie and say to G what he thought G wanted to hear. L pointed out that if the candidate were programmed to tell the president what he wanted to hear, if the president didn't level with him, then the candidate would have to guess. At least with G's strategy the candidate would have more valid information. Moreover, added A, "I think we can tell somewhat when these guys are handing us a line."

Several of the presidents felt that G's proposal for an open discussion with the candidate was dangerous because it could put off the candidate. "Moreover," added B, "how does the candidate know that G is attempting to live in a Model II world?" G responded that he was not, as yet, living in a Model II world. "I'm saying that I live in a Model I world but that I want to change and to learn. And I will need his help."

E then pointed out that the group had approved A, B, E, and F returning to their companies and trying to create some Model II relationships with their immediate subordinates. The same people were apparently resisting the proposal that G do it with an outsider. "Is our logic," he questioned, "that G should be more candid *after* he hires the individual?" "And," he added, "let me say I've been sitting here boiling. Before this session I would not have raised the question the way I just did. I would have said something like, goddamit, we haven't learned anything this week!"

Several presidents responded that they were not against the idea. They simply felt that it was too risky to do with the final candidates. G was not adequately skilled. It might be best to try this out with the semi-finalists. F agreed but reminded the group that the best way to interview any candidate is to be as open as possible. "The more open we are, the higher the probability of getting valid information. If the guy is new, he will never forget the first interview and the fact that the president strove to be candid and open. I think this is the way to start."

B then laughed, shook his head, and remarked how mistrustful all of them were about the probable negative reactions of people to Model II behavior. "And I'm as mistrustful as anyone, if not more so." Yet he continued that he had just hired a new young executive who worked for a firm much larger and more powerful. When B asked the candidate why he was interested in a smaller company, the candidate responded that he was tired of working in an organization in which the top people fought each other, lied to each other, and in which he might become a pawn in a power struggle. B then asked him what evidence he had that it would be different in this firm. The candidate responded that he had done some research and found out that B was willing to look at and change his behavior.

C then asked G if he had considered asking the younger executives about their views of an executive vice-president. G could involve his top team in diagnosing if and when they needed an executive vice-president. G said that he wanted to do something like that but was concerned because he doubted if the men presently there were capable of being the president. Although he realized this was inconsistent with Model II, he simply did not feel he wanted to say that to the men.

C responded that there is nothing in Model II that says that one must communicate something he is anxious about. What Model II does ask is that the president test publicly, with the people involved, the views that he has about them. A added that as president he had an obligation to keep his top people informed of his evaluation of them. C recommended that G consider being candid if he were willing to have his evaluations confronted and tested. If he were not willing, then any kind of candidness would be a facade. G decided that this made sense to him and that he would think it over seriously.

ADDITIONAL LEARNING

21.   The participants learned that it was possible to develop a model of their theories-in-use that they could use to organize their learning, to store their learning, and to begin to invent new behavioral strategies. As they thought about producing them in the back-home situation, they began to become aware of doubts and fears that were part of their theories-in-use that they did not include when preparing them.

22.   The participants developed a clearer view of how deeply they felt they would be mistrusted by their subordinates if they stated openly that they wanted to experiment with Model II interventions *and* that they felt unsure and lacked confidence in their ability to produce effectively the behavior they intended.

23.   The participants became aware that they were uncomfortable about owning up to their sense of incompetence regarding producing Model II behavior. They preferred "instant effectiveness" along with "complete trust." Why should they set such an unrealistically high level of operation regarding their performance and why should they require complete trust?

24.   In the presidents' view, a strong president was one who was competent, manifested few, if any, insecurities, did not strive to learn in front of others; in short, a person who minimized personal vulnerability.

25.   But how did they know that describing reality to their subordinates would make themselves more vulnerable? The facts were that these fears had never been tested publicly. The presidents concluded that they tended to mistrust the motives of their subordinates. They saw their subordinates as ready to embarrass them, and/or expecting them to be "strong," and/or mistrusting any genuine attempt by the presidents to alter their behavior toward Model II.

26.   The presidents learned that they held (untested) deeply pessimistic views about changing human behavior, especially about their subordinates' encouraging change in their (presidents') behavior. Once these views were made explicit, the presidents realized that it raised a

whole host of questions about the quality of the relationships at the top that could not be ignored.

Nevertheless, they all committed themselves to some public experimentation and a reporting back when they met again in four months.

Four months later, seminar 4 was held. It began with the presidents' reports on their experimentations in their back-home settings. Each had invented and produced a different set of experiments. Most of them felt that the results were mixed. They reported that they did not behave as effectively and consistently Model II as they had wished. However, they also reported that subordinates tended to react much more positively than they had predicted. Since detailed descriptions of back-home experimentation will be presented in Chapters 9, 10, and 12, we summarize the early experiments in the form of reports given by several of the presidents to each other.

E and D represent examples of people reporting that they began to learn about themselves in their back-home setting. E apparently generated the learning by trying to be a more effective observer of his and others' behavior. D, on the other hand, utilized his group to obtain feedback. He told them what he thought he had begun to learn about himself and asked for their confirmation and disconfirmation.

A, on the other hand, reported that he was still having trouble detecting whether his subordinates were leveling with him or not. He asked for the other members' experiences on this matter. They, in turn, said that they might be of more help if they could hear an actual case and react to it. When A gave such a case, it led to an interesting discussion of the problem of advocating one's position without being unilaterally controlling. F reported a case with X in which he behaved in ways that the group interpreted as Model I, a conclusion that F had apparently not reached. B reported that his major discoveries were related to his own ambivalence and his credibility with his subordinates.

Interestingly, the competitiveness among the presidents while they were reporting on their back-home experiments was beginning to be reduced. When E appeared to have advanced more than others, instead of A trying to compete with E, he admitted that he had not been as successful. B focused on his ambivalence, A on his increasing awareness of how much people may not be as candid with him as he had thought. All these actions would not have been produced earlier because they might have been interpreted by the members as signs of weakness.

E began by noting that he left the previous session with five specific strategies in mind. They were derived from his theory-in-use and selected because, "I felt they had the greatest probability of being changed in a constructive way." Looking back and focusing on the present E believes:

> *I think that I've had pretty good success with some of the five elements (but I still have many more to go) and less success with others. I used to think the task of changing required some minor adjustments because I had already made quite a few adjustments. I'm no longer convinced that is true.*

E described, in detail, a meeting he had with the top group of his company that was, in his view highly successful because he threw away the old, unilaterally defined, efficiently honed agenda and involved the entire group in developing the agenda.

E then specified the five behavioral strategies on which he had focused. For example:

1. *I strove not to retain or withhold my definition of the situation, or my fears, as far as projects in which we were engaged. I've learned, I believe, to be more of an advocate without being controlling.*

    I could be kidding myself because the others may be role playing, but I do not think so (gives several concrete actions that had never occurred before).

2. *I realized that I was open only with the people that I respected and admired. I have spent time recently in becoming genuinely more acquainted with subordinates who affect my life whom I didn't respect. In some cases, I found that they sensed the lack of respect, which made them up tight when they talked to me, which made them less effective, which confirmed, for me, that they were not very bright.*

3. *I found that people had concerns about our projects that they were not surfacing because of the corporation's preoccupation with my directions.*

    I am still prominent in setting overall corporate goals, indeed, now it's more open and unconflicted. This seems to have encouraged more confrontation of my ideas and more developing by others of their ideas.

4. *I had a friend say to me, and intended it as a compliment, although I thought it was rather devastating, "E, you're the most completely logical person I have ever known. I can't imagine you're doing anything that wasn't carefully thought out, analyzed, turned up."*

    He was correct. Everything had to be thought through. Everything was rational. Now I realize that I simply denied emotion as a proper and constructive force. Other people could "lose their heads" but not I.

    I think I now recognize more of my emotions; I am more accepting of them, so I am more accepting of others' emotions.

A reported an incident in which the top management group attempted to decide what to do about a particular division that was in financial difficulties. A felt that the discussion had been more open than if he had not attended the seminars. The other presidents responded that they had no way of confirming or disconfirming that assessment. However, by reading parts of the transcript that they received, they were able to point out episodes of straight Model I behavior on the part of A, and episodes that began to show movement toward Model II.

B reported that the most accurate description of the results of his initial and very small experimentation was ambivalence. He said:

> I have become much more aware of how controlling I was. Basically, the question is, how can I advocate a position without controlling the situation? Sometimes I wonder if I am still manipulative but only more covert than overt.
>
> Some of my people are wondering, you have an opinion and you are not stating it; you are not being honest. And that is the fundamental thrust of my frustration. Yes, I do have an opinion but if I say it will I impose control? I don't know which elements are easier and more difficult for me. I'll just have to experiment.
>
> I have also begun to see that my executive committee is made up of subgroups. Some are more open than others.
>
> I expressed to them that I intended to experiment; that I would like to be confronted; that I would strive to ask for disconfirmation; that I probably would not ask for it effectively because I wasn't very good at it yet.
>
> Another thing that I have concluded is that the individual should establish his purposes (as closely as possible) but invite disconfirmation of them; then, I at least, am freer to advocate.
>
> I've done this in the last month, and I've gotten very positive reactions from the people reporting to me.
>
> I still have a long way to go. I am trying to behave according to Model II in the budgetary process, and that is difficult. But, I'm saying it, and so far, from most I've gotten a positive response.
>
> I still have troubles with C. I still think that I am more in the stage of oscillating Model I with him than Model II. (Then D described a successful dialogue with C.)

After D described some of the misunderstandings between himself and C, B commented:

B: We are all wrestling with the fact that our behaviors set certain standards for the company. We have to become conscious of these standards.

E: Yes, there is a constant danger that, by our behavior, we give the wrong message; for example, as to what is good performance.

D: And that we must involve the others in defining good performance.

An intense discussion developed regarding the behavior of the president. Did he have to behave the way he did? Why did the subordinates set such budgets in the first place?

E: I think that we may be missing something that's fundamental. It is a Model I
      world out there, and that's the kind of behavior it respects.
          I think what X got was a round of applause for being a Vince Lombardi.
      We have a Vince Lombardi cult in this country, and I think it is unhealthy.

"That's the key to the problem," added G. "How do we retain the respect
of our culture when we do not use the uniform of the culture?" The
question hit home for most of the presidents. They felt the quandary.
On one hand, they were expected to be Vince Lombardi, and on the
other hand, if they behaved according to Model II, they would be seen as
Mr. Milktoast. But, as we have seen, Mr. Milktoast or Mr. Withdraw are
behaving according to the opposite of Model I, *not* according to Model
II.

The presidents were beginning to make experimentation part of their
leadership style. The experiments were being conducted under real life
conditions and involved central issues rather than peripheral ones. The
risks were substantial but so were the pay offs, because most of the learning was at the double-loop level.

Providing directly observable data was becoming part of their
theories-in-use. This had profound effects on the presidents as human
information creators and communicators. Knowing that they would be
asked to describe complex situations with directly observable data meant
that they had to become more accurate observers of reality. Also, they
would be requested to describe more of the complexity of reality, and
they would be permitted to get away with fewer generalized, incomplete
descriptions.

Communicating with directly observable data meant that they could be
more easily confronted about their meanings as well as be required to be
more precise in defining the concepts that they used. Finally, they have
been, and will increasingly find themselves being, confronted about their
inference processes from data to concepts.

It was developments such as these that affected the quality of the contributions during the seminar. No longer were the contributions glowing
(especially about self) and condemnatory (especially about others). The
descriptions were full of statements that limited the generalizability of
what they said they were learning, that invited confrontation of the validity of their statements, that acknowledged that they may be receiving
distorted feedback, and that pointed out that they were just beginning to
learn.

There was an increase in the presidents' seeking to learn more about
their personal responsibility and their personal causation in different situations. They no longer took the position that the causes of most of their

problems lay outside of themselves. This did not mean that they blamed themselves fully for all problems. It meant that they wanted to see their responsibility as well as the responsibility of others more clearly and accurately.

As a result, the presidents saw their respective top management teams more clearly. Several reported that they had begun to see that their teams were composed of different subgroups or coalitions. The coalitions appeared to vary with the nature of the problem. Also, several presidents who had doubts about the quality of their teams had, in the past, kept that evaluation secret and publicly made such comments as "I am very proud of this fine team." They were not only curbing this kind of deception, but they were realizing that it fooled no one (since their theories-in-use did not jibe with these glowing abstract statements) and, indeed, might have harmed the teams' ability to confront difficult issues.

These learnings surfaced the dilemmas of power. Some of the presidents wondered how they could advocate without controlling. Some thought that the way to solve the problem was to withdraw. However, they realized that this was a Model I response because it denied them the opportunity for advocacy and inquiry. Part of their problem was to learn to advocate and inquire more effectively. Another important part of the problem was related to the expectations that the subordinates had toward people in power. These issues would have to be faced and, as we shall see, they were faced in later experiments.

There is another, perhaps more insidious, weakness in the strategy of withdrawal. It creates anxieties and ambivalences within the president that could result in his becoming less effective. For example, B admitted that he was withholding some very important valid information from certain subordinates. He felt conflicted, unsure; he felt that he was playing games with his subordinates; moreover, he believed that his subordinates also felt that he was playing games.

A noted that if B's subordinates sensed that B was withdrawing they would know that this was new behavior on his part; they might wonder if this were a new fad; they might predict that B would be having a difficult time with the new behavior. B also wondered about these issues. He too questioned if his new behavior was not a fad; he was having a very difficult time in behaving as unconflictedly and effectively as he wished. B realized that if he were to follow Model II, he would surface these issues with his subordinates. To date, B has not chosen to express his dilemma because he does not have a relationship with his subordinates in which he feels free to express the dilemma.

A deeper dilemma of power has surfaced, and is expanded in later sections. It is the realization by the participants that, since their concept of a strong president was one who advocated and controlled, they found the Model II concept of advocacy and inquiry as "weak." Part of the problem was that, since the presidents did not know how to be skillfull in advocacy combined with inquiry, they had experimented, as mentioned above, with withdrawal. This would be a "weak" leadership strategy for several reasons. First, the subordinates did not tend to trust it. Second, it was a "weak" strategy in the sense that it appeared that the president had no opinion. Third, if the president did have an opinion, the strategy was a punishing one to the subordinates because, for the first time, the deception was indirectly surfaced, by the president, implying that the way to get their ideas was to withhold his initially. This meant that he did not trust their strength to be candid.

Finally, we have also seen the surfacing of the presidents' genuine question about the role of the presidency under more Model II conditions. What would they do if they did not advocate and control? As they explored these questions, they also unearthed another doubt, namely, whether subordinates wanted to or were capable of taking the initiatives that would be required under Model II conditions. These doubts, as we shall see, formed the basis for further inquiry and experimentation.

CHAPTER

7

INVENTING AND PRODUCING MORE DIFFICULT INTERVENTIONS: THE GROUP BECOMES MORE OF A RESOURCE

The members began seminar 4 with a discussion of some of the back-home problems they were experiencing in attempting to apply Model II in their back-home settings. They soon realized that, to problem solve effectively about these back-home problems, they had to resolve some here-and-now issues that existed among themselves. In this chapter, two examples are presented of how the group attempted to help its members. The first is a problem A had with a senior executive in the back-home situation. How could he confront his subordinate constructively when the issue was important yet full of potential for embarassment, rejection, and anger? The second example is a similar problem, but it dealt with a particular member of the learning group.

CASE 1. A told the group that he had the following problem. Mr. Z is a senior officer in his company and in a key position. Several years ago, A was thinking of Mr. Z as a possible replacement for him. Lately, however, he has had second thoughts about Z. Nevertheless, he still thought very highly of Z.

The other day, an informant whom A trusted told him that he had heard Mr. Z was seeking another position. A was concerned. He did not want to lose Z, or, if Z felt that he had to leave, A wanted adequate time for the transition process.

"As I see the situation," A stated, "(1) I could confront him. (2) I could ignore it and start looking for his replacement and solve the problem on my own terms. (3) I could try to develop some data without revealing that key point."

A said that he wanted help on how to find out how Z feels about the company and about A. He wanted to find out if he (A) was a cause of Z's apparent dissatisfaction.

A: I think whatever the problems, it is partially caused by my behavior. Also I have to find out whether he intends to stay. If so, is he still presidential timber?

C: How can you find the answers to these questions?

A: Well, I'm caught. I'd like to be open with him. But I am uncomfortable about doing so. On the other hand, if I act that I do not know, that too is phony.

A then said that he would like to role play what he might say to Z. He began by asking Z about the disposition of certain large orders and Z's views on certain organizational problems. A's strategy was "to work slowly into the problem," lest Z become upset.

C asked A to try the role play given with the assumption that Z was relatively secure and confident. Given this assumption, A developed a more candid yet constructive dialogue.

A: I would start off right away and say, "I have heard (Z) that you may be unhappy here; that you see conflict in the organization and you are looking to get out. If this is true, it may be too late for me to change it; if it isn't too late, how can we get some of these things on the table?

C asked A what it was about the present situation that discouraged A from saying the above. A responded that he was worried that Z might "try to give me a snow job." The group then helped A to understand what existed in his relationship with Z that would lead A to have those fears. After several role-playing episodes, it became apparent to A that he was worried about Z giving him a "snow job" because he was not sure that he could cope with it effectively. A was helped to invent and produce appropriate behavior by role playing how he (A) would respond. Finally, as the result of the role playing, A realized that another fear was that, if he did not deal with the situation effectively, Z might become angry and leave, thereby creating a gap in the management of the company. Again, he was helped to invent strategies and given the opportunity to produce behavior to deal with the problem effectively. A sample of the product is:

A: If you are going to stay, then I feel good about that. So there is no issue here except maybe finding ways to work together more effectively. If you're going to leave, then (and it's a decision you have already made), I can accept that. In fact, if you're going to leave I can perhaps help you find something else, give you a good recommendation for what's appropriate. And the *quid pro quo* only has to be that we do it on a basis where I know what your intentions are and you know what mine are. If you do want to leave, and feel a necessity to leave, fine; I accept that. I'm not angry. I think you should do what you can to further your career, but let's do it on a basis that gets us prepared for your leaving and let's help you get the best possible. . .

F: I cannot see any other way of doing it but that. Any other way you're going to get killed, and to me that's the absolute only way. It's the only way you can pull off, also, A, because you're honest about it.

A: I hear you, and I guess I have to agree with that. Certainly the way I would be most comfortable would be that. I've tried that system with another V.P. and could never get any honesty out of the guy. Maybe I shouldn't relate that experience to this one.

E: Let's assume you didn't get honesty from this guy. So what? You're still in a better position; you still can evaluate more clearly whether he is going to leave or isn't.

A: You know, I've confronted this guy several times. The problem that I have is if he says, "I'm going to leave," I have a terrible problem running the company with a guy in a key job who's a lame duck.

Let us pause for a moment and note that A began a discussion about himself, and without any prompting he began by first focusing on his personal responsibility for the problem with Z. Next, he attempted to be as realistic as he could about Z's responsibilities in the situation. Unlike his early behavior, A invited confrontation of his views. Whenever A expressed doubts about Z, he included directly observable data, which made it easier for others to confront his diagnosis. The degree of competitiveness on the part of A and others continued to remain lower than in the early seminars.

B then said that he would like to role play Z. Consistent with his basic themes in all of the previous sessions, B role played Z, behaving in ways that B would find difficult if he were faced with a similar situation. This helped B to test the limits of the validity of a Model II approach; it also helped others to do the same.

The next morning A stated that he had been thinking about the learning from the previous night. He asked if he could take some time to try out once more an attempt to deal with Z. The group agreed.

A: Z, I know we have a meeting set up this morning to go over some loose ends from last week, but before we get to that I've got something I'd like to discuss with you. A few days ago I got some feedback from someone who was at a party who supposedly is reliable—I'm not much on rumors, but this one sounded like it had something to it, and I'd like to tell you what I heard. Let's see if we can discuss it. The story went something like, Z is very unhappy at our company. There's a lot of antagonism between him and me; conflict in the company; and he's become generally detached from the business. He's looking to leave, and go someplace where he can have a more secure future. I just wonder if in fact you are looking for a job, and if you are, whether you think it would be worthwhile for us to discuss it?

Obviously I don't know whether this is true, and if I thought it was just loose talk I would brush it off. I'm not brushing it off. When you joined our company six years ago, I had great hopes for your future. In the first year, I think it went along very well. You learned our business rapidly. People seemed to relate well to you. You were a good leader. In this period of time, we've gotten going in Alaska, which you started, developed some good managers, and have some pretty good results. To tell you the truth, if the story is true, I'm disturbed to find that you're thinking about leaving. Also, I know that if that's true, at least part of that situation has to be as a result of our relationship and my part of that relationship. If in fact your decision is not irrevocable, I'd like to see if there's anything we can do about improving our relationship, and specifically do you think there are some ways that I can improve my behavior vis-a-vis you?

D: I think that's sensational.

F: Yes.

C: Are you planning to talk with Z?

A: Oh, yes.

B raised another important and potentially embarrassing issue. A responded to it, which, in turn, led B to raise even more embarrassing questions. A did not hesitate to reply. The reader is asked to keep in mind that A had no idea what B was going to ask until he did so. A appears to have begun to invent and produce responses that approximate Model II, and to do so under on-line conditions when B played the role of a smooth but mistrustful and perhaps lying subordinate. A had never done this before, and he reported that he could not have done it without the learning experiences that he was having.

B: Suppose Z hasn't looked for another job at all?

C: Why don't you role play? Be Z.

B as Z: A, you know, what you're telling me, I'm kind of shocked at this, because you know I'm not that happy, and there are some problems, and I'd love the opportunity for us to surface those, but the farthest thing from my mind is to look for another job. Now, I'm a little bit concerned whether maybe this is your way of putting an idea in my mind that you have somebody else in mind, and just in case I'm not very happy, then you'd like to ease me out, but you don't feel very comfortable about doing this. I'm a little concerned whether I'm getting some kind of a message here from you, because really it isn't all honeymoon, but in any kind of business. . .

A: Well, to tell you the truth, Z, I thought about whether or not I should confront you with this. I visualize you as a mature manager. Not much loose talk gets out of your mouth, at least that I've been able to observe, but the source was, I thought, quite reliable. Then I began to try to see if I could confirm it, whether it was a logical story in my mind, and I thought back just a few months ago to the conversation we had about your taking on some additional responsibilities in the company, and my impression of that conversation was that I left the next move up to you and these months have gone by and nothing has happened. Then I thought about a few other things. (Lists other cues.) If in fact it isn't true, well, fine, then we can go to work on some of these points, and maybe you've got some you'd like to put on the table, and we'll have some constructive meaning from it. If it is true, I really think it would be best for you to come clean with it, and I'd like to encourage you to do that; if you've decided that you want to leave, and you haven't got the job lined up yet, I'd like to see what I can do to help you, and I'd like to see how you can help me to get your job structured into the company so that it would do the least damage to our company.

B as Z: I'm sure glad you said that, because there is something on my mind. This has bothered me, and I'm so glad you gave me this opportunity, because I kind of felt that half a year ago or so you waved this executive vice-presidency at me. I really didn't think you meant it, and it really hurt me, because you know, that's really what I want, and you just said to me . . . after all, I didn't bring it up—I can't make myself executive V.P., only you can, and you didn't follow through. I've been hurt by this, and I suppose that . . . I'm not the kind of guy that deals in rumors, and so on. I'm kind of surprised that you're saying what you've heard about this party or that party, and that kind of bothers me. So if you want to get into it, I really feel that I could be executive V.P.

A: Well, to tell you the truth, Z, if you recall the conversation that we had about the position of executive V.P., and I do, at least my recollection of it, I said that I had one problem with that job, and that is that in order for the job to be done successfully, I have to really feel secure that the incumbent there is going to follow through all loose ends and do all the follow-up work that I now feel responsible to do. I'm talking about the total, day-to-day, week-to-week operation. I think I expressed my feeling that that was something that you and I had been having some difficulty on; there had been a lot of loose ends. I felt uncomfortable with the loose ends. I've tried to express that to you. I thought you had all the potential to have the job; that you weren't ready for it. That's why I was hoping you'd come back and say, "Listen to how I plan to handle this follow-up."

B as Z: I really need the job now, and I think I've proven myself in these years just by the example of the marketing V.P. And now I hear you say, "Well, maybe in 18 months, etc . . ." That's my problem. This is where my dissatisfaction is—I want to become executive V.P. right now.

F: This guy is giving me a heart attack; he's breaking me up.

A: F, you're not helping me learn.

F: I'm sorry.

B as Z: I'd like to meet this issue and work it out with you. And I think we ought to talk about specifics. I think we ought to set up a time frame. I'm thinking right now, and you're thinking 18 months or maybe a year. Maybe we can compromise this out, you know, set a date in 3 months with this announcement made.

A: Let me respond to that by saying I don't think that we have enough of the data on the table to decide how much time it should take. Why don't we set up a meeting, or even start right now on the open items between us. You make a list of the things that you think you should accomplish, and when they should be, before you get the job—if there's nothing on the list, OK. If there is something on the list, you develop a time frame for it. I'll make a list of the things that I think you should accomplish, and we'll go over the lists, and when we've come to agreement about what a reasonable time frame is for that, I think you'll be satisfied with the time frame we set, and if you beat it, I'll be delighted to have you in the job sooner.

B continued the role-playing by asking and later almost demanding that now was the time for him to be given the new assignment. "The time is right now; either I am, or I ain't."

A: Well, I'll tell you the truth, Z, if you put it to me that way, you ain't. Because I've got to feel comfortable when you get into the job. I think it's my responsibility as president of the company, and in dealing with myself, to be comfortable when you're in the job. I'm not saying that you haven't done a good job. What I am saying is that there are some things that I think are still very important that haven't been done.

Both men received warm praise from the group: B, for his role playing of a cagy and persistent individual; A, for his own on-line response to some very difficult pressure. A felt that he did quite well and was going into the meeting with Z with a deeper sense of confidence in his abilities to cope with it effectively.

CASE 2.   F had become an increasingly difficult problem for the group. On one hand, he was very bright, and he was able to conceptualize issues quickly and effectively. F was also competitive, and he used these skills to "win" in front of his colleagues. Moreover, F maintained that he had learned Model II and he had developed such a relationship with a new president that he had selected for one of his companies.

On the other hand, the group kept experiencing F as suppressing his feelings, as remaining at the abstract level, and as distancing himself from learning by producing very little directly observable data about himself. His descriptions of the back-home problem rarely included scenarios. The tapes that he submitted were recordings of meetings in which he played a minimal role.

During one day of the seminar, F made several glowing statements about the degree of Model II relationships that X and he had developed since the previous seminar. The members responded that they could not comment usefully in the absence of directly observable data. F responded by nodding his head understandingly and continuing the abstract description.

L raised the issue to the surface by saying:

L: (As we were discussing our back-home experience) I felt the credibility issue with F rise again, especially with A and B.
A: You're right about me. I found F's description diffuse. He spoke mostly about X. I wanted to learn more about F. Can't you give us examples about what you have done?
F: Maybe you're right.
B: Sometimes you sound more like an adviser to the group; you're not one of us having difficulties.
E: I don't sense he is an adviser. But, I agree we're not learning very much about his learning.

A: You (F) haven't put yourself on the line, so far, in this meeting.

F: But, I think my position *is* different. I'm now chairman of the board and don't have day-to-day operational problems. I think I'd be kidding you if I said that everything is going beautiful for me. I guess I'm saying that I've been very comfortable the last three or four months with Model II behavior. I'm astounded by how well it is working. But I also say that I don't have (the operational pressures that you do.)

It is interesting to compare this dialogue with the examples presented from the earlier seminars of how people attempted to give each other help while they were limited to the presenter's perception and had no directly observable data. If the group members had not begun to change, their behavior toward F would have been, as one president said, "To tell you, you're full of shit, and to get into a long-winded argument about whether or not you're experiencing Model II."

F agreed and said that he would like to present a case. He asked for time to write a scenario of a meeting with X on a very important subject. The next morning F presented his case. It was almost completely in scenario form and he was a central figure in the case.

X, who is president of one of the companies F owns, asked F to meet with him to discuss an important issue. X was beginning to have doubts about a new product that he had approved. The doubts stunned F, because X has "impeccable logic and positions" and never approved anything until he was completely certain it was the correct decision. Moreover, X represented the height of the introduction of professionalism in the firm. The firm had been started by F and managed "intuitively" for years. F realized that the firm had grown so large that it could no longer be managed by himself, and therefore he introduced professional management, especially at the upper levels. F was surprised and taken somewhat aback that the professional experts were doubting themselves and were turning to him.

F did not reveal these feelings to X. He attempted to reassure X and reassure himself that (1) the decision was a good one, (2) everybody made mistakes, indeed (3) F had made some very big ones while he was chief executive officer.

For example, X asked F, "Are we really believable in this new market?" Instead of F helping X surface his fears, F responded, "Our share of the market is significant and growing." Later when repeating his fears, F said, "Let us put that issue aside for a moment." (And then F reminded X of some success stories.) Still later X said, "I'm not sure what is bothering me about this decision." F responded, "I'm trying to be as open as I can about why and how this decision came about. I don't think it is bad judgment." And later F asked, "Are you doubting your professionals?" (A fear that F had but was not communicating to X.)

When F finished, L asked him to give his views of the case. F's response included:

1. *It was an exciting challenge from the start.*
2. *X was obviously troubled.*
3. *(Normally I would have) kidded him by saying, OK, X, where is your impeccability today?*
4. *I tried to be more constructive by trying to answer his questions.*
5. *He was asking for help.*
6. *I guess what really troubles me is (with all this professional intelligence we have hired) here was the captain of the professionals somehow having doubts. I was saying (to myself) "Good god, after two and a half years, the captain is saying that we're playing the wrong game." But I did not say that because that would turn him off.*
7. *So I said to myself, OK, the captain can be wrong, but let me help him find out why and how and take the risks involved.*

The ensuing discussion pointed out:

1. *F's dialogue with X was intellectually honest.*
2. *F never communicated any of his fears and feelings.*
3. *F never helped X to explore his feelings or fears.*

The quality of the conversation was loaded, for the first time, with some degree of anger and impatience toward F. It was as if the group members had evidence that F *was not* behaving according to Model II, and they would badger him with the data. Also, F rarely expressed feelings or was sensitive to others' feelings; thus, the group members badgered him with theirs and made it difficult for him not to be sensitive to this feeling.

L pointed out to F that every time X expressed some doubts, he was responded to by F with marketing answers. "Your theory-in-use toward X," suggested L, "was the way to help X become more logical so that then you could attack logically; to force him to become more logical." Someone added that if he were X, he would not feel allowed to have feelings, just to be logical. Someone said, in a disparaging voice, "Look F, X is a human being." Another added, "You're treating him, because he is a professional, as if he is not allowed to feel."

C interrupted and asked if anyone felt that F was not trying to learn, and if he were not a human being. Several members relaxed, returned to their chairs, and a few said they were sorry.

The discussion continued with A, who knew F best, telling F that he doubted that F had really turned over the company to X. Another said to F, "You have such an incredible investment in professional management and when it didn't pay off, it rang your bell."

As the attribution and the anger increased, C asked if the group members would talk to each other about helping F and act as if F were not in the room. "What are we trying to communicate to F?" "How are we trying to help him?"

The members began to surface views that they had about F. First, several believed that, although F was a great spokesman for professional management, he appeared to be neither patient nor comfortable with it. Second, X may be president in name but not in fact when it came down to key decisions. "The market place is not X's boss, F is." "From the data we were given," added another, "I would infer F is the oracle and X is coming to the oracle."

C said that he had heard several say that F was insensitive to X's feelings. Would someone give F some examples of what he might have said? The tone of the conversation shifted. The participants began to role play suggestions, some of which were like F's and some of which were not. Moreover, they began to refer to the notes of the scenario F presented, and they admitted that F had produced some valuable and helpful interventions.

These comments apparently helped F, because, for the first time, he admitted that he was baffled with the episode because he did not know how to behave more effectively. As he listened to the comments, he began to think of different scenarios. For example, F wondered what would have happened if he had said, as some suggested, "I'm glad that we have such a relationship that you can express your doubts with me." "And, you know," F continued, "that is how I felt but I never said it."

F began to see that if he could be more in touch with his feelings, under real time conditions, several positive "skills" could be developed. First, he could make comments like the one above. Second, he could talk about his fear about the value of professionalism—a fear which, apparently, X realized but was unable to surface with F. Third, by suppressing his feelings, F made it difficult to help X express his. If, for example, F had helped X express his fears about the new product, it could have led to an examination of the decision-making processes that led to the decision in the first place. Such a discussion risked the possibility that the issue of the value of professionalism would be raised—an issue that F had decided to suppress.

A discussion of such an issue might have helped F begin to understand that some of his "overemphasis" on professionalism (in speeches throughout the country) could be an attempt to convince himself that he had made the right decision. But an overemphasis on professionalism included making professionals deliver more than they could deliver, which could cause others to develop an unrealistic level of aspiration, could frighten them, could lead them to develop even more unrealistic levels of aspiration (as they did in the example cited previously regarding budgets) that could upset F. We then have, in motion, a circular process that would be self-sealing and heading toward increased ineffectiveness.

F said that, after producing this theory-in-use, he decided to focus on one of his behavioral strategies that was cutting people off. He had left the previous seminar angry with himself for cutting people off too often. So, in this scenario with X, F was proud because he didn't cut off anyone. However, he was becoming aware that effective change did not occur by focusing on a specific bit of behavior (such as cutting people off) or a specific outcome (such as double-loop learning) without also focusing on the governing variables. In his case, the Model I governing variable of maximizing the intellectual and minimizing the emotional was still operating. This governing variable would have to be altered to give feelings prominence—when they were prominent—if the new behavioral strategies were not going to become gimmicks.

To summarize: F represented an individual who tended to suppress awareness of his own and others' feelings. The suppression of feelings was counterbalanced with an overemphasis on the intellective aspects of life. He even hired a president who had intellectually impeccable positions.

F understood Model II quickly and, given his sense of competitiveness (I want to be one of the first in the group to report success in Model II), he (1) focused on changing bits of his behavior (e.g., cutting people off), (2) focused on double-loop learning which, for technical problems, may occur by applying his superior intellectual abilities, and (3) reported to the group the early modest successes but (4) behaved in the group in ways that led everyone to doubt his successes, which (5) led others to become annoyed at F and eventually (6) to confront him with their feelings, the area in which F needed to enhance his competence, and (7) with the help of the faculty the members found that F was willing to learn, although he admitted it was very difficult. The session therefore helped F to see the factors that he must work on if his behavior, as a total human being, was to match his ability to create maps of effective leadership.

CHAPTER

8

QUESTIONING THE APPLICABILITY OF MODEL II

The final theme during Seminar 4 was dealing with the recurring question of the applicability of Model II in everyday life. During this seminar, the presidents focused on this issue with greater deliberation. It appeared that they wanted to bring together and organize their doubts in order to begin to invent strategies and hopefully practice producing them. Perhaps it was no accident that this confrontation occurred in the seminar in which they had several successful experiences in helping A and in confronting F with his participation within the group. Given the new sense of confidence, the group members were able to face the applicability issue more earnestly.

As we shall see, the presidents felt that they faced a difficult problem of credibility. Would their subordinates believe that they (presidents) were trying to alter genuinely their own theories-in-use? How would they, and the subordinates, cope with the problem of credibility? Would it not be an embarrassing issue to both the superior and subordinate? If so, there was the dilemma that, as Model II becomes, in the eyes of the presidents, more achievable and applicable, it also becomes potentially more embarrassing. Thus there is a new dilemma of striving to learn Model II theories-in-use while hoping that they might not become as applicable as their potential appears to be.

CREDIBILITY PROBLEMS

It appeared that B's confrontation of anxiety about, and ambivalence toward, Model II helped to surface these issues. It began during E's description of an experiment that he attempted in changing his leadership behavior. E decided to become more candid about his views, to admit that he had controlled others, and to request the vice-presidents to confront his views. B questioned whether the subordinates would feel free to express themselves candidly. He used this opportunity to challenge again the applicability of Model II and the credibility of E's description. Unlike Seminar 2, neither type of question was condemned, shelved, or denied. Although few of the group members openly shared B's mistrust, they encouraged the discussion.

A word about E's case:

A critical decision had to be made in E's company. E saw three possible alternatives. The first would have been to make the decision personally and send out memos announcing it. E rejected that strategy outright. The second alternative was the one he had been using until the experience in Seminar 3.

E: I would have called a meeting, concealed how I felt about the issues, let the discussion go, but I would have made darned sure that the group came to the conclusion that I intended. It would have been a group decision, on the surface, but really my decision.

The alternative that E chose is an illustration of the president being both candid about his views and facilitating genuine discussion.

E described how he told the group of the personal dilemma (if I remain silent, I may manipulate covertly; if I am open, I may be disbelieved or people may tell me what is consistent with my views), the internal conflict (can I behave effectively? is this the right way to behave as president?), and then asked them to have faith in him (that I was really trying to change my behavior). The issue, as E saw it, was, could he be unconflicted about his views, state them, and yet get a genuine discussion in order to tap the resources available for the best end result for the company. Their input would be very important to the quality of the decision.

E: What happened was that they relaxed (because they didn't have to figure out when I would pull out my views or be concerned how I might manipulate them); they felt some sympathy for me; and they saw their role as vital. The discussion was the freest that I have ever experienced. I did not sense any cues that they felt that I pre-empted the decision or subtly controlled things (as I used to sense).

   If someone had told me to do it this way, I would have said, "I can't do it." If I tell them how I feel first, they will all say, that's the way we want to do it. To use your words B, "If that's the way we want to do it, boss, that's the way we'll do it." There was none of that. It seemed as though, since everything was above the table, they played by those rules with all their energy and intelligence.

A added that he too had been thinking about this issue. If the vice-presidents were involved and concerned, they were dealing with the same data that he had—indeed, they created the data for him. "If they're dealing with the same data and they're having the same sleepless nights as the president is, then I think they can be very helpful."

B asked if he could take the opposite view. He stated a scenario in which the subordinates were thinking:

B: That S.O.B. He's telling me that he wants my input but he will make the final decision. He is using me as a playboard for his satisfaction and telling me ahead of time. I have very little control, and he's got all the control, and I resent that.

E admitted that this was a possible scenario, but he did not think that it was valid in his case because he could not have predicted the decision as it was finally made. Others pointed out that B's fears were also theirs. The way to deal with fears was to have discussions in which subordinates had a genuine influence on the decisions. It should be possible that an objective observer could report that the president did his best to generate valid discussion and to encourage confrontation of his views.

Slowly but surely the group members were learning that Model II did not mean that the president should hide his views because that implied mistrust of the vice-presidents, the relationship between the president and the vice-presidents, or the relationships among the vice-presidents. If these mistrusts existed, they should be surfaced and worked through. The president, or any member of the group, should display the behavior that he expected others to model if the group was to be effective. If the president wanted others to be candid and influenceable, he should behave likewise. If the dynamics of the group were such that he could not behave in ways that he was asking others to behave, this dilemma should be faced.

L helped B and the group to explore another reason for the fear and mistrust B (and others) had about the strategy attempted by E. First, he asked B, "Why is it that after E reports that when he tried it, this is what happened; B, who has never tried this strategy, insists that the consequences as described by E could not happen?"

B agreed that L's question was important.

B also agreed that he not only lacked directly observable data but that he was making global assumptions, such as that E would not tolerate emotional confrontation of him. Interestingly, instead of cutting B off or condemning him, the members began to present directly observable data. They cited examples, within the group, in which E had brought cases to be discussed in which subordinates were confronting him, cases in which E expressed mistrust of his own leadership style, and examples of experiments in which E was trying to alter his behavior.

L then said to B:

L: Let's start with the assumption that E (is the kind of person who) goes into a meeting with ideas about how he wants (decisions) to come out. (Let's also assume) that you (B) do the same thing. You know how you want it to come out. Am I right so far?

B: Yes.

L: Would you guess that your subordinates realize (your stance)?

B: Yes.

L: Now what I consistently hear you saying is that if I (B) were ever to be more clear and honest about what I am doing, that people already know I am doing, they would mistrust me more.

B: Yes. That is consistent.

L: Could not another alternative be that they might say, OK, he is finally owning up to what we have known all along, that indeed he does make the decisions, he does have points of view.

   What I don't see is the data (other than perhaps your own fears) you have for the proposition that if I become more honest that will increase the mistrust.

B: I think that's very helpful. Very well put. I guess the underlying issue here is a matter of my strategy to control.

   I guess what I'm coming to grips with is that it is hard for me to believe that a subordinate could sit in a meeting, give input, and not feel that I can exercise some control on how that's going to come out.

The group agreed with B's beliefs about the subordinates because B admitted that he did try to control the decision. Thus B's beliefs or fears were self-fulfilling prophecies. B agreed that the discussion made sense, and he wanted to think about it.

E asked, "My question about all this is, Why was something that seems so simple, in retrospect, so difficult to do?"

THE SOURCE OF "STRONG" LEADERSHIP

B then added that this discussion partially represented a struggle to define the role of the president. "I see the role of the president as giving leadership and direction, to set goals and objectives, to see to it that the goals and objectives are reached."

A: That's a beautiful Model I definition of the president.

B: Yes, I think so. But that is not what I want—or is it?

C: It is not a question that can be answered simply and for all times. It is a question to be worked at throughout our lives.

B continued to explore the issue by role playing with C. B took the role of the subordinate who questioned seriously (as does B) the applicability of Model II. G took on the role of the president. He attempted to show that B's questions (as president) were valid *and* discussable with even highly skeptical subordinates (as played by B).

B: (as S, subordinate) What does he (president) want from me? He's giving me his ideas and his feelings. He has the power; he is controlling me. Who in the hell is he kidding?

C: (as president) What you say makes sense, especially as I have dealt with you in the past. I mean what I say, and I realize the best way for me to prove it is through my actions. If you see me doing anything that contradicts what I am saying, let me know.

B: Really boss—you have all the power, who are you kidding?

C: If you are saying that I cannot be trusted, I can understand, given the way that I have acted in the past. Again, I ask you to confront me.

B: Yes boss, but putting myself in your shoes, I can't imagine a president meaning that.

C: If you were boss, you can't imagine yourself doing what I am doing.

B: No, why would you?

C: Because I am committed to see if it is possible to have more effective decisions; more involvement in, and commitment to, decisions that we make.

"OK," said B. "I guess it can become believable if we work hard at it. But the trouble is we keep slipping and then they must be saying, That son of a bitch is playing games with me!"

E then said that he had left seminar 3 with the promise (to himself) to attempt to change his behavior and to explain to the subordinates why he thought the changes were necessary.

E: I lost my courage to tell them partially because I was not sure I could deliver (the new behavior.) The more I thought about it, the more skeptical I became of my loss of courage because it might have been related to my need to win and excel as well as the fear of failure.

So I decided to try to alter my behavior without stating that I was trying and without asking for help.

L: To what extent are we questioning whether the president should have doubts and whether he should ask for help with his doubts?

The response was quick and almost unanimous. The presidents were comfortable neither with having doubts nor with asking for help. They also admitted that doubts were valid, especially in the transition from Model I to II. One function of this learning group was to help them work through these doubts. C suggested that doubts never go away and that it may be important for them to have people with whom they could discuss their doubts. C also suggested that this could be one genuine way of involving their vice-presidents in the idea of taking a trip toward Model II.

The discussion about expressing doubts led to another discussion about expressing feelings. F, one member recalled, was seen by the entire group as expressing few doubts, as being intellectually agile, and as coming on strong. Yet none of them trusted the image of intellectual impeccability and interpersonal coolness. They saw him as a person who had difficulty in dealing effectively with important organizational problems that were heavily laden with his own and/or someone else's feelings.

F: All this is very interesting because I consider myself a very emotional person. But that isn't the same as saying that my feelings are transmitted to other people.

C: And my guess is that X may also feel the same way.

D: I experience you as very emotional on a narrow spectrum. Where you are talking about a financial deal or a concept, I find you very expressive (gives an example).

G then asked if he could raise a general question about the advisability of expressing feelings when someone is the president. He had tried it with mixed results.

G: I think there is a fear on the part of the top executive that somehow the captain of the ship has to appear as if everything is under control even though there are rocks and storms—here's the guy you can have confidence in. The thing that concerns me about Model II approach is that expressing feelings seems to diminish, to a certain extent, the confidence of the subordinate to their leader.

C: How do others react?

A: I disagree.

B: I agree.

A: It depends. I find that if I express my feelings, then they get into the decision-making process and people can deal with them. I know that I make inferences about how emotional others are about a decision.

B: There is a big difference between the president saying that I don't know where we're going as compared to saying that he was concerned about whether the right decision was being made.

Recently, I leveled with what I was concerned about, and several of my people came right back and said why they were not concerned. They identified reasons that I had never thought of.

C asked the group to explore the differences between the two approaches. The first one seemed, to the members, to cut off the president from further feedback. C agreed and added that in the first approach the president may be experienced as a frightened person. The subordinates may not wish to deal with a person who is frightened *and* who is either unaware that he is expressing fear or, through past experiences, has shown that he is fearful about expressing his fears.

Several of the presidents identified other causes of fear, such as feeling alone, seeing no solution to a difficult problem, fearing that others could not handle the problem, or others expecting the president to handle all issues effectively.

All of these conditions could understandably produce fears in anyone, but especially in someone held legally accountable for an organization.

However, the presidents also concluded that the above conditions did not have to be the only options available to them. It could be possible for a top management team to be so effective that the members shared the

responsibility for solving such problems and that they did not expect the
president, or anyone else, to be always a calm, confident individual.

E: Why can't a president say (if it is true), "I'm scared as hell," or, "I'm ex-
    tremely concerned about this."? I'd like to explore this with you (to his back-
    home group).

A: That would be positive to me because I would feel that I can be part of solv-
    ing the problem.

C: My guess is that the open expression of fear can be very helpful and have
    the impact A just expressed *if* the top management group is effective, if its
    members are not uncomfortable with expressing feelings.

Someone then asked whether Model II implied passing the buck to the
subordinates. If you are sharing your responsibility aren't you reneging
on your job as president?

A lively discussion ensued, concluding with the idea that no one (at
any level) shared responsibility. It was possible, however, to share
power. C noted that sharing power did not necessarily mean that A
gave up power to B, because the pie (of power) was not fixed. It was
possible to enlarge the amount of power subordinates had. The reason
for enlarging the subordinates' power was to create the best possible
conditions for them to fulfill their responsibilities.

E: (to B) Do you have vice-presidents in your company who can perform at the
    same level of excellence as you?

B: Yes—I would hope so.

E: If that is so, then why is it so important to jealously guard the prerogatives
    of the president?

B: Well, I suppose if you lose control you create uncertainties.

The group discussed this issue. F gave an example to illustrate the point
that his big fear was not losing authority. His big challenge was to enter a
discussion and not care if he turned out to be wrong. F added that what
he tried to focus on was the quality of information and problem solving.
As he became more comfortable with this focus, he also became less concerned with power and so did the vice-presidents.

B wondered out loud that perhaps he feared that he could be
replaced—a fear of which he was not aware and which he denied by
creating an executive development program whose objective was to have
several replacements for him. E agreed with B's musing and added that
uncertainty was always in the air, that B must have been full of uncer-

tainty when he started his company, that uncertainty will always exist, "as long as we are learning."

The session ended with the group agreeing that Models I and II were not mutually exclusive leadership strategies. It is possible that each model may be appropriate for different conditions. C suggested that Model II is more relevant for the difficult, unprogrammed decisions that have long-range implications and require much monitoring and therefore internal commitment.

E added that he preferred to operate as much as possible under Model II because the decisions that they, as top people, make, are precisely the more unprogrammed, long-range decisions. However, he also felt that under emergencies he could conceive using a Model I approach and that his subordinates would expect him to do so. He then added:

E: So the minute I could be unconflicted about the use of authority in an open manner, then I didn't have to depend upon my old techniques which tended to be more ambiguous and manipulative.

L: Moving toward Model II does not mean that I (or anyone else) eliminate my capacity for using Model I.

C: The point is to develop, jointly with your group, decision rules that stipulate the conditions under which Model I and II are appropriate for anyone in the group.

SUMMARY

27.   In the last two chapters we see how the dilemmas of power become highlighted. For example, there is the dilemma of advocating without controlling. And if this skill is acquired, there is the dilemma of the subordinates believing that their superiors want to change to advocacy with inquiry rather than unilateral control. That raised the dilemma of how to encourage the subordinates to express their feelings toward the superiors when both have assumed that to express feelings is to express weakness or to generate chaos. Then there is the dilemma of expressing dilemma because the expression of a dilemma is seen, in a Model I world, as a sign of hesitancy or weakness.

28.   Moreover, there is the dilemma that is caused by the presidents' awareness that they have mistrusted their subordinates but have acted to communicate opposite information (We are a fine team). Given the Model II requirement of working through the mistrust of the subordinates' competences, the president is also faced with the requirement to discuss openly his years of covert, deceiving strategies. This can produce

righteous indignation on the part of the subordinates. More fearful is that it can surface the fact that they have been doing the same to him *and* to each other. Cannot having all this information come to light act to erode the legitimacy of leadership and the credibility of the group sense of cohesiveness?

Also there is the dilemma that Model II theory-in-use will lead to the president being less aggressive. Might this not be interpreted as a weakness by the subordinates? How does one surface this possibility in such a way that one can obtain genuine feedback and not some pap to keep the president happy?

29.   The above dilemmas exist because the subordinates are also programmed with Model I theories-in-use, and all exist in organizations whose policies and practices are congruent with Model I theories of action. There are certain dilemmas of power that would exist for the presidents even if their subordinates suddenly behaved according to Model II or if their organizations were designed according to Model II values and strategies. The dilemmas are related to their own discomfort of expressing fears and asking for help. Their concept of a strong leader was one who hides fears, who works compulsively in order to be on top of issues, thereby lowering the probability of experiencing fear as well as the need for help. To explore the fear of expressing fear or asking for help is a dilemma with a recursive quality. It is a cure that requires the asking of help and the exploration of fear. These requirements could make the problems worse.

CHAPTER

9

SEMINAR 4.
THE BEGINNINGS
OF A
MORE INTEGRATED
LEARNING CYCLE:
THE CASE OF F

A new level of discovery-invention-production-generalization surfaced during this seminar, whose beginnings probably occurred during the previous seminar. Recall that the group members had begun to deepen their discoveries about their theories-in-use and to connect them causally with some of the major organizational problems that plagued them. As a result, they invented and produced samples of solutions to the back-home problems which, when they returned, they attempted to implement. The results, although mixed, indicated progress.

The resulting feelings of success helped to continue the spirit of inquiry. The experiments raised new and deeper questions for the presidents to deal with. This led, for example, to helping A deal with the problem of confronting a valued vice-president with the rumor that he was leaving. It also led to F being confronted with the discrepancies between his assertions of his competence and the way in which he was actually behaving. The group members participated heavily in these discussions, and behavioral data were liberally produced to show that A and F had been helped. These feelings were confirmed several weeks later when A and F sent scenarios to all of us of how they dealt with the problems back home.

The development of a more integrated learning cycle could be illustrated by taking examples from all the presidents' experiences. Because of space limitations, and for the sake of continuity with Chapter 7, the case of F has been selected.

The reader may recall that the members had confronted F, during the early phase of seminar 4, for not having brought a case, in scenario form, for them to discuss. It especially irked them because F continued to remark during the seminar that he was comfortable with Model II behavior; indeed, he was astonished how well "it" worked. The members confronted F with their doubts. They experienced F as a person who operated primarily at the intellectual level, who suppressed and denied his own feelings, who was highly competitive, and who acted as if he preferred to use his admittedly superior intellectual abilities, "to try to squirm out from seeing his own inconsistencies."

This confrontation resulted in F developing a case and presenting it the next day. The case described an incident with X, the president of his (F's) company, who had committed an error that stunned F because it was in X's area of managerial strength. The conclusions of the discussion were that F did not have an honest relationship with X because he had not communicated his true feelings to him, nor did he help X explore his feelings about his own effectiveness or his relationship with F.

F commented to the group, after the session, that the discussion was "an eye-opener." He realized now that he was a long way off from behaving in accordance with Model II. This admission, as one member of the group said, "placed him right among all us humans, who also had a long way to go." Moreover, pointed out several other members, the very fact that he did not try to talk his way out of his theory-in-use was an important step forward.

In terms of our model, F had begun to become aware of aspects of himself that were hidden from him but were known by most of the people with whom he interacted. For example, many of his friends and peers felt that F had overreacted and unfairly downgraded the positive aspects of the intuitive qualities of an entrepreneur like himself. They also felt that F had overvalued the qualities of "professionalism" that were related to running the business in a rational, programmed, plan-ningful manner. In talking with YPO presidents who learned that F was to be a participant in the group, they were unanimous in describing him as brilliant yet a nut on professionalism. Yet no one had com-municated this to F.

As we have seen in the two previous chapters, F saw himself as a very emotional person and was proud of the fact that he had found X, whose main quality was "impeccable logic," to replace him. The group, how-ever, experienced F as distant, overrational, and suppressing his feel-ings. They were able to explore these discrepancies effectively by focus-ing on the inconsistency of F maintaining that X and he had a perfect Model II relationship, yet F rarely produced Model II behavior within the learning environment. When F responded that the reason he was having quicker success than they was that he was now chairman and no longer into the day-to-day operations, the group members asked him for some directly observable data. This led F to produce the scenario that became the leverage for the session that he described as an eye-opener.

When F returned home, he brought with him a new set of lenses with which to see the world, a new set of ideas with which to experiment, as well as a partially learned set of skills with which to experiment. During the period between the previous seminar and this one, F began to see some of X's typical behavior in a different light. X had managed the company expansion in a way that made it necessary for the company to borrow substantial monies from the banks, something that this company had rarely done. F had foreseen this possibility, but he had refrained from stating his concern lest X feel that F was interfering with the every-day running of the business.

F came to this seminar with a very long scenario describing different key episodes with X. This scenario presented further evidence that X had some serious limitations, that F had foreseen these limitations, *and yet* F was still reluctant and hesitant to confront X. Indeed, as we shall see below, X provided F with several direct opportunities to be candid about his (F's) doubts, but F chose to remain "discreet" and "careful" lest he be unfair and/or upset the key officer in his company. For example, in a meeting with the bank officials, the bank officials said (1) that they were not highly confident of X as president, (2) that they wanted F to guaran-tee the loans with his personal resources, and (3) they suggested that F reenter the company's activities in a more active manner. The scenarios also suggested that X behaved, at times, somewhat naively in front of the bank officers, perhaps harming his image with the key loan officers. I quote from the case.

F: So am I. A bank loan officer asked very penetrating questions, and I think very right questions. But you have to understand, X, when you told him you were now bringing in a comptroller to bolster Mr. M and our financial planning, that in effect you were saying, "I, X, did not have sufficiently good financial planning," and that "I, X, let the inventories get out of hand."

X: I agree with what you are saying. We have taken on a lot of things, and what I have found out this past year as president rather than vice-president for production is that I don't have my fingers on things quite the way I had in production. There was another layer of management to get to the solution of actual problems. And if things go wrong, I just cannot push buttons to get them corrected as quickly as I could before. I also find that if I begin to get immersed in marketing or finances or production, then I am just dead, because I can't be overlooking everything and getting immersed at the same time.

F: I keep asking myself whether I have given you the freedom to do your job, or interfered too much. X, do you feel that I have given you the liberty you need to do the job?

X: Yes, I do. But as long as we are being so candid, I should like to say that some members of the top management group have made references to the fact that you may be sorry you turned over the company to me, and that you are in fact anxious to get back into the management of the company.

F: I would really dread that for a number of reasons. While I feared you overstaffed the company last year, and it is probably fortunate for the company that one of those people was as bad as he was (because he was released), I do feel with the steps you have taken and. are taking that you are no longer overstaffed. But if I were to take over command of the company, people like Z would expect me to begin working with them again, and I think the company could not operate this way any longer. We have grown beyond this.

  I don't want to get into running the company. While you have made some mistakes, I think we are both very cognizant of what they are, and I still have implicit faith that you can run this company, and perhaps make it into something I could not. I don't know what you meant by your earlier reference to some of the officers in the company thinking I want to run the company.

X: I don't either, F. I must say that in all my relationships with you, you have been very straightforward and very honest.

F: I don't know how to say it more honestly to you. I think perhaps the only mistake that I would suggest to others so that they don't make it is moving somebody directly from head of a functional area to president. In retrospect I would have liked to have seen you as vice-president for operations for a year or two.

X: I am not sure about that, but perhaps it would have been better if I had had a year where we were not trying as many things as we were this year. I was constantly balancing how important was my first year versus my second and third years, and now the banks are pulling us up hard on my first year's performance, and in fact it is my thought that I spent too much time on the first year as compared with the second and third. I agree—it has been costly. In Scandinavia we call this kind of thing "learning money."

F: We have used up our learning money, and I surely hope we learned.

The group explored other incidents in which F indicated a lack of confidence in X yet did not seem to be saying it openly.

A: (You said to X) in retrospect, I would have liked to have seen you as vice-president for operations for a year or two. That's hard for X to accept now that he is president. He responded, I'm not really sure about that. What else could he say?

G: Also, you wind up by saying that he's used up all the learning money. That would be threatening to me.

F: OK. How would you have responded if you felt that way?

C asked F how he felt X felt about the issue. F said that he knew X felt that he had used up the learning money. "Then," asked C, "what is the objective of telling him something you believe he already feels?" A suggested that another approach might have been to ask X if he felt he had used up his learning money (in order for F to check his attribution and assuming that X responded as F predicted). Then F could confirm X's response. C added another possibility. After X made his comment about learning money, F might have commented, "Am I sensing correctly that you feel you have used up your learning money?"

B wondered if one of the underlying issues was that F had turned much of his life's work, as well as his financial assets, to X, and now he was beginning to be unhappy with X's performance.

F: Yes, I was and am really feeling this. Maybe we tried to do too much in one year.

F then described a dilemma with which all of the others immediately empathized. On one hand, X was made chief executive officer, and F withdrew to make certain that X, and the others, felt that X was president. On the other hand, there were times that F felt X was making errors, but he did not want to interfere lest he undercut X's position.

This problem, as we shall see, is a basic problem for most of the presidents. How can the superior help others to be autonomous and have full responsibility for their work without the president's valuable resources becoming suppressed? Moreover, F added that, under these conditions, his preeminent concern was how to make a suggestion without implying to himself and to the others that he (F) was reintroducing himself into the company. "So, I would raise a question but then add (to X) that I had full confidence in him which was not true." X, on the other hand, began to wonder that, if F had full confidence in him, why did he have to say it? Also, as we shall see below, how could F have full confidence in X when X did not have such confidence in himself?

A series of episodes then occurred during the conference that helped F to become more aware of the halo that he had placed over X's head. They are presented in order of occurrence.

F: A asked me if I were disenchanted with X. I replied no. He is a very bright guy. He's made a few stupid errors and has done many things right. I think the inventory and overstaffing problems have passed; there are no other difficult tasks ahead.

C: As I hear that, I would interpret you as having been, or still are, somewhat disenchanted with X because you say that you have full confidence in him now that the future presents very little challenge.

F: Little what?

C: Little challenge.

A: Little risk—yes?

LATER

A: F, did you not overreact to your appointment of X by staying the hell out of his way?

F: Yes, I agree, now.

C: What is it that you could have done to keep yourself active in the company without threatening X's position?

G: This is a dilemma that all of us are in. Here's a new bright guy who is confident and he wants to demonstrate that he can do things without help. As a result, he bends over backwards to get as far away from F as he can.

F: You're right. He wanted no part of me.

LATER

F: Yes, I am more clear now that I had placed a halo over his head. X is very good, especially as a production man. But he needs more experience to be an equally good president. I don't think that I told him my doubts about him (as I experienced them). In fact, at times, looking back, I didn't tell myself.

F: I sit in my office and say, how can I give X a sense of confidence in himself without saying things like, "X, I really believe in you."

C: How can you give someone else a sense of confidence? Also, if this were possible, how could it be done if you are ambivalent about him?

F: No, no, don't misunderstand me, this guy is terrific in operations.

C: Yes, but as president, how did he handle the bank and financial problems?

F: Not as well.

F: OK, let me be clear. Here is a very bright perceptive guy. You're right, I do not have complete confidence in his present performance but I do have complete confidence in his potential. OK? But, I haven't seen it, in fact, come true.

A: Would you say now that what you see ahead is a process of several years of helping him to become an effective president? If so, is not the next step to see if he agrees? And if he does, to design jointly a process by which this education can go on without his authority as president being undermined?

F: Yes, that is what I see now.

E: But the way you try to bolster him up (in the scenario) is something like saying to X, "I have to bolster you up and let me tell you how good the financial results were for April and May . . . etc. But, if I were X I would begin to wonder.

G: To put it another way, I would think that you are still assuring us that you have confidence in X when in fact you do not.

B: We do not see any observable data that confirm a sense of confidence by you in X.

F: Yes, I see that. I have no qualms about going back and saying to X that one of my mistakes is that I tend to place halos around those I select; that I did that to you and get his reaction.

F: I am concerned that I may have harmed X by building him up (in my eyes) too high and now not supporting him in ways that are healthy and effective.

C: What's your best guess as to how X would feel about all this?

F: I think that he would be ambivalent. He might see my attempts to help him as a reflection of weakness.

C: Perhaps this may be the first problem to deal with.

F: You know what I am feeling about myself. I am feeling that I am a gutsy guy, I'm going all the way to be of help to X; but do I have the confidence that I can do it well, I'm not really sure. This will not be easy. Once I told X that he delivered everything that he promised. He responded that his record was not that good. And I said, "Oh, yes, you were, can you give me an instance when you weren't," in such a way as to say that he'd be the world's biggest smuck if he did!

There are some interesting patterns in these episodes. F began all but one episode with a discovery. The discovery was usually about X's limitations as president or a more candid ownership by F that X may not be as effective as F thought. The group members then selected an inconsistency within what F had said that led him to explore further and deeper into his relationship with X and with himself. Discovery produced, with the help of the group, further discovery. Moreover, whenever it was relevant, the group members generalized the discovery to their own problems. For example, there was the dilemma of leaving a subordinate alone yet desiring to give helpful input in key decisions. There was minimal attribution, competitiveness, and punishing of F. As F was learning about himself, the others were learning to help others with problems that were important to all. The episodes may be said to have the quality of building up a message to a crescendo that F has been conflicted about X, unaware of the scope of his conflictedness, and not truthful with X about the concerns that he (F) had.

INVENTING AND PRODUCING ACTIONS

F began the session by saying that one way to begin to discuss the issues with X would be to begin with the issues of withholding his views about issues that were laden with feelings. F would say to X, in effect, that he (F) tended to suppress many of his views. For example, X had remarked how unemotional F was during the bank loan procedures, yet F was actually feeling many emotions. Also, F had not expressed all his feelings about X but, as just illustrated, the suppression of feelings was part of F's theory-in-use and not caused by X. F, in short, began by focusing on those aspects of the problem for which he accepted a major share of the responsibility.

F: I've got to get into the question of how honest I have been with him . . .

A: How might you do this? (Note that A asks for directly observable behavior.)

F: Well, I would say exactly what's on my mind. On one hand, X, I think we are both unhappy about some things that have happened and on the other hand I believe that I do have a lot of faith in you, perhaps less faith than I had a year ago, but there have been a lot of things that I think you've learned from. And I begin to spell out those things.

A: And what are those things? (Continues to ask for directly observable behavior.)

F then provided the directly observable behavior. In doing so, he raised questions in E's mind about the degree to which F was accepting responsibility for his part of the problem.

E: I don't think that adequately assumes the responsibility that you ought to assume, for the expectations you had of him a year ago. And the fact that your expectations now are not quite as high as they were a year ago, because the expectations you had a year ago weren't his promises to you that have been unfulfilled, they were *your* expectations of him that were excessive. And I think that somehow you have got to—if you are going to say to him that you have a lower expectation of him now than you had a year ago, you have got to also say, "But, X, it's more realistic. A year ago I had an expectation of you that was wish fulfillment, out of relation to fact and your experience and what was practical. And I've got to accept the responsibility for that."

B: X may have had the same unrealistic expectations.

G: Yea, that's an interesting one because I would just bet that he could come back with that remark too, that—you know—I've learned a lot this year. I thought I could do it all and I've also become more realistic.

F: He's already said that to me.

Note that F appeared to include both the happy and unhappy events in their relationship. He owned up to his decreasing faith but did not, as E pointed out, assume adequate responsibility for the unrealistic expectations F had of X. On the other hand, it might have been more effective if F had asked X to list the mistakes as well as the successes (or that they do this jointly); then F could confirm or disconfirm them. E, on the other hand, focused on F's personal responsibility, but did so in a controlling manner. He told F what he did wrong and did not invite confrontation of his views.

F then added a second scenario that would follow after the above issues were resolved. The second scenario was related to the new role that he wanted to play (that the banks were also requiring). F wanted to design the new role with X in a way that did not give cues to X or to the other officers that X was not the president. Again, the group members asked him to produce the second scenario.

F: OK, X, I expressed to you even before the banks did that I thought it
would be beneficial for the company and for me to take a greater involvement. We just defined that as my sitting in on more meetings and spending
more time with you. And then because of the pressures, we didn't take it any
further than that. But I would really like to ask you how you feel I can be of
the greatest benefit to you and the company?

B confronted F with a difficult question that X could, in all probability, raise.

B: OK, then he said to you, "Well, why do you want to sit in on these meetings?"

F: He made reference to the fact. I said I'd like to sit in on more meetings, but
maybe that isn't the right approach. And that's why I'm opening this up for
very open discussion. OK, the bank and you and I have talked about my
having greater involvement—that can take many forms. How do you think
my involvement can most benefit you and the company? That's what I
would like to discuss.

E wondered how realistic and helpful it was for F to maintain that X was
to have the final say in how F was to reenter. Why should not this new
role be designed jointly and monitored jointly over a long period of
time? E also encouraged F to consider using the entire top group as a
resource. F again maintained that this would threaten X, but he added
that he would test it out with X.

B asked how F could react if X decided that he wanted to keep F's new
role vague? Would he agree?

F: OK. I would handle that by saying, "Well, X, I don't know. Maybe we can't
design, at the moment, a role that mutually satisfies us, but I think we ought
to start off then by saying we are going to spend an hour and a half a day
together. And let's begin to talk about the problems that are here."

A: That makes you president. And that's—in my opinion—that, he might accept that as a face saving device, although I don't know why I should assume
he would. But I think you are rejecting out of hand this—the man who
needs help in a job that's too big for him—needs help from someone who
has more expertise in an area.

E: Aren't you putting so much on X, who at the moment has got to be going
somewhat scared? You're really throwing it all on him. Why are you
withdrawing instead of helping him?

F: I haven't thought of it that way. I could see myself approaching and saying, "OK, X, we could look at this on the basis of a mutual design of my
role, and we could get into that by exploring a trip that he is taking to
Europe.

Note in both responses that F produced directly observable data without being pressed (as was the case in the previous session).

C: When you first appointed X, you then bent backwards not to be in his way. You did everything you could to give him as much freedom, and he's confirmed that. He's not succeeded without your help—I think the challenge is how do you stop bending backwards and how does he start being more open about the kinds of help he needs, and how you can create—let's say you two together—the office of the presidency or of the chairman and the presidency together.

B picked up C's comments by surfacing a problem that he and others worried about not only in F's organization, but in their own. Note again that the objection is raised by including directly observable data.

B: But isn't X thinking that he is not in favor of an interdependent relationship with F? He might say, for example, "I'm not comfortable with that. I don't know if I want to take that risk of F taking over. That's certainly what the banks are thinking."

C felt that B asked the question directly of him. He attempted to reply by producing an answer in the form of a scenario.

C: Let me be F for a moment. I'm trying to think what would I do if X said that to me. I think I'd say . . . I think I'd say something like: "X, that raises a question in my mind that I'd like to discuss with you. Looking back in our relationship I began by communicating an unconditional faith in you. I'm now more and more clear that an unconditional faith is neither reality for you nor really healthy for the organization or for me. An unconditional faith could, in fact, control people rather than free them up. And so, I would like to see if we can design a relationship in which I can be more interdependent with you, more help to you."

A: That's pretty good.

F: Excellent. I wrote it down. (asking C to continue) Well, F, what do you have in mind?

C: (role playing F) I haven't thought it through and I don't know what to do. What I do know is that I don't want to get back in and be the chief executive officer. I'm not interested in handicapping you in front of the other vice-presidents. So if you ask me what I have in mind, it is that I need a lot more data and I need it from you—your views, and I'd like to hear it from the other vice-presidents as to how can we design an office that in fact will create the kind of team that this company needs, which, for example, X, after things get better I can leave it, but a new member can come on that team so that the office of the president may still exist.

F: What if the group says, "All right, F, we understand that, but you know, we really have learned our lessons, we're very confident of what we're doing now, and we appreciate that you want to help us, but we really don't need your help. We're very comfortable.

C: OK, well what I would say to the group: "I'm willing to accept evidence that you are ready. Why don't we set some criteria that we could use to monitor the effectiveness of the top team."

F: OK, this has been helpful. I'm ready to give it a try.

F'S ACCOUNT OF HIS ACTIONS

Several weeks later all the members received a memorandum from F describing his version of what happened. The memorandum included much information in scenario form:

1. F began his memorandum by expressing his feelings about having the session with X.
2. F began the session by discussing his predisposition to place a halo over X's head.
3. Although the document illustrated some change in the way F conducted this session, it did not at all times indicate that he behaved according to Model II. There were times when he was unilaterally attributive and evaluative. There were episodes in which F could have encouraged X to be more confronting of F or in which F could have accepted more responsibility for his way of relating to X. Also, F's comment that "all points had been made, and a sense of relief on X's part" may have been overoptimistic. Thus we see a human being who is learning, who is experimenting, and who has, as he suggests, much more to learn:

> Before I update you on my situation I want to thank you very much for your assistance. I think it was extremely (formerly would have said 'tremendously') beneficial. My wife and I listened to the tapes on Sunday, and she kept saying, as did you, "That's not enough involvement." She was pleased with the final outcome of our session. On Monday morning I felt like Gregory Peck in Twelve O'Clock High, and put aside my pipe, and sat down with X. The dialogue went pretty much as follows:

F: I think I have a habit of putting super halos on new people or old people in new responsibilities. It's perhaps very unfortunate that I do this, and perhaps I should be very careful not to do this in the future, but I have a habit of buying size 8¾ halos, and I think this is what I did when I made you president. Since then, that halo has become somewhat tarnished, and has resulted finally in the bank asking for my personal guarantee. Through all of this, I have been saying to you that I have implicit confidence in you, and I guess the words that would be more apt would be that I still have a great deal of confidence in your ability, but that in a way saying that I have implicit faith must have a somewhat hollow ring to you, and that you must sincerely question the degree of faith that I have in you.

X: I agree with what you are saying, F, and you are correct in saying that the words "implicit faith" bothered me. I think it is natural that you are questioning the faith you have in me.

Commentary. At this point I had the feeling that X was rather agreeing, somewhat because of reality, but also because he was not certain what direction the conversation was taking, and appeared to be somewhat frightened.

F: I think, X, that I have given you a very free hand, and I think there should be little question in your mind that I have given you a free hand, and we have recently discussed this. There is now a new set of circumstances because of the bank guarantee. I have spent a lot of time thinking about this the past few days, and it's my feeling that because of the bank guarantee, for the very sound reasons of protection of my own property and integrity of my family, it's necessary that I become a very active chairman. "Very active chairman" can mean many things—at the moment I see this as no longer being a "consultant" but actively participating in the management of this company. I am not, at the moment, exactly certain what role this should take. It's something I want to work out with you and the group, but basically I want to bring my talents to bear where they can do the most good and be the most valuable.

X: Could you elaborate a little more on this? I cannot disagree with the fact that the personal guarantee, and what you have said about protection of property and integrity of your family are justified and correct.

F: At the moment, X, I see myself going where the risks are greatest, and I immediately define these as the Plant E problem, pricing and marketing. And then I suggest our forming an "office of the president," where we air this to the entire management group, and I say very sincerely that any actions I take, or plan on taking, I am perfectly willing to be confronted on by the group. I am open to confrontation, and I want the group to feel this very sincerely. I realize that the group may say, "X, we told you so," but the bank and I have agreed that when our tangible net worth equals our liabilities my personal guarantee will be removed, and this should be in a period, according to your plan, of less than two years, and as soon as that occurs I am willing to step out. So there is a specific point at which it is clear to the group that I shall step out.

X: I am not disputing that it is wise for you to become involved in the area of greatest risk, but what, for example, do you believe you can bring to the Plant E situation that I cannot?

F: I guess I looked at the Plant E situation yesterday afternoon very differently
     than I had before. I suddenly said to myself, "F, if this were your problem,
     how would you handle it?" And walking through my garden thinking about
     this, I realized that we had a potential source without a backup source, and
     that I felt strongly, when I recommended last November that we seek
     another source and was voted down, that this was a bad tactical error,
     because we no longer had any kind of a stick. But rather than get into this,
     X, why don't we do a little role playing? You be X next Monday morning,·
     and I will be John Smith.

Commentary. X and I then did a little role playing, in which he was basically saying
"you see the importance of this," and I was saying "we are doing everything we
can." I then suggested to X that we reverse the role playing, that he be Plant E
director, and I be us. I then introduced two scenarios, one in which, if we didn't
get the production we suggested, we take castings out of their factory for
finishing, which clearly says "if you cannot help us, we will help ourselves
through somebody else, and that somebody else may end up with this business."
In short, it's no longer a threat; it's a positive action on our part. Second, I would
just stay there until production reached the necessary figures.
    I felt that the point had been made, and there was a sense of relief on X's part.

F: I realize that the managerial group is dispersed at the moment, but as
     quickly as possible I would like for us to have a group meeting, where we
     discuss my involvement, and I am willing to have it open for confrontation.
X: That's not possible now because we are spread apart. And while I agree that
     you like participation, I am not sure we have the time for it.

*I was very pleased with the way X took this whole thing, and I am pleased with the
way that part of the group that is here has taken it. I would hope that by the time we
come back from Europe we can have an open meeting.*
    *We had a meeting on retail stores yesterday, and during that meeting X asked me a
number of times "what is your feeling about this or that?" The group came to some
very satisfactory conclusions, and when the meeting was over, X said "I think it's important that we establish exactly how meetings like this are going to operate—that is to
say, who is going to make the final decision?" I replied that I thought this meeting had
gone very well—that X had proposed the final decision and that I had nodded approval, and that in the future, until we developed the overall openness between all of
us that I should like to see, that if there were an obvious disagreement between X and
myself, I would suggest that we think it over for a day, and he and I could argue our
position in private. And this is something on which I should welcome any comments
from you, because I think the "office of the president" is fine up to the point where the
two people occupying that office may have disagreements, and the question is, should
these disagreements be aired publicly or privately, and to what degree does the active
chairman, who is the principal stockholder, override the president, who has the title of
chief executive officer?*

SUMMARY OF LESSONS LEARNED

In this chapter another important dilemma of power is surfaced. How can a superior create conditions for autonomy for a subordinate yet provide whatever input he may have that could be helpful? The dilemma was not solved permanently; it cannot be, for it is a permanent dilemma of power. However, processes were invented and produced to deal with it more effectively.

The source of this dilemma is the misconstruction of progress from Model I toward Model II. An individual programmed with Model I theories-in-use will tend to conceive of progress toward Model II as behaving in the opposite direction of Model I (Argyris and Schon, 1974). Thus autonomy is now conceived of as no advocacy and no control. F therefore strove to leave X alone. He withdrew from the business. X conceived of the meaning of autonomy in the same light. So did all the other vice-presidents. Indeed, several were taking bets that F could not keep his hands off the administrative tiller for more than a few months.

But Model II is not the opposite of Model I. A Model II relationship provides *anyone* with the opportunity for advocacy. Under Model II conditions, F would not withdraw and keep to himself the valuable information that he kept hidden. F would feel free to advocate whatever ideas he felt were relevant, but he would do so with inquiry.

This is an important distinction because, as we have found in our research, most subordinates (in schools, business, government, unions, etc.) tend to conceptualize being trusted and respected as equivalent to being left alone by the superior. The negative consequence is that it discourages the superior from having an interdependent and contributing relationship with the subordinates. Since the subordinate equates trust with a superior leaving him alone as long as he (subordinate) performs, the subordinate tends to take a more controlling stance with the subordinates. Finally, in order for the superior to keep a distance from the operations of the subordinate, he has to believe that he has a subordinate who is very strong and manifests few weaknesses. This acts to prevent the superior from becoming aware of the subordinate's weaknesses and the latter remaining ignorant of important aspects of his theory-in-use.

CHAPTER

10

DISCOVERY—INVENTION— PRODUCTION AT THE BACK-HOME SETTING

In this chapter and the next one, the focus is on the activities that the participants generated in their back-home settings. In the cases of A and G, they were carried out with no help from the members or the faculty beyond that which was given during the seminars. In the cases of B and D, they did have help from Professor Bolman.

The objectives of this chapter are to show that Model II theories-in-use can be used to deal with very difficult decisions as well as to explore issues that are rarely discussed, yet require open exploration. Examples of the former are A's group cutting their operating budget significantly, their discussions of new modes of organizing and operating their business, and G's discussion of the role that division Y should have in the total corporation. Examples of the latter are D's and G's discussion of the ineffectiveness of the problem-solving activities of their respective top management groups, and B's confrontation of the same issue plus the issue of his credibility with the key executives.

151

The presidents kept detailed notes of the inventions and productions they attempted in the learning seminar (indeed, most obtained tapes of all the sessions). Most also tape recorded their experiments, and the recordings were sent to C and L as an official record. C and L would then listen to the tapes and send preliminary feedback to each president. The tapes were also used to create new case material for the next seminar. (The tapes were also used in the conduct of the research.)

In this chapter, we illustrate four different back-home experiments carried out by A, B, D, and G. Because of the space limitations, all we can do is select samples from the tapes. The samples have been selected to illustrate the successes and difficulties involved. The emphasis is on the difficulties partially because it is those data that the presidents used as a basis for further discovery—invention—production, and generalization.

A

A sent tape recordings of three important problem-solving sessions with the top management group in which he had attempted to experiment with utilizing a more Model II theory-in-use to guide his behavior as well as his thinking about long-range policy for the company. The first session represented A's first attempt to communicate the theory of practice that he was learning in our sessions. Case B represented a highly tense and involved meeting in which over $700,000 had to be cut off the operating budget. Case C was a session in which the top group explored new models of organizing and managing the company.

CASE A.   A began the session by saying that he wanted to take a few minutes to describe what he was learning in the seminar group. "I hope you'll find it worthwhile because I think the *real* effectiveness of our meeting depends on how effective we are as a group." He told the group that, after he began, if they didn't find it worthwhile, to tell him, and he would stop. It appeared that the invitation to stop him was given with the hope that it would not be accepted. Thus the session began in a Model I, unilaterally controlling process.

A began by emphasizing that one of the biggest learnings the presidents developed was, "No matter how well we all thought we behaved, (when we took a close look) we saw how ineffectively we behaved. One president had a case that all of us were convinced was an example of a good case. When we finished the analysis, we realized how controlling this guy had been." And later, "The six of us thought we were the world's greatest presidents, but we learned that we were pretty bad from the point of view of opening up the group."

As A began to describe Model I, he began to use directly observable data or examples to illustrate the concepts in the model. He used his own behavior to illustrate the concepts. For example:

1. If I already have decided what I want to accomplish, I become controlling in our meetings.
2. If I want to win, then all my arguments are aimed, not so much to understand you, but to win the argument.
3. In trying to help T, I often had made up my mind as to what he should be doing. Then I would get angry if he didn't.

Question: Were there any of you who didn't react (defensively)?

A: No, I don't think so. All of us got where we are because of experience and charisma. I guess that I would say none of us would qualify as being effective (according to Model II). Other (presidents) didn't want to face the issue. That is how the group got so small. It's not easy to change your values and behavior.

When A spoke about a Model I strategy as controlling the task, he added:

A: I hope in this group we all develop the inputs. I really feel that I would like to encourage everybody to put their ideas on the table and particularly when my behavior might be inhibiting the results of the company. I realize that I'm not as sensitive as I should be. I'm spending a hell of a lot of time trying to become more aware. You can help me by letting me know how you feel.

After he finished describing Model I, several people asked questions about the meaning of the model. He replied that he would try to answer the questions, but he did not consider himself to be an expert.

The underlining theme of the questions was how free and open people should be. A responded that they should feel free to say anything that was relevant, especially if it was in disagreement with him. His encouragement of the subordinates to be more open and confronting included an invitation to tell him when they felt he was crazy, off base, and unrealistic. A seemed to be struggling so hard to encourage confrontation that he did not focus on the fact that feedback characterized as crazy and unrealistic could increase the concern of the individual who received it. A was assuming that the model of confrontation that he was suggesting would apply only to himself.

The members realized that the analysis and behavior that he was suggesting was relevant to the vice-presidents (as peers) as well as to their subordinates. The group members began to illustrate the concepts of Model I by their behavior with each other.

Sub A: There are two ways we put guys down in this group. One is to say no and just cut it off. The other is to say, "I've never heard that before," when in fact everybody at the table knows you're saying, "that's crap, I really have heard of that before, but I'll be nice to you."

Sub B: Yes, we also use the ploy of saying, "That's a good idea but . . ." and then ignore it.

Sub C: Yes, we do all these things. One reason is that we're in one of those goddam win-lose situations. That's one reason creative ideas get squelched.

The group members returned to an example of A's behavior that they found controlling.

Sub A: You began the meeting by saying, "I'm sure everybody has something that's going to cost a lot of money." When you said that, I said, "oh, oh, be careful what I say."

A: You're one thousand percent right. I was really zipping in there with Model I. You're right! Boy, you learn fast!

Two members added that they did the same thing with their subordinates. "We probably kill a lot of ideas from our subordinates." Another added that he found it fascinating to watch what happened to others when they got attacked. He had never thought of helping or supporting anyone.

Sub B: It is terrible to be totally on your own in this group . . . terrible! When everyone is against you, you know it!

Sub C: Imagine how bad it can be in other meetings.

Sub D: I'm sitting here and thinking about meetings that I have with subordinates. I mean, there are two guys that I cut off something awful, and I do it all the time.

Sub E: How can we improve ourselves if others don't tell us what we're doing to them?

Sub B: It's not easy (because Model I states) we're so damn competitive. If you have an idea in my area, I would have a tendency to try and shoot it down.

Sub C: We also protect each other. If I sense that I have hurt any of you, I back off.

Sub D: (laughter) The trouble is you don't sense it!

Sub A: The president of this company always has a secret agenda. And he had
         one today (discussing Model I). This time it was a good one. But I still
         think that our agenda items shouldn't be laid on.

A: I agree with you. I hope in the future when I do this, you'll let me have
         it. Don't worry. I won't collapse.

Again the president was inviting confrontation. However, the behavior
he was inviting could be punishing. Although it might not upset him (the
data suggest that it does), such an invitation might be taken, by the vice-
presidents, as a model for behavior toward each other and toward their
subordinates. Such behavior is still Model I. In effect, A was moving
from a unilateral Model I relationship (in which he was in control) to a
model in which the subordinates may become controlling. The result
was an oscillating Model I, not Model II.

This discussion led into a detailed analysis of a particular case. Most of
the group members felt that A had behaved terribly toward Sub B. A
said he did not recall doing so and asked for directly observable data.
The more the members tried to recall the data, the clearer it became that
the president was not at fault. In fact, he had behaved in a very effective
manner, and his actual behavior had been forgotten or ignored. This led
to a discussion of how the group members could, unrealizingly, distort
the president's behavior and motives.

A responded that, although he had much to learn, he was very thank-
ful for the discussion because there were moments when he felt he was
misunderstood, his behavior distorted, and his motives maligned. In a
Model II world, the subordinates must learn about the care and feeding
of superiors just as they expect the superiors to become more sensitive
about them.

Assessing A's First Intervention

A began the intervention in a unilaterally controlling manner. He described Model I quickly, as if communicating that he was aware that he
was taking time for an item not on the agenda. Nevertheless, whenever it
became appropriate to illustrate the concepts of Model I, he used examples of his own behavior with them. He also accepted and confirmed
examples of his own Model I behavior.

A invited and encouraged confrontation of his behavior. He invited
others to punish him (e.g., tell me I'm crazy), and he assured them that
he would not be hurt. The advisability of such invitations may be ques-

tioned for several reasons. It may be difficult for some subordinates to act so aggressively. Also, it may be that the subordinates would feel uncomfortable because of the implied reciprocal invitation. If they let A have it, he may let them have it. Indeed, it may well be that A's invitation is a way for him to maintain his competitiveness (a consequence of which he may be unaware).

The group members used the opportunity to explore their relationships with each other and with their subordinates. There was a high degree of agreement that they behaved in a Model I manner with each other and with their subordinates.

The discussion returned to the behavior of the president. The group members focused on a case that, they unanimously agreed, illustrated unfair and punishing behavior on the part of the president. The president did not accept their view. Instead of punishing or condemning, he, for the most part, kept asking for directly observable data. As the subordinates attempted to retrieve such data from their memories, they found that there was little agreement as to what had happened. Finally, all agreed on one bit of datum (a memorandum). It was retrieved, and it showed that the president had not behaved as charged by the group.

The president's response was to say that he felt good about the end result, but he did not want to gloss over the fact that he did, at times, behave in ways that might not be helpful. He reiterated that he felt he had much to learn and invited them to help him. They asked the same of him and of each other.

Listening to the tape, I felt that A was anxious about giving the lecturette and about describing the concepts. Yet he appeared to express no discomfort when he stated that (1) he was not an expert on Models I and II, (2) he might easily botch things up knowingly and unknowingly and asked for patience, and (3) he needed their feedback to alter his leadership style. The interesting point about this is that it was these kinds of issues that the presidents had initially stated they should not make overt, because it would make them appear weak. The presidents had learned to behave in ways that, two sessions ago, they had doubted they could do and that they were sure would create anxiety within them and among their subordinates. These fears never materialized in any of the cases.

CASE B.   The top group had to cut about $700,000 from their operating budget. This was not an easy task for several reasons. Cost cutting is not an easy task for any group. Attempting to do it openly with the top group members present and confrontable by each other compounded the difficulties. Moreover, as indicated in case A, this group had only recently begun to explore its own problem-solving processes.

A managed the meeting with a mixture of Model I and Model II behavior. Several vignettes are included from the lengthy transcripts that highlight A's behavior and indicate the quality and quantity of the involvement of the group members.

A began the cost-cutting meeting by making his proposals to the group. He invited them to disagree and "shoot me down." The invitation encouraged win-lose competitive behavior. Indeed, the beginning of the session was composed of several important Model I episodes. A appeared much more competitive than in the previous session. Interestingly, this increase in control did not appear to hinder the expression of disagreements by the subordinates. For example:

1. The subordinates began to question certain of A's views. One tried to convince A not to cut their salaries as well as the salaries and commissions of the sales personnel.

A: I just don't believe that anyone will think we're tightening our belts if we don't cut our salaries.

LATER

A: The things you cut out of the salesmen's (perquisites) are going to lead them to squawk.

SILENCE

A: I don't buy your approach to the problem.

2. Several subordinates attempted to make the point that cutting people was not a good strategy.

Sub A: If business goes up then you are going to have to put people back in. This will cost more.

A: You can't tell me if you are able to keep —. That's what's crucial for 1975.

Sub B: But you don't keep good men by cutting salaries. You keep bad or mediocre men that way.

3. A then suggested a pay cut for everyone in the room including himself.

Sub A: I'd like to dig deeper before we go to pay cuts.

Sub B: I'd like to make a comment on pay cuts. As far as I am concerned, this is my personal reaction; I would not like to go to someone and tell them to absorb the work of others and get paid less for it . . . More-over, people simply *can't* live for less than $25,000 a year.

Sub C: You're one hundred per cent correct.

Sub D: Especially with this inflation.

Sub E: (Pay cuts) should be a last resort. Let's find the damn $740,000 in real savings, and I think this group can do it!

A: I feel satisfied with that.

LATER

A: You cannot go to the salesmen and tell them they're going to get cuts in commissions without saying that we are taking a pay cut. They're abso-lutely related.

Sub C: I'll tell you, godammit, we've got to find $50,000 to cut. We set the goal, and it's there. It *is* a shame (if we don't reach it).

A: If we don't make the $55,000, OK, we're not going to go bankrupt.

Assessing A's Second Intervention

This case was discussed by the presidents during the sessions. The sum-mary of A's behavior will be abstracted from their evaluation of his inter-vention.

The presidential group focused almost immediately upon A's compet-itive win-lose behavior and his attempts at being open to confrontation. They illustrated it with examples from the scenario given to them. Some examples were:

You can't tell me . . .
I just don't believe that anyone will think . . .
You're not going to get that (amount) out of—so forget it.

Examples of owning up to his feelings and attempting to encourage confrontation:

I'm trying like the devil to tell you how I feel . . .
Have I been clear? Also, have I come across as being open and not holding back?

The members of the seminar felt that A came across as desiring to behave according to Model II, but his theory-in-use was still primarily Model I. A agreed and added that it was not easy for him to alter some of his unilateral, controlling behavior. "Somehow I seem to feel that I must hit them over the head in order to get their attention. How long will it take for me not to do this?"

This comment led the group members to discuss what level of change they were undergoing and what level of change would be required. Were they focusing on changing their leadership styles? Their personalities? They answered their own questions by concluding that leadership style and theory-in-use may be consonant. Moreover, maybe there was no such concept as "personality." Human nature was very complex, and it could be viewed in many ways. They were viewing it as equivalent to changing their theories-in-use. A more detailed description of the discussion would show that it covered many of the critical issues that scholars confront when they try to understand the conditions under which personality-oriented concepts or situationally-oriented concepts are more effective.

Equally important for the purposes of learning how to learn, the presidents also surfaced the problem of becoming more effective about their behavior. They were just beginning to realize how difficult it was to become reflective about their behavior while they were accomplishing their tasks. This was an important insight because it helped to give "on-line" reflectivity priority in their lists of competences to be learned.

"I'm impressed," said E, "with how unaware I am while changes are going on. I seem to see them after the fact." "For example," added C, "there is much less attribution and competitiveness and much more use of directly observable data in this group. Yet no one had mentioned it until we focused on the issue of our change."

"Moreover," added F, who had recently become more reflective of his own behavior and that of other presidents who serve jointly on several boards of universities and companies, "I have become aware of how much I and others were saying out of competitiveness and how little I and others were adding to the discussion. No wonder groups are not very effective."

"As I see it," stated B, "I believe that we are all trying to design our own personal development and trying to speed it up." "Yes," remarked several members.

"But why," asked A, "is there this tendency to hit people over the head? Clearly, I did it during the budget meetings, but it was unnecessary."

E said that he wanted to venture a hypothesis about this group of presidents. "Whatever we do—we do it too much." "Yes," added F, "we all seem to exaggerate, to magnify, to overemphasize." "That's me," added A, "I come on too strong."

One reason for this tendency may be that the presidents' theories-in-use to motivate others was to use fear and evaluation coupled with very high levels of aspirations. They also used such theories-in-use on themselves. They all overworked, and overcontrolled, overchecked, overevaluated, and underrewarded themselves.

The presidents also concluded that they did not want to tackle these behaviors as "personality issues" to be explored with clinicians. This strategy, they concluded after lengthy discussions, should be used with behaviors (1) that they seemed unable to change with competent help from each other or their immediate subordinates or (2) with behavior whose negative impact the subordinates could not help them to neutralize while, simultaneously, designing new behavior. The presidents felt that they had just begun to utilize each other as resources and had a long way to go before they could use their subordinates as resources.

A returned to his behavior. He sought ways to change behavior that was recurrent yet ineffective.

A: I'm having a tough time changing that part of my behavior. It's an ingrained habit, at home, everywhere. I find it is a constant matter of remaining conscious of it.

E: But maybe our groups (back at home) can help us remain aware of our impact.

G: And there is another issue. You (A) appear to take the edge off of some of your needles by causing others to laugh. When you do it here, I interpret that as you're being nervous. I assume that you believe you are thinking more clearly when you are joking. But I may not think more clearly under those conditions.

A agreed and added that this comment reminded him of his uneasiness when C (an officer in his company) give his Knute Rockne speech, admonishing the group to achieve the total cut in budgets or consider themselves a failure. A felt ambivalent. On one hand, it seemed absurd to him to agree that the excellent progress should be judged a failure because the last $50,000 was not found (it was found several days later by two vice-presidents). On the other hand, he always was worried that as president he didn't hold people's "feet to the fire" once they made a decision. He did not want to appear weak.

F reminded A and the others that this seemed to be another theme of all the presidents. On one hand, they wanted to be fair; on the other hand, they did not want to appear weak. Yet, the parodox was that their level of aspiration was so high, their compulsiveness to work so strong, that it was difficult for them to make some form of objective assessment of what was weak and what was fair.

CASE C. As we have seen, A worked diligently to help his top group become a more effective team, to behave more like a group of equals, and to become more aware of the possible benefits of being more reflective about their problem-solving processes and their interpersonal relationships. This had led to increased problem-solving effectiveness with difficult problems (the major cut in budgets) and enhanced reflection and confrontation of their win-lose, competitive group dynamics.

Also, A and the group members raised some long-range questions about the company's future. A began by asking the group how they viewed the idea of his selling the company.

Sub A: We run the company for the owner.

Sub B: I think you want to sell the company, and you must have a purpose.

Sub C: The president sets the direction for the company, *totally*.

Sub D: I think you will stay until (you decide) to go public. Also, I think you will allow your executive group to participate (in the benefits of going public).

A admitted that at one time he thought that the ideal would be to sell the company or turn it over to someone else to run it. However, he now believed that he had to remain involved.

A: I don't mind staying private. It gives us some advantages. I'm ready to create, with your participation, a profit-sharing plan. Make it as if you were a stockholder. Even if the market was beautiful, I still don't think that I want to go public.

Sub D: No one would blame you for selling————times earnings.

A: The profit-sharing plan is absolutely open to change. I am open to any formula.

LATER

Sub B: You said that we don't have any investment in this company. Boy, we do! Blood, sweat, and tears.

A: You're right.

Suddenly, A made an unexpected statement. He suggested to his group that they drop the experiment toward participation:

A: Maybe we have had too much participation. I was disturbed (at the cost-cutting meeting) that we could not take a top-management view.

The group members began to give examples of the positive results of the participation. They included (1) cutting out certain products that no one had dared cut off, (2) they had begun to work more cooperatively, (3) they had jointly produced savings of expenses by different departments helping each other, and (4) they were beginning to feel a sense of cohesion and a sense of increasing trust. They asked A why he had made such a suggestion.

A: I suppose it was not a feeling of the inadequacy of the group that led me to make the proposal; it was how tough it was going to be to make the ten percent cut. The bigger the group, the more difficult to come to a decision; the more participative you make it, the longer it will take to make a decision. Results are what counts in 1974.

Sub A: Results are what count every year.

Sub B: The value of a group making certain decisions is that we may be able to control costs better.

Sub A: I don't see the advantage (of cutting participation).

A: It will save peoples' time.

People give examples of how A has overruled them.

Sub B: Maybe we are finding out that only in a meeting we can change your mind.

Sub A: Right. I think that A listens to me better in a meeting than in a one-to-one relationship.

A: Maybe you are right.

Sub D: This group has a better and more honest, more open relationship. It is the best in the history of this company. We may not agree. We are basically honest and we trust each other more.

Sub E: One thing that no longer exists is people going to A for brownie points. There is a greater sense of cooperation. (Gives examples.)

A agreed with the vice-presidents that the participation should be continued since the group was so committed to it.

In thinking about his suggestion, A commented:

A: I think everybody felt pretty good about participation, and I'm not sure whether subconsciously this wasn't a sort of testing procedure on my part to make sure that this group held together. I really, I really, don't have an answer for why it happened.

AND LATER

A: I realize that if what I said above is true, it is manipulation. But, participation seemed to me to be a painful process, terribly time consuming . . .

G: But, according to your own description, they not only cut the budget in
record time, but they were committed to carrying it out.

A: Yes, they were committed. That was absolutely great.

AND LATER

At the end of the meeting one of the officers came up and said, "Goddamit, I could not understand what the hell you were trying to do. But I
can say that it generated even more commitment on the part of everybody to work together as a team and to make our meetings more effective."

A's hypothesis that it was an attempt to generate more commitment
seems plausible if the attempt is seen as being unconscious or tacit.
Listening to the tape would not give the reader the impression that A
was expressing part of his ambivalence about Model II. The company
was going through some very difficult financial problems. Under these
conditions, he may have wished to "take over" and simply tell everyone
what to do.

Another hypothesis is related to A's confidence in his abilities to be
"strong". As a young man he watched his father "give in" to many of his
subordinates. A would become angry that his father did not "keep (the
subordinates') feet to the fire." Indeed, one of the sources of his ambivalence was related to the possibility that he was interested in learning
Model II in order not to keep people's feet to the fire. He discussed this
issue with some of the members of the group and soon came to the
conclusion that if that was his (unconscious) motivation, learning Model
II was not a valid response. Model II meant increased responsibility on
everyone's part.

D

In D's case, another transaction problem is illustrated. All the presidents
who were experimenting with Model II behavior in their executive committee meetings were meeting with mixed success as well as genuine
resistance. This was expected; the presidents well remembered their
own early resistance.

The material taken from D's tapes illustrates the bewilderment and resistance subordinates generated as well as his attempts to respond to their questions.

D had experimented in several ways with trying to behave according to a Model II theory of action. First, he periodically reviewed his model, his theory-in-use, to check what kind of changes, if any, he could identify. He also asked for confirmation or disconfirmation from a few of the vice-presidents and from all of the members in the presidential learning group.

He reported varying degrees of success with himself and with others. As for himself, he reported that he had reduced hiding his feelings, focusing only on facts, seeking to win while modestly increasing the conditions for valid information and free choice. Moreover, he believed that he had become less judgmental about self and others and had striven to set more realistic levels of aspiration for himself and to be more tolerant of others who do the same. He also reported that he believed that he was reducing the distance between himself and his subordinates while increasing his striving for public testing of issues and double-loop learnings.

D had taken several transcripts of key meetings and reviewed them, noting whatever feelings and ideas he had that he did not express during the meetings. He sent these transcripts with the comments to the two faculty members and the other presidents for their reactions. Also, he invited both faculty members to visit his group to help him in the process of becoming a more effective president and to help the group members learn more about Model II. L was able to make several visits.

These transcripts served as very useful learning devices for D and the group members. D had been very frank in his comments about his behavior. The frank comments plus the transcripts helped the group members provide helpful feedback to D.

Looking back on the history of the group, sending such a transcription was another important sign of the progress D was making in designing his own learning experiences. What seemed natural for him to do was a sign of the degree to which he had begun to internalize Model II learning conditions.

That the top group (in D's company) was beginning to explore these issues was illustrated by a transcript D sent to all the members of the presidential group. The transcript was of a session in which the group discussed some of their transition problems. (No faculty members were present during this session.)

A: I think when you (D) stop a meeting in midstream and ask someone why he did something, that puts the person on the spot. I think this may cause some people to shut up because they don't want to explore why they said that. If you want to find out, make a note and ask them afterwards.

D: I hear you saying that it doesn't help and that people are defensive. I'm wondering, perhaps it is the way I do it. Or could it be that I don't create the defensiveness? I may be making an observation that is correct, but the individual is defensive. I'm not saying that your observation is right or wrong.

B: It may be partially the way you do it. You imply a value. (Unable to give example.) I feel as if you are making a judgment of some sort. It makes me defensive.

Note below that M began by saying he was not prepared to explore group processes. Moreover, he did not want to be asked, nor did he want anyone else to be asked, to explore the group's problem-solving processes. He recommended to D that, if he wanted to learn, he should do it privately afterwards. D responded by checking publicly if he had heard M accurately, owned up to the fact that his behavior could be troublesome, and tested this publically. J then added that the quality that bothered him most was the value judgment that he thought D was making. Such a feeling would be partially a projection by J on D. However, it could be a valid attribution. Recall that D described himself as highly evaluative and judgmental of himself and others.

   K then added the possibility that the discomfort might be transitional. "Once we've learned more about Model II then we'll feel freer. At that point such comments as yours may be helpful. I'm saying that during the learning process (your interventions) may harm the flow of the meetings. Does that make sense?

D: Yes, but if people become defensive then communications may become distorted.

P: Another possibility is that when you ask people why they said or did something they might clam up.

M: I think most everybody in this group says what he thinks.

L: I don't agree with that.

Q: I don't either.

D: If we could minimize distortion and be more open, would this not help us in operating more effectively?

M: I think in my group people get pissed off, but there is a high level of trust and they forget it.

S: I don't agree.

D: It may be true for some meetings and not others.

The group was beginning to explore important issues, especially about these problem-solving processes. There was partial agreement that everyone was open. D helped to differentiate between meetings that were more and those that were less open. This helped to develop a discussion of the causes of the differences in effectiveness. Incidentally, the subordinates were correct in suggesting that "why" questions were not very helpful. First, they usually developed espoused theory answers. Second, people programmed with Model I theories-in-use will not tend to be reflective about their behavior. The "why" questions would tend to bewilder them.

The discussion soon turned to an exploration of D's behavior. The subordinates did not seem to hesitate to tell D about his impact on them. They were quite confronting. D listened to their views, acknowledged their validity, and also asked the group members to explore these issues further.

D: I'm very uncomfortable at our Monday meetings because I don't feel that we're really leveling with one another, trying to surface a problem and comment on it and trying to solve it. I sense a lot of defensiveness, and it may just be strategic action on everyone's part. As a global evaluation, I see a great amount of defensiveness, protectiveness.

J: I'd like to suggest why that's true, as a theory. I think it comes through in this transcription, although I don't think it's as clear here as it is in other places. I sense that in these groups that you tend to dominate these meetings, D, and it's partially because you're generally the leader to the group. Maybe it's somewhat natural. I sense that—trying to level with you as you're suggesting that we do—that in looking through this transcript, almost every other statement is an expression of your opinion. D participates more than anyone else. Correct? I sense that very often I am uncomfortable too. I'm uncomfortable because I feel that you expect us to play the role of being

receptive to your opinions, and when we're not, we're suddenly given the label of being negative or thought of as being an obstacle to decision making, and as a leader of a group, your opinions certainly are valuable. You might also think of yourself in the role of trying to solicit the opinions of others and toward reaching a group decision. That's one way of looking at it. The other way is just to convey information to us, in which case we'd be a lot more efficient and effective by just, you know, spelling it out. I know that's not what you want to do, or at least I sense that's not what you want to do. What I sense is, that's what's being done because you're so forceful in expressing your opinions. When someone starts to express a different . . . I get the opinion that I'm being viewed as a real pain in the ass, an obstacle to the smooth going forward and making of the decision.

D: I'm sure that I feel all the things you are saying. But I would appreciate your letting me know the next time that I come across that way to any of you.

G

The material below was also excerpted from transcripts of G's top group. G had not invited any outsider to help him in his attempts to bring about a more effective top group. He believed that some members would experience an outside consultant as a "shrink." He also feared that the group could become too easily dependent on an outside consultant. Finally, his strategy was not to begin by introducing the concepts of Model I and II. He wanted to introduce these concepts by attempting to model them during the meetings.

The transcript that the group read of G's group was about a meeting at which several members disagreed with G on a basic investment strategy. G wanted to put more money in area A, but they felt such an investment would harm division Y.

G defended his position and insisted that the executives who disagreed were not giving him documented, well-thought-through arguments. They, in turn, felt that the president was not documenting his case. Going into area A was always his baby, and he never seemed open to genuine confrontation of his views.

G: What bothers me is that you people believe that I do not have a strong desire to be first in Y business. And I give you six things we are doing to be number one. I then ask you to challenge the view, and I get statements without facts.

H: I can list facts. For example, let's take the working capital . . .

G: Where are we cutting expenses to keep us from being number one?

B: I'm saying that you do not want to be number one in Y business. You want to be number one if it can be shown in advance that it is going to have a 16% return on assets used.

G: Right.

B: I wonder what your impact is on the people of division Y. I think that they doubt your commitment . . .

G: What did you observe in my actions that supports that? I think that I do get across to them that I want to be number one.

B: I don't want to answer that off the top of my head. I will think that out and observe you from here on in.

G: That would be helpful. If I'm doing what you say, then I should learn because I would be doing something that I do not intend.

Note that G did not condemn or argue against B's confrontation. He asked for directly observable data. However, his comment that he did get across to the subordinates in the way that he wished did not encourage B to confront G. G was able, however, to maintain the position he was advocating while at the same time B felt free to say that he would observe his (G's) behavior more closely.

The presidents felt that G expressed some strong reservations about the professional competence of some key members of his top group. For example:

G: When we speak of marketing effort, B (head of marketing) wants to talk about manufacturing. We're more concerned with the other guy's problem than with our own.

B: In six months do you *really* see *real* tangible progress? When I say tangible, I mean in the bottom line? (asked with disbelief)

G: (Thinking back about our operations meeting) I asked myself, "Well, what did we accomplish? Are there actions being taken to solve the problem?" And in my mind, I was saying that I don't see results. I hear that things are being done, but I've been hearing that for the last six months. Like we take one step forward and one step back.

G agreed that this was a problem. He did not feel that the operations group, as a group, was as effective as it should be. He also felt that the meetings were not very effective. G was also concerned that A, a senior corporate officer, disagreed with the basic policy of the company, was loyal in carrying it out, but his vocal disagreement might have negative impact in the organization below.

B

As in the case of D, B had invited L, one of the faculty members, to visit his top group at their headquarters. In his introductory comments to this group, B said that he was interested in exploring new managerial practices, increasing the possibilities for individual development, and increasing the number of talented people who could rise to the top of the organization. He also said that he had learned, in the seminars with the other presidents, that these ideas, if they were to succeed, required internal commitment from them all. Internal commitment meant that they would have to decide, for themselves, whether these ideas were useful and whether L should be invited to work with them.

B also talked frankly about the kind of learning that he was getting from the presidents' seminar. Samples of his comments to his subordinates included:

I learned that I was doing quite a bit wrong.

What I thought was a superb job in managing a meeting turned out to be a horrendous job.

I have a long way to go.

I don't get much consultation from others—I need it.

How can an open relationship be developed where management is not controlling, where there is not the feeling that management is manipulating? Conversely, how can I state what I believe without that becoming controlling?

B also surfaced some of the doubts that he had expressed in the presidents' seminar. He wanted, as president, to express his view without that being overcontrolling. He wanted to be viewed, indeed, experienced, as not being manipulative. He wanted to help create a setting in which people could say what was on their minds *and* in which inquiry and problem-solving effectiveness were high.

The group chose to meet with L, without B present, and with L encouraging the expression of negative votes against his becoming a consultant. The biggest concern the vice-presidents had was related to L's professional behavior. They made it clear that they expected him to be a consultant to all and not a private communicator to the president. L not only agreed, but had made that requirement part of his coming for the visit.

Intensive discussions ensued that indicated that B's perception about subordinates' mistrusting his motives of participation was in question. Furthermore, they saw their president behaving in manipulative ways. For example:

Sub A: I still question whether B really wants to change, what his motives are. He wants us to get involved in such a personal thing, yet he'll sit down and pick apart a price point . . . I could never understand why he'd come back from one of these sessions, and every time he'd come back, he'd be a different person almost. And we'd all think, 'Oh my God, that YPO is going to ruin our company."

Sub B: We never really knew what happened at those seminars. We'd get just enough to be confused, really.

Sub C: B has said many times he'll respect a person who will stand up to him and tell him that he's wrong. That's his espoused theory. Now, I know two things will happen if I do stand up to him. He's going to get his feelings hurt, and he never forgets anything and you might have repercussions for a long time afterward. On the other hand, if I don't stand up to him, then maybe he won't respect me.

Sub D: On some of these task forces, some people felt he was going through the motions and saying it's democratic, but he's already got his mind made up, so it doesn't matter what we come up with. I think sometimes he asks for input when he has his mind made up, and sometimes I think he's looking for allies.

Sub E: A lot of times, I may disagree (with someone from another department). We got a difference. OK, we'll fight it out. But B sees this and decides it means I don't understand that other person's needs. So it gets blown out of perspective. Yet sometimes something that really does represent a major difference doesn't get dealt with.

B's group developed a summary of their perceptions of B's leadership, and this became the basis for the first discussion of B and his subordinates on these issues. This session was taped, and about 15 typewritten pages of transcript became the case to be discussed by the presidents at the learning seminar.

Excerpts from these transcripts included:

B: Last night, L gave me this paper, which I read. I understand you had some discussion about whether you should give this to me. I felt a little surprised at first at the concept that I would be hurt. But there was one thing that did have a tendency to hurt me, which was the feeling that I might be hurt, rather than that there could be free communication so that people can talk straight to each other, rather than saying, "Gee, he probably can't take it." That was probably the only thing about it that did hurt. Isn't that about the essence of the way I explained it to you, L?

L: No. The part that's different is that the other place I thought you were feeling hurt was—one of the comments on that paper had a comment like, "I wonder if he really wants to change."

B: In my mind I was relating those two together. What are people thinking about if they say, "He talks about all this, but I wonder if he's really serious." Inasmuch as this is something of a painful process, and it's not the easiest thing to be dealing with, and changes in behavior are hard to accomplish, it would seem to me that most people would have seen me wrestle with it. I could take it much easier if people said he fumbles a lot, and he really doesn't come off too well. But really questioning whether I want to change, that is a fundamental question, and that would hurt me.

The presidents, as a result of reading the case material above, felt that B had expressed himself candidly, but in doing so, he confirmed some of the subordinates' fears—that the report might hurt B. They did not wish to imply that B should have withheld his feelings. Rather, B might have acknowledged the dilemma that he was experiencing. On one hand, he valued highly what was happening; on the other hand, he was surprised and hurt by certain comments made by subordinates, and he knew that saying this might act to inhibit others.

A and E pointed out that immediately after B's comments several vice-presidents tried to soothe B's feelings. However, they noted that Sub C raised this possibility during the discussion.

Sub C: I wonder if we're not using Model II somewhat as a scapegoat. I wonder if I hadn't seen Model II whether I wouldn't feel the same way. My question would be: OK, he's been exposed to Model II, so have I. How do we both perceive that Model II?

B agreed that his comments might have had that effect, but his intention was the opposite.

B: I wanted to convey that they feel perfectly at ease to confront me. I wanted to convey, you know, speak right up. I mean, whatever is on your mind.

L pointed out that in one sense B had been more open than was usually the case. It was probably the first time the group had heard B talk about being hurt (although many saw him as a person who could be hurt). What was missing was B's inviting feedback, even if it hurt at times.

Then B added, "Yes, I suppose there was also some degree of anger. I was angry that they doubted that I wanted to change. And I said to myself, why in the hell do you think I'm doing all these things if I didn't really mean it."

C then noted that B, in his role in the learning seminar, had been the most vocal doubter about anyone changing. Also, if B were feeling angry about his being viewed as play acting with change, these feelings would be relevant.

B: I can see what you mean. I am already withholding information when, at the same time, I am asking them to be fully open.

You know, I thought that I was being open and aboveboard. But listening to this, I can see that I wasn't.

AND LATER

Perhaps I am not as aware as I should be of the degree to which I am not open.

CHAPTER

$$11$$

SEMINAR 5. EXPLORING "UNCONSCIOUS" FACTORS

There was another level of learning that was going on with F during the session (see Chapter 9). Recall that he entered the session viewing himself as an intuitive, emotional individual, while the group members experienced him as cold, distant, and rational. Recall also that F believed that X was an excellent president with impeccable logic and "naturally" Model II in his theories-in-use. Yet the group, on the basis of the cues F was giving them, questioned whether X was an effective president with Model II theories-in-use.

By the end of the session, F learned that he was viewing himself differently than others; the differences were crucial because he made important decisions based on his views, such as hiring a president who had the qualities that F felt he himself did not possess. When F was describing the excellent relationship he had with X, the group members were inferring the opposite.

If we examine the dynamics by which F began to change, they appear to be consistent with Model II learning actions. When F said something that the group members disagreed with, they would ask him for the directly observable data. When F said something that was inconsistent, they would point out the inconsistencies. When F described his impact on X in ways that they believed were not congruent with the data, they would surface the data and the incongruities. Recall the six mini-episodes presented in Chapter 9 (pp 141–143) to illustrate the changes F went through as a result of this process of inquiry. In each episode, he learned an important lesson, usually an inconsistency or implication of which he was unaware.

For example:

In episode	he learned	the inquiry surfaced
1	I trust X because there are no big challenges ahead.	What is the nature of the quality of trust in X if it is based upon the presumption that X will not face difficult challenges in the future?
2	I agreed to a relationship with X in which he wanted no part of me.	What is effective about a relationship in which F idolizes X and X wants no part of him?
3	I did not level with X nor with myself.	What is it about leveling with X that threatens F?
4	I want to give X a sense of confidence.	What leads F to appoint and support as president an individual in whom he has to inject a sense of confidence?
5	I placed a halo around X.	What is F protecting himself from by placing a halo around X?
6	I inhibited X from exploring an issue (his record of failure) which I knew was an important issue.	What aspects of F is he protecting himself from when he encourages X *not* to examine issues that F believes must be examined?

The theme that underlies the learnings and the inquiries just listed is that F had been unaware of them, yet this was not true of the other members. Moreover, the unawareness was not due to the lack of availability of knowledge or the lack of experience. As the transcript showed, the participants worked hard to help F become aware of information that they knew. F was unaware because he was defending himself. Unawareness that is related to self-defense is usually connected with unconscious factors. Psychodynamic clinicians would argue that the lessons F learned require a therapeutic encounter. The answers to the inquiries raised require digging into F's history, especially his early childhood. They would relate these issues to the unconscious.

A theory of action does not deny that there are factors that individuals push out of their awareness. What we were able to do was to bring them into awareness by using an inquiry approach consonant with Model II. The members kept asking questions, which F answered. With each answer, he built a consistent picture, which he could not ignore, of inconsistencies, incongruities, and gaps in his position. As he became aware of these factors, he began to see himself and X differently. He returned to the organization with his perceptual filters altered. He could now see X differently and more accurately. As a result, he learned new things about X during the interactions with the bankers (to cite but one example). These new insights, in turn, reinforced in his mind that the group members' perception of him had validity and had to be faced. The way these issues were faced was (1) to question himself more completely and (2) to deal with X more openly.

It may interest the reader to learn that several months of continual testing with X, of examining X's performance record and of receiving feedback from others led F to decide that X should be terminated as president. Instead of calling X into the office and firing him, which would have been his strategy before these experiences (and which was the advice given to him by several of his board members), F decided to talk openly with X about his diagnosis, to request confrontation of it, because he realized that firing X unilaterally could be a defense of himself. X reported that he valued the discussions but was somewhat bewildered by F's openness and patience. Shortly after what was described by several vice-presidents as a fiasco by X, he (X) was terminated. The termination was also discussed with the key vice-presidents. As a result, F learned not only that they were in agreement, but that they wanted to contribute to a new reorganization of the top that would save substantial costs. Moreover, the morale and cohesiveness of the top group, which is usually impaired under these conditions, was actually strengthened.

C and D also experienced learning that may be described as becoming aware of defenses such as projection.

In G's case, the learning began when G said he had a problem with a vice-president who we shall call T. Briefly, in G's view, T was not performing adequately as a vice-president. G believed that T could make valuable contributions at jobs that were beneath the present job level that T held.

After a lengthy discussion, it became increasingly apparent that T had performed ineffectively in three key episodes and that G was protecting T by doing some of the work that was in T's domain.

E asked G why he did not confront T more forcefully. For example:

E: . . . As a result of our discussions, I have decided to restructure your job. I will not condone the present level of performance.

I know two things. We can't continue as we are, and there will not be any restructuring of your job without active participation . . . etc.

G: I'm uncomfortable with that because I haven't been fair enough with T up to this point. It would be a total shock and surprise to him.

L asked G how valid he felt E's comments were. G responded that his gut reaction was that E was right, and some day what E said would probably happen. L asked G if he could invent an appropriate response. G seemed to hesitate because on one hand he had tried countless times and failed, yet, on the other hand, he did not wish to move too fast. G saw the inconsistency and owned up to having ambivalent feelings. As he explored his ambivalence, he discovered that one source was his fear that T might quit and that there was no immediate replacement.

This led A, B, and D to help G see that to go out and look for a replacement for T, on a covert basis, was a Model I response. Moreover, to seek a replacement without testing T's capacity to change (assuming for the moment that the major fault was with T) was also ineffective.

E wondered if G was fulfilling his obligations to the organization. How could he keep an ineffective vice-president?

G: Well, OK, I see the point. I have not recognized myself whether T is or is not salvageable. I haven't faced up to this issue, even though I've said I should many times.

C then said that he was now beginning to see another problem for G. G was not able to communicate difficult issues to T, and perhaps the group could help G to develop the competence required to do so. Someone recalled that G felt E's intervention above was like a "two-by-four." Now he wondered if, by G seeing E as a "mean bastard," he could have prevented himself from seeing his procrastinations with T.

E supported his view and gave an example of a senior officer who was fired because of incompetence. E also said that the officer had given great service to the company, and he was given very lucrative separation benefits. E was willing to accept any hostility from others about the lucrativeness because he felt that the officer's incompetence was partially the organization's responsibility. The point that was stressed to G was that E seemed to be willing to make these tough decisions and defend, when he felt they were just, the lucrative separation arrangements.

G: Yes, I'll accept what is being said. I haven't come to grips with this situation. I don't know how to do it.

L: I am struck with some parallels between the concerns you have about T and some of our concerns about you. For example, T, as I recall, proscrastinated at making difficult decisions; and you appear to do the same. You believe T should get rid of some people, and you get perturbed when he delays. Yet you delay.

This led G to ask if others saw the parallels. All the members confirmed L's view. C added that this discovery would reformulate the problem as follows: "I, G, have a problem. I do not feel competent in confronting T with his incompetence that I believe I can document." Such a statement of the problem was different from the one with which G began, which was, in effect, "How do I deal with a subordinate (T), who is ineffective?"

G: I see the problem more clearly. What is in me that makes it difficult for me to deal with people like T?

C: And one response is that I, G, have some of the same qualities and theories-in-use as T does and of which I am unaccepting.

Again we note that a similar type of inquiry as that used with F helped G examine the degree to which he manifested the same qualities as T, as well as the possibility that his procrastinating in dealing with T openly was a defense of himself. The fact that he condemned T for the same qualities that he had and that he kept this connection suppressed led G to develop insights into the defense, commonly called projection.

The reader might be interested in learning that G discussed the issues openly and candidly with T. A discussion, for example, was held between G and T after both listened to the tape recording of the first discussion. With T's permission, G sent the transcripts of all the sessions to the writer. If space were available to present them in detail, they would show that, during many key interventions, G approximated Model II theories-in-use.

For example, G opened one of the sessions with T with the following points:

I hope we can use this as a learning experience.

I was bothered when you said, "Well, one thing is that I don't have to report to you anymore and maybe that solves the problem."

The more I thought about your comment, the more certain that I became that this action did not solve the problem; it just postponed it.

I should like to learn, not only because I value the relationship with you, but whatever I am doing with you, I may be doing with others.

During the session, G owned up to information he withheld ("I should have told you the truth . . ."), clarified his intentions as requested by T ("As I recall, I was trying to express . . ."), advocated as clearly as he could the difficulties he had with T ("I felt that I kept repeating to you that I did not see such and such results. You would tell me not to worry because you were on top of things, yet nothing seemed to change"), asked T if he had sensed his (G's) frustration and other feelings, described how he, as president, did not want to overcontrol people as he did before, etc.

When T, in anger, made statements that would have sent G through the roof (e.g., "I was a loyal employee and it didn't work to my advantage. In the future, I am going to have to take an attitude of what benefits T"), G responded by asking, "What has led you to that conclusion from our discussion so far?"

One of the results of these meetings was that T was not fired. He was able to design a different job for himself that he took and is presently performing very well. There have been several discussions between T and G because, as one might expect, T had serious questions about G's new version of effective leadership and about his future relationships with G. Again, the transcripts show that G handled the situation effectively.

The reader may recall that D had a vice-president identified as C (not to be confused with the faculty member C) with whom he was having very difficult relationships. Again, through a similar process of inquiry, he became aware of several of his defenses, including the defense of projection.

For example, D rethought his relationship with C. He was able to identify more clearly his (D's) personal responsibility in the situation, as well as the self-sealing destructive processes. He developed a written statement of his diagnosis that is quoted at length.

I discuss with others their behavior that is similar to mine if I do not recognize it in myself or if I have accepted it in myself. I avoid discussing with others their behavior that is similar to mine if I recognize it in myself and do not accept it. I do not want them to feel free to confront me on my behavior that I do not accept.

For example, I am angry at C because he does not establish and monitor a completion date for a project. If he recognizes but does not accept his behavior, he will change the subject. If I persist and he feels guilty, he will attack me to try to stop me from punishing him. He will probably attack me in an area in which I have a shortcoming that he has and is blind to. He will tell me I delay making decisions. If he's blind to his shortcoming, I'm probably blind to mine. However, I don't admit my shortcoming to myself or to him, so I think he is stupid and defensive. He thinks I am stupid and defensive. At this point I feel guilty about my inability to teach him and to manage our relationship. Consequently, I attack him again. And so on . . .

At some point I withdraw because the situation is painful for me. He withdraws for the same reason. Neither of us has been forced to recognize shortcomings to which he is blind or deal with shortcomings he recognizes and doesn't accept. We do not deal with our own anger or behavior. We deal only with the other's anger.

This led D to take an old memo that he had written about his relationship with C and alter it. The words on top were words that he inserted *after* he had generated the new insights into his relationship with C.

Memo on C

    I   his   me

C may have a high level of concern with my evaluation of him and the effect

                       his   I   I

this incident will have on my evaluation. He may wonder how he can influence

                        not   I   his

these evaluations. I have   been as explicit as I know how. He seems to reject my

basis.

          his

A part of my evaluation is how someone works with others, helps others, man-

  I   me

ages others. C may lay great weight on the evaluations of others in regard to him-

                me   I

self and those who work for him. If so, he would overemphasize the effect of others'

    his   I

opinions on my evaluation. He may not have developed usable standards for judg-

                                           I

ing effective managerial performance. This may be one reason he performs so

               I don't   I   my

poorly as a manager. If he doesn't have usable standards, he can't help his people

establish objectives and meet them.

    I   him, etc.

Yet he will tell a draftsman he has to improve, fire another, tell me M. isn't in

His   I
the plant. My experience indicates that at times he will pick capable people; at

I   him   I
others mediocre people. He seems to indicate to me that every person he picks and

retains is capable and will do an excellent job without guidance or discussion of

I have   I
standards of performance. Yet he has said someone isn't doing too well but he (C)

I   I'll   he leaves me
can't find anyone better. C tells me he'll do a much better job if I leave him alone.

He   I   I wouldn't   him/my father   I
I think C believes he would be president if it weren't for me,   he

he's   (if I were dependent on him)
would do a much better job because I'm not adequate (and I'm dependent on him).

He   I   me
I think he feels fate has kicked him once again.

He thinks he's   is   His
I think I'm doing a good job and have become an acceptable manager. (My

My   him   I don't
standards suggest excellence.) His disagreement is indication to me that he doesn't

I'm not   I
recognize good management, additional evidence that he isn't a good manager. He

him   he's   me   he evaluates me
must attack me, because if I'm capable of evaluating him and do evaluate him as

my   I'm   I'm
ineffective, his self-concept is destroyed. More simply, if he's wrong, he's inade-

My   his
quate. His constant attacks emphasize the disparity between my performance and

he is   he reacts to my
objectives. The more satisfied I am, the less I react to his attacks.

He   me   my   his
I may be angry at C because his mediocre performance reinforces my concerns

he   father   He   me   I am
that (I may not be a good manager). I can't manage him. The worse he is, the

he is   His   me   I am
worse I am. This is self-reinforcing. My alternatives are to accept him as he is,

me   leave me   He doesn't   he   me   me
isolate him, or to fire him. I don't think I can help him change. Can I help him

me   he thinks
operate more effectively? Would it be productive to tell him what I think and get

my   me
his reactions? It's probably worth the risk. It may even free him to do a better job.

I   him I   he is
He told me he wants to learn from work with L on Model II. At times I am in-

me   he   he
furiated with C. Why? During the period of time when I didn't think (I was doing

he   me   him   me   My
a good job), I let him control (punish) me. Dealing with him was miserable. His

my
refusal to set completion dates and his lateness and partial solutions of develop-
                    him   *My*
ments and problems seemed to me to be a form of aggression. His dogmatic repeti-
  my   *myself*   *I*
tion of his viewpoint or extended defense of himself disrupted most meetings. He
                                                   he
would rarely agree with a position that I took or a decision that the group made.
My   *he tells me   he has made a de-*
His arguments were interminable. Currently, I tell him that a decision has been
cision   he won't   I have   he tells me
made and I don't want to review it unless he has new information; or I tell him I
he   my   I'm   He   he's
understand his point and he's being repetitive. (I could ask the group, but I'm
                                                      He   his
afraid they will be uncomfortable and won't respond. I could express my fear to

them).
  He   he   He
I may be afraid that I can't find an adequate replacement. I may be unhappy
     he doesn't   it   himself
that I don't want to spend the time finding and training someone to take his new
              he's   He's
position. Therefore, I'm not a good manager. I'm afraid to run the risk. Therefore,
he's   He's   He doesn't
I'm weak and can't make decisions. I'm afraid of competition. I don't have guts.

What's the difference between J and C? J was clearly not making a contribution. C

is a clever engineer and from time to time makes an important contribution. Yet

the cost is great.
  He's   himself   me   him
I'm angry with myself for letting him take advantage of me and others, not
                          his
doing a good job. It is my responsiblity to have good people who operate effec-
        he doesn't, he's   He hears   him   I'm
tively. If I don't, I'm not managing well. I hear people telling me that C is not
                      I   He does   I have
doing a good job and that he should be fired. I do not agree. C has a contribution
        He   me
to make. I should explore with him and our management group how to organize
              me   I am
and staff so as to let him make the contribution he is capable of and at the same
        my   his   me
time minimize his negative impact. On the one hand, my experience with him in-
        I haven't   me
dicates he hasn't changed much. Can we structure a productive role for him exactly
  I am
as he is?

It should be pointed out that in all cases, as the members began to work through their projections and other defenses, they reported an increased sense of inner calm and a decreasing sense of internal conflict. They also reported, and these reports were confirmed by tape recordings of actual sessions and by interviews with the relevant individuals, that they were more open and more willing to problem solve these issues than before. Moreover, they entered such discussions significantly less interested in fixing blame, punishing the other, or winning out. The transcripts showed that they invited the others to confront them because they were aware that their views were highly influenced by defensive filters.

Whenever the issues were not worked through, as in D's case with C, D worked hard not to punish C for D's projections. At the same time, with the cooperation of C, D has developed ways to evaluate C's performance and to confront C with his inadequacies. (D wants to keep C because he is an excellent engineer.) Also, D is aware of the conditions under which he might not hear C accurately and has told this to C and encouraged C to permit a third party to attend those encounters that promise to be difficult.

There are examples of defenses that have not been worked through as successfully as those above. A, for example, can still be highly controlling, attributive, or competitive. Although he is confrontable on such behavior, he does not yet appear to be able to manage it so that he can prevent it from occurring. During the discussions, he has related his overcontrol of others to the fear he recalled of experiencing his father as a weak president who could not "keep his vice-presidents' feet to the fire." A realizes that he overreacts to these issues. At the time of this writing, A is working on these defensive actions by utilizing the group to alert and question him in the same manner as was described with F above.

In all these cases, important insights and changes have been begun to evolve in the theories-in-use and in the degree of internal conflict of people without exploring the historical roots of the defenses. In all cases, the issues have been worked through by using present-day, here and now examples of these problems.

This suggests the following conjecture. If defenses do develop early in life, they may be maintained through an elaborate network of propositions in one's theory-in-use that are internally inconsistent. The inconsistencies are kept out of one's awareness through the development of a second order of defenses that are maintained by our cohorts, who, being programmed with Model I, do not tell us the inconsistencies and incongruities as they arise.

It may be possible to become aware of this elaborate network of defenses by examining the inconsistencies that people manifest when they deal, in the present, with problems that are related to these defenses. For example, F's inability to accept his own coldness and rationality was reduced when he had to deal with X, who had similar qualities. G's inability to confront T with his poor performance had to be dealt with because T was not confronting his subordinates with their poor performances.

It may be, therefore, that the metaphor "deep" problems is not always an accurate metaphor. It may be that certain deep problems are actually "wide" ones in the sense they exist because a wide interrelated net of inconsistencies and defenses is built around them that are so complex that they appear unchangeable. For certain types of problems, a theory of action approach may be at least as successful for the individual as the more traditional approaches. The advantage of the theory of action approach is that it tends to involve many people in systemic relationships. Hence, others learn, groups change, and eventually, organizational living systems may be altered.

CHAPTER

$$\boxed{12}$$

ORGANIZATIONAL LEARNING

LEE BOLMAN

Individual change has repeatedly failed as a strategy for producing organizational change (Katz and Kahn, 1966, ch. 13), and earlier chapters have shown that significant change in adults' behavior requires a substantial investment in time and energy. But why go to that much effort? Why should we expect that presidential learning, even if it occurred, would lead to significant organizational change? This chapter attempts to respond to those questions by presenting a model of organizational learning and describing the effort to apply that model in an organization headed by one participant in the presidents' seminars.

Why go to the effort? Basically, because organizations are universally victims of a decay process that is predictable from the analysis presented earlier in this book. It has been shown that human are programmed around core values of unilateral goal achievement and self-protection. Those core values lead to strategies that produce (1) deterioration in relationships, (2) gaps between self-perception and behavior which in turn prevent individuals from seeing their own causality in the problems they create, (3) inability to solve those problems, and (4) the fatalistic as-

183

sumption that the problems are unsolvable.

The same thing happens to organizations. Organizations, like individuals, have both espoused theories (embodied in descriptions by organizational participants of the nature and purpose of the organization) and theories-in-use (embodied in the structure and norms that govern behavior). Model I individuals create organizations whose structures and norms reflect Model I assumptions and produce Model I consequences—including organizational decay. Such decay is characterized by a set of symptoms that is predictable from Model I:

1. Decreasing efficiency—the organization requires increasing amounts of energy and resources to produce the same output.
2. Decreasing satisfaction—organizational participants (employees, customers, clients, etc.) become less and less satisfied with the organization and their role in it.
3. Simplistic, self-defensive diagnoses of organizational problems—people see the problems but not their own causality and project responsibility onto convenient targets.
4. Increasing investment in protecting one's own turf—individuals and groups see themselves as a positive force in the system and see others as the cause of the problems; they therefore see it as legitimate and necessary to defend their current activities and to maintain or enhance their power in the system.
5. Failure of efforts to reduce the decay process—since they are based on inadequate diagnoses of the problem.
6. Fatalistic assumptions that the problems are unsolvable.

Model I acts as a paradigm that shuts off exploration of and learning about the paradigm itself (i.e., inhibits double-loop learning). The problems that are inherent consequences of Model I governing variables cannot be solved without going outside that paradigm. That means that organizational decay is inevitable unless the organization's theory-in-use can be changed in the direction of a theory like Model II, which emphasizes valid information and double-loop learning.

Where does an organizational learning process begin? A paradox emerges: it is difficult for individuals to learn Model II behavior when organizational norms support Model I, but it is difficult for an organization to have Model II norms unless individuals within it have learned to behave in consonance with Model II governing variables.

The paradox implies that individual and organizational learning need to be simultaneous and mutually reinforcing. Increasing the number of people who have competence in Model II behavior increases the likelihood that such behavior becomes the organizational norm. Such learning is most likely to be self-maintaining if it involves groups of people who can facilitate and reinforce one another's learning. Since existing educational methods limit the number of people who can be involved in an educational process, a selection has to be made. Success is most likely if the change process begins at the top of the hierarchy, since individuals at that level are most able to influence and are least imprisoned by existing norms and practices.

The strategy of "start at the top" has been criticized on the grounds that (1) it is conservative (e.g., "People who have power will never give it up voluntarily."), (2) it makes change agents servants of power who are coopted by the establishment, and (3) change may never reach the bottom. Examples can be found to validate all of those criticisms, but the examples involve change strategies that reflect Model I governing variables, even though the change agents may have espoused different values. Moreover, the criticisms do not suggest a viable alternative. Starting at the middle of organizations has failed repeatedly. Starting at the bottom and using confrontational strategies may succeed in altering the distribution of power (although often it does not), but the processes used are based on and reinforce Model I governing variables.

The arguments above suggest an organizational learning process that begins with a group of key executives at the top of the organization and helps them to develop effectiveness in Model II behavior. If the effort with the initial group is successful, they will begin to reinforce one another's learning and to reexamine existing organizational norms. If other organizational participants perceive positive outcomes from the learning process, they may also choose to participate. As more and more people develop the necessary behavioral competence, Model II governing variables will increasingly become embedded in the organization's culture.

There are many reasons to expect such a strategy to fail. Any process that is consistent with Model II governing variables must seek to provide people with a free and informed choice either to seek or reject such learning. If they are fully informed, individuals will know they are deciding whether to embark on a learning process that will be long, difficult, and at times stressful. (Faced with the same choice, some chief executives rejected the opportunity to participate in the presidents' seminars, and two of the original participants dropped out after the initial session.) A second reason the strategy is likely to fail is the slow pace of learning. Outsiders could look at participants in a learning process and say, "They aren't learning anything," or "They've learned some jargon, but I don't see any real change." Such a credibility gap is not only possible but likely in the early phases of learning.

The organizational learning model can be effective only if the barriers are outweighed by people's awareness of the existing problems in their organization, by their desire to enhance their ability to behave congruently with their espoused values, and by their willingness to trust Model II as an espoused theory long before they are able to enact it.

THE CHIEF EXECUTIVE AS CHANGE AGENT

Can a chief executive serve as a catalyst for such a process in his own company? The president has several advantages in such a role. His subordinates usually accord him a legitimate role in setting organizational norms and influencing the culture of the company. The prominence of the president's role means that his behavior serves as an important behavior model—a source of information to others about how people are supposed to behave in the organization. The president is also spared the necessity of fighting uphill battles against entrenched authorities.

Despite the advantages of the presidential role, there are equally significant obstacles. It takes a long time to reach the point at which he can consistently generate Model II behavior, particularly in stressful, real time conditions. Thus, the behavior model he presents is likely to be inconsistent and variable. He finds himself in many situations in which he is unsure how to apply Model II, or unsure how effective his behavior is. His subordinates have usually adapted themselves to the president's historic, Model I management style. When he attempts to change, they are likely to be mistrustful, puzzled, or confused, but unlikely to confront him openly. Since the subordinates' own theories-in-use are Model I, they are unlikely to be effective even if they do confront. The help they offer is more likely to help the president revert to Model I than to facilitate his learning.

President B encountered all of those obstacles and became increasingly frustrated at the slow progress he felt he was making in his company. He concluded that he needed outside help to help him develop a more effective learning process and asked the seminar faculty for help. Since we were anxious to test the possibilities for organizational learning, I agreed to work with B in his company.

THE SETTING

B (for the purposes of this chapter, he is given the pseudonym of George Peters) was the president of AA Stores, Inc., a company that he and his partner had founded as a single retail store, and that had evolved into a growing, geographically dispersed retail chain. B's partner, Bill Hanson, held the title of chairman of the board and headed the operations end of the business, while Peters was responsible for merchandising and marketing.

Peters' commitment to learning—both for himself and his company—stemmed importantly from his perception that he had been successful in developing his business, but notably unsuccessful in developing his subordinates. That disparity would, he felt, eventually produce a crisis as the company reached a size at which a strong, second level of management was essential. He doubted that his organization's existing climate would permit such managers to develop or function.

INITIAL STEPS

The model of organizational learning described above calls for three initial steps: (1) offer to a group of key executives the opportunity to participate in an educational process, (2) if they agree to participate, conduct a series of seminars designed to help them move through the learning phases from Model I to Model II, and (3) if the educational process is successful with the initial group, expand it to additional groups.

The first problem was to create conditions in which the key executives could make a free and informed choice to participate or not. That was difficult for several reasons:

1. The outside consultant was invited by the president, who hoped his subordinates would choose to participate in the learning process.
2. The president wanted his subordinates to make their own decision, but the credibility of the message was undermined by the subordinates' long history of being pressured and manipulated by the president.
3. Having lived in a Model I world, the key executives were likely to expect that the consultant's primary goals were to sell his services and do what the president wanted done. That makes it difficult for the consultant to communicate that his goal is to help the group make an informed decision (either for or against what he is offering), and that he considers the group to be his client (including but not limited to the president).

The strategy was to hold an initial one-day meeting with the key executives to provide them the opportunity to decide if they wanted to participate in a learning experience. Ten key executives were invited to the meeting—seven who reported to George Peters, two who reported to Bill Hanson, and one (the company treasurer) who reported to both. Hanson indicated that he did not wish to participate in any subsequent seminars, but was interested in attending the initial meeting.

Peters and I collaborated on an agenda that included three major phases:

1. An opening statement by Peters on why he had invited the consultant, his own learning experiences, and his feelings about the executives' making their own choice. The opening statement was to be followed by questions and discussion.
2. A discussion (by the author) of objectives, goals, and methods of the learning process.
3. In the afternoon, Peters and Hanson would be absent, and the group would discuss what decision they wanted to make. I was to be present to answer questions and to facilitate the discussion. (I suggested that I leave for part of the discussion, but the executives insisted that was unnecessary.)

George Peters' opening statement included discussion of his own learning experience in the presidents' seminars, of his hopes and aspirations for himself and for the company, and of ways in which he thought learning experiences could be useful for the executives. He closed by indicating both his own stake in the subordinates' decision and his hope that they would be able to make a decision to which they felt committed:

PETERS: I do have a selfish interest. If you know I'm committed to changing my behavior, and if you know more about what I'm trying to learn, you would be in a better position to say, "hey, you're not doing what you said you would." I'd like you to be able to confront me, because that's the way I'll learn. But just because I believe in this doesn't mean that other people will.

Hanson responded almost immediately by referring to an anecdote Peters had used in his opening statement. The anecdote referred to another chief executive who decided to withdraw from active management because of the difficulty of changing his leadership style. Hanson asked:

HANSON: George, do you subconsciously imply to people in the room that they might be subject to leaving the company?
PETERS: No, I think I started by saying there are different choices people make. Fundamentally, I'm saying I believe this approach will help our company become professionally managed. I feel the key execu-

tives need to have choices. I assume there will be a variety of management styles. I did not mean to imply think the way I do or get out.

L: I think the issue Bill raises is important. How easy is it to say no when George is saying yes?

GEORGE: People may be hesitant to surface their fears. They might be thinking, "He says it, but he doesn't mean it." I'm not sure I have the skill to give information that people will believe. I'd like to open this up, but I don't really know quite how.

Peters was able to be open about how he felt and to acknowledge a powerlessness chief executives often feel—the inability to be sure that he is credible or that his subordinates are fully honest. Peters' apprehensions were justified by the cautiousness in the subordinates' responses. Their initial reactions consisted primarily of expressions of confusion and requests for more information. I responded to those requests with an extensive discussion of the learning model and the theory underlying that model. The executives indicated they found the information helpful, but it was not until the afternoon session (when Peters and Hanson had left) that they began to discuss more openly their feelings about their organization and about the learning activity that was being proposed.

They discussed the special problems created by the dual leadership in the company. Hanson had a reputation as a colorful, but very aggressive and authoritarian manager. The executives who reported to him indicated that they expected more conflict with their boss if they really began to change their management approach. They expected that they might find themselves having to switch back and forth between management styles, depending on the situation and pressures from Hanson. But they were dissatisfied with their own managerial effectiveness and with the relationship they had with Hanson. As they saw it, there were risks, but there was more to be gained than lost.

Discussion of the leadership situation in the company led to discussion by marketing executives of their concerns about George Peters. They had often experienced him as changeable and inconsistent. They wondered whether he really wanted to change his behavior, and whether he could if he wanted to.

A [1]: I still question what Mr. Peters' motives are. How can he want us to become part of such a personal thing, and yet he'll sit down and pick apart a (rela-

---

[1] Letters A, B, C, etc. can refer to any member of the learning group, and are not assigned to specific persons, except that L always denotes the author. The chapter is written so as to protect the anonymity of individual participants.

tively minor decision). He's so variable—one thing this morning, something else this afternoon.

B: That's one reason I'd like to go ahead. I hope it will help me understand him better.

C: Is that a valid reason? I've known him a long time, and I still don't understand him.

That discussion surfaced another concern: might the program actually be harmful?

D: I think during the time Mr. Peters has been working on his own behavior, he's left a lot of us puzzled. Will we do that to the people who report to us?

I said that the risk was real because the transition process from familiar modes of operating to unfamiliar modes is difficult, and that there probably would be times when the executives would feel confused or be confusing to others. That led someone to ask what the group could expect to gain from a two-day seminar. I said that people could probably develop a better understanding of their existing management style and a sense of their own "learning agendas." But a short experience would be unlikely to produce significant changes in behavior, and such change would require additional learning. The executives were not particularly discouraged that so little was promised from an initial learning experience. Instead, they were reassured that (1) I could be trusted, (2) the program did not offer the alarming prospect of completely remaking the humans who participated in it, and (3) I was not repeating the practice so common in our culture of promising miraculous improvements in no time at all.

As the afternoon discussion proceeded, the executives showed considerable interest and energy in discussing the leadership styles and impact of the two top executives, but showed little inclination to discuss their relationships with one another or with me. When questioned about that, the group twice responded by going back to talking about Peters and Hanson. Eventually, the group was able to acknowledge that there was mistrust of one another, that they were reluctant to confront each other, and that conflict among members of the group was often resolved by going to "Papa Bear" (either Peters or Hanson). The group began to see the connections between their difficulties with one another and with top management. If, for example, they continually appealed to the top to resolve conflict, they invited the very intrusions from top management that they disliked. After several hours of discussion, the group concluded that they wanted to proceed. That decision was carefully tested with each member, and each indicated that he or she saw it as a worthwhile experiment.

KEY EXECUTIVES: INITIAL SEMINAR

Once the executives had agreed to proceed, an initial two and a half-day seminar was scheduled. Each member of the group agreed to provide a case situation that would provide data relevant to both espoused theory and theory-in-use.

Two hypotheses seemed reasonable for the initial seminar:

1. The case papers would show Model I theories-in-use in every member of the group.
2. In an initial seminar, it was possible to help each individual:
   a. develop an understanding of theories for action, and the distinction between espoused theory and theory-in-use.
   b. develop an intellectual understanding of Model I, and an ability to use it as a diagnostic map in analyzing behavior.
   c. attain an initial understanding of one's own theory-in-use and of the degree to which Model I was an accurate map of an individual's behavior.
   d. develop the beginnings of an intellectual understanding of Model II.

The plan for the seminar included five phases:

1. Initial conceptual input on Model I.
2. Group discussion of several individual cases, using Model I as a diagnostic framework.
3. Discussion of Model II.
4. Discussion of additional individual cases, using both models as a diagnostic framework, and attempting to generate Model II alternative behaviors.
5. Closing meeting with George Peters, to review progress at initial seminar, and to plan for the future.

As the group moved through the individual case situations, their understanding of the concepts in Model I and their ability to use Model I as a diagnostic framework increased steadily. Individuals found it easier to see the Model I behavior in others than in themselves, but there was a gradual increase in each person's ability to see the disparities between his or her intent and behavior. Members of the group discovered that they continually withheld relevant information from other people in an effort to protect self and other and to control the relationship. They gradually learned how often their behavior was based on untested assumptions, and how easily such assumptions could become self-fulfilling prophesies. For example, two individuals presented case situations in which they entered a meeting with the president anticipating that the situation would be win/lose, and that the president would win. In each case, the subordinate had behaved in ways that helped to fullfill his pessimistic prediction, but each had attributed the negative outcome to the president. Only after discussion of his case was either individual able to see his responsibility for some of the things he disliked about the relationship.

As the participants became clearer about the ineffectiveness of their behavior, they also became more frustrated that they did not know what to do differently. The group was clear that they needed new ideas, and welcomed a presentation of the theory underlying Model II. The group found the model intuitively appealing, but also found that the concepts in Model II were much more difficult than those in Model I. Consider, for example, some early statements provoked by the concept of valid information:

> *The problem we have in a lot of situations is that some of us are armed with assumptions, others with facts.*
> *But if you're sure of something, it's not an assumption, it's a fact.*
> *Well, it seems to me that X provides valid information in the case when he says, "Every time I come in the store, Jane is always in the back room instead of out front selling."*

None of the quotations recognizes that certainty of belief is not a sufficient condition for validity. The importance of making information testable became clearer only as participants began to realize that they could not be certain of the validity of their perception nor that others would validate their perceptions without testing.

The difficulties of Model II became even more apparent when the executives tried to generate Model II behavior in response to case situations. The first case for which this attempt was made involved a situation in which the case writer, A, was talking to a subordinate, Mary. A's purpose was to persuade Mary that she needed to take immediate action to confront one of her subordinates. A found the issue difficult to raise with Mary for two reasons: (1) he saw Mary as sensitive and defensive in response to criticism and (2) he felt that Mary's personal relationship with the subordinate inhibited her from confronting the problem. A's approach was to be diplomatic and try to lead up to the issue gradually through a series of leading questions.

A had no difficulty seeing that his behavior was Model I, but could not invent any other approach. Other members of the group thought that they could, but their suggestions for improvement were highly abstract—for example, "The only way you can do it is to be open with Mary." When they tried to translate such advice into observable behavior, they could not. The following simulated transaction between a group member (who counseled openess) and Mary (role played by the writer) is an example:

B:
Mary, I have the feeling that perhaps our relationship could be improved. I'd be interested in hearing how you feel about our relationship.

MARY:
What makes you feel there's a problem in our relationship?

B:
(Dropping out of role) You're a rip aren't you? (Returning to role) Well, it seems to me that there are areas where you haven't come to me for counsel where you might need counsel.

MARY:
When you say I need counsel, are you saying there's something wrong with how I'm doing my job?

B:
Hell, be that way, Mary!

C:
Yeah, Mary, who gives a shit about you anyway.

B's espoused theory was to be open with Mary, but his behavior rested on the Model I assumption that the way to get someone else to be open is to be evasive about one's own feelings while "drawing out" the other person. When Mary responded by asking for evidence for B's assertions (which would have required B to behave his espoused theory), B became frustrated and blamed Mary for being difficult.

Others also attempted to generate Model II approaches to Mary, but every attempt made the implicit assumption that the superior needed to be diplomatic, to stay in control, and to get Mary to be open. The more they tried, the more clearly the executives saw the difficulty of generating Model II behavior.

The final phase of the initial seminar was a meeting between the executives and the president. The meeting was preceded by an evening meeting of the seminar group to discuss what they wanted to do when they met with the president.

As the group discussed the forthcoming meeting, they found themselves again facing their mistrust both of George Peters and of one another. After one and a half days in the seminar, they were aware that much of their behavior was ineffective. They were attracted to Model II governing variables, but limited in their ability to behave according to them.

As they continued to discuss the meeting with George Peters, the conversation took on a quality of, "If only he would change, everything would be fine"—if only he would stop pitting subordinates against one another, if only he would get off our back, if only he would stop sending reminder after reminder for the same meeting. What was missing was a consciousness of the group's own contribution to problems in the relationship. No one asked, for example, "If the president is too aggressive and intrusive, could that mean that we are too passive, that we don't confront enough, that we're not performing as well as we ought to be?"

Because Model I acts to prevent individuals from becoming aware of their own contribution to problems in their human environment, it makes it easy to believe that problems would be solved if someone else would change. But that diagnosis placed the subordinates in a dilemma. The action strategy suggested by the diagnosis was to blame the president and persuade him to change his behavior. But no one expected that to work. Indeed, they were very fearful that their meeting with the president might cause him to feel hurt and resentful. The other alternative was to withdraw from confronting the issues, but that would perpetuate the problems. The group could see no way out of the dilemma, and found it difficult to be optimistic about the meeting with the president until they began to explore their own responsibility for the problems. Then they could begin to see the meeting as one in which they could try to learn from the president just as they hoped he would try to learn from them.

In the actual meeting the group was able to begin the exploration of some basic difficulties in the relationship between the president and the executives. Particularly at the beginning, the group was politer and more cautious with the president than they had been the night before when he was not present. For example, in the previous evening's discussion, some members of the group expressed the view that the president was wasting his time by visiting the company's retail stores, but that view was never expressed in the following conversation:

PETERS: Now, I was in store X yesterday, and someone had decided it's a sophisticated area, they don't need item Z. Being there, it was clear they did need Z.

A: Because we own a lot?

PETERS: They sold the few they had, and wished they had more.

A: We could sell a lot of things if we had them in the store.

PETERS: Yes, but there was a discussion that it's a sophisticated market, we don't need item Z, and the business in that item is no good. I'd just spent some time in New York and learned that wasn't true. That helped me, and put some wheels in motion that we might have prejudged a market too fast.

F: Your theory makes sense, but so often in the past, this was not a sensible theory. The reaction was, 'He wants Z, we'll put them in.' There were a few and they sold them, and that qualifies him to make that judgment.

C: In the past, when George has come back with a note saying something like that, how many times have we come back and said, 'Wait a minute. What's your rationale for that note?' Rather than just getting them there to please him?

H: How many times did we directly approach him? Probably not enough. That's exactly right.

The interchange captures the spirit of the meeting. The president and the executive group were discussing important issues about one another's roles and relationships that had never been discussed as openly in the past, but it was still a very cautious confrontation. The discussion was important because it surfaced many important issues and concerns, and helped to clarify some of the problem dynamics in the company. The meeting also suggested that the learning process was making it possible to be more open than previously, without producing the punitiveness and acrimony that the executives had feared.

But everyone realized that it was only a beginning—they needed more time to resolve the substantive issues they were discussing, and they needed more learning before they could make any substantial changes in their behavior. The group was unanimous in wanting to continue the learning experience they had begun, and a decision was made to schedule a second seminar experience later in the year.

At the end of the seminar I shared my diagnosis that the group had made considerable progress in its ability to analyze behavior in terms of Model I, and that each individual was clearer about some of the Model I elements of his or her own behavior. The group had discovered that they could be more open with each other than they had been previously, and that learning could result. But they had not obtained a very clear understanding of Model II, nor of how to use Model II. That implied that the group would find it difficult to transfer their learnings:

L: I think the only way you currently know how to get things done at AA Stores is using Model I approaches to management, and for the near future, I think that will still be the only way you know how. So I think you will find many situations where you will feel you have to use Model I, even if you don't want to. One danger is to expect too much of yourself or of others. If you expect too much of others, there's a good chance you'll become discouraged or frustrated when they're not as open as you think they ought to be.

No one quarreled with the diagnosis, but some executives felt it might be too pessimistic about the possibility for improvement in their relationships with one another. We agreed that we would have more evidence in several months when the next seminar occurred.

KEY EXECUTIVE GROUP: SECOND SEMINAR

I asked the participants to do two tasks in preparation for the second seminar: (1) write a second case paper and (2) write a brief note describing what their experience had been in trying to use what they had learned, mentioning any significant problems or concerns.

Each individual's experience was unique, but there were two widely-shared concerns: (1) people were not very clear about what Model II was, and found it hard to know when they were being consistent with it, (2) when they were (in their view) behaving Model II, they encountered problems. Among the problems were: (a) things were taking too much time, (b) it was hard to use Model II with people who were not members of the seminar group, (c) there were variations among members of the group in how open they were being and how much they were attempting to apply what they had learned.

For several individuals, one of the first discoveries in the second seminar was that their behavior in the case they presented was less Model II than they had thought:

A: (to B) Did you feel that your case was Model II?
B: I thought it started that way, but I don't think it came out that way.
A: That's what I'm wondering. At first, I thought mine was Model II.

B: I think mine came out with control. I tried to change it and it wouldn't change.

A: C looked at my case and said it's Model I.

C: Well, I could have been wrong.

A: No, I looked at it again and could see you were right. But until then, I thought I handled it beautifully. I gave myself a gold star.

Although the participants had described several problems they felt were happening when they used Model II, further exploration showed that the problems could not yet be blamed on Model II because the behavior that produced the problems was still Model I. The problems were occurring as the participants tried to do the opposite of their old behavior (e.g., avoid controlling). That often resulted in behavior that was less effective, but no closer to Model II.

The primary emphasis in the second seminar was on helping the participants develop a clearer understanding of Model II. The basic learning cycle involved repeated cycling through the following: (1) an individual presented a case situation that illustrated his or her behavior, (2) the individual received feedback from the group about the Model I aspects of the behavior, (3) the individual tried (with help from others) to invent a Model II alternative, and (4) the individual received feedback about the new behavior. The participants developed a better understanding of the meaning of Model II and of the difficulties in using the Model. They found it required time, repeated experimentation, and (usually) help from the consultant for them to generate Model II strategies. The second seminar did not appreciably alter their ability to generate Model II behavior in real time conditions, but they were more aware of the difficulties and had a much clearer intellectual understanding of the concepts in Model II.

At the end, the group concluded that they wanted to continue their learning process, and to invite George Peters to become a participant in future learning activities. Prior to the second seminar, the group had been fearful of having the president as a regular participant. They feared that George Peter's presence would complicate a process that was already difficult, and make it very hard for individuals to be as open and willing to take risks as was necessary. They also feared that the president's advantage in terms of his greater experience with Model I and Model II would add to the imbalance in the relationship, and increase their dependence on him. At the same time, they felt that the president's experience in trying to alter his own behavior could be of use to them, and everyone in the group felt that it was essential in the long run to build a bridge between his learning process and theirs. After the experience of the second seminar, the participants felt secure enough about their own learning that they were ready to invite the president to join them in the future.

Still another significant consequence of the second seminar was that the executives began to acknowledge more directly their own historic pattern of passivity, dependence on the top, and lack of felt responsibility for the overall health of the organization. That realization was brought home vividly during one afternoon meeting of the seminar in which the group was trying to reach decisions around agenda for a forthcoming meeting with George Peters. I made an explicit decision not to lead that discussion, and the executives were appalled by their own ineffectiveness and inability to reach decisions when they had no authority on whom to depend.

An immediate consequence of that learning was the "October 1 memo" from three members of the group to the entire management group of the company. In the memo, they presented some of their views about problems in the company's management:

1. There exists a lack of confidence in (one another's) professionalism between different areas of the company.
2. There is a need to acquire one AA Stores thrust by coordinating merchandising (i.e., part of the business reporting to George Peters) and operations (that part reporting to Bill Hanson).
3. There is a communications breakdown caused by closed minds and mistrust. We need to encourage the exchange of valid information.
4. There is a lack of confidence between (executives at the second level in the business).

The memo represented an important milestone in the company's evolution—for the first time, the second level of management was taking independent responsibility for diagnosing the health of the company and for trying to do something about it.

KEY EXECUTIVE GROUP: THIRD SEMINAR

A third seminar for the key executives—the first in which the president participated as a member of the group—took place six months after the second one. The group met prior to the seminar to develop an agenda, and individuals took on assignments to develop case materials related to the agenda. The group decided that the case materials need not include observable behavior.

The decision not to include behavioral evidence (similar to what the presidents had done at a parallel point in their learning) partly was aimed at simplifying the task of preparing case materials. But it also indicates how difficult it is for people to get beyond Model I assumptions that people can learn about their behavior and increase their effectiveness using only evidence of espoused theory. In a Model I world, it is considered superfluous, impolite, and intrusive to ask someone to provide observable evidence to document their self-descriptions. In previous seminars, the group had repeatedly seen major descrepancies between behavior and self-perceptions, but that experience had not produced fundamental revision in historic assumptions about the conditions under which adults can learn.

When the group began to discuss the cases they prepared, the conversations were meandering, unfocused and unsatisfying. The group repeatedly tried to get a picture of what had actually happened in a particular case episode, and found themselves continually running after a train that was pulling out of the station and always just out of reach.

Although the group knew that people's behavior tended to be stable over time, they were slow to see the here-and-now behavioral evidence of the seminar as a useful substitute for the evidence missing in the cases. In one dialogue between A and B, the two were discussing a historical incident that had left both of them dissatisfied with the relationship. As they discussed the event in the seminar, they were also recreating it. The same problems that had occurred in the past were recurring. After A and B both said they were having the same feelings now they had had previously, C asked, "Well, did you have a valid dialogue back then?" The question was another attempt to catch the moving train, and C asked it because he had not thought of the possibility that the behavior he had just seen was better evidence than A and B could provide by trying to reconstruct the past. After I suggested that it was unlikely that A and B had a productive dialogue in the past if they were unable to have one now, the group began to use the behavior in the seminar as a way to explore what was occurring in the relationship between A and B.

Much of the learning in the third seminar occurred in a similar process. The group began to discuss a case, but found discussion unproductive because of the lack of behavioral evidence. They then discovered they could learn more from an examination of their behavior in the discussion than from the espoused theory in the case.

Most of the major substantive issues in the third seminar were not new ones. All of them had surfaced before, but had been left unresolved.

The group re-experienced their difficulty in producing Model II behavior. They explored again the differences between a person's intent and his behavior, and became clearer about the difficulties of making valid attributions about another person. The group returned to the question of the role of the president in setting norms and standards, an issue that arose in the context of subordinates' feeling that the president overemphasized working hours as a basis for evaluating them and their subordinates.

The question of working hours was symptomatic of several deeper issues that had not been addressed: (1) the process by which organizational norms are established, (2) the extent to which the president's inferences (like the inference that longer time at the office means better performance) are confronted and tested, and (3) the degree to which subordinates implicitly supported norms that they did not like (by not confronting the president, while telling subordinates, "You have to get in by 8:30, because that's what the president wants.").

The difficulties the group had with the issue are reflected in the following excerpt from the discussion of working hours:

PETERS: Isn't this whole conversation around the question of initiative and its effect on the company?

B: I would challenge that. I think it's around the question of whether we have an evaluation process that everyone understands.

PETERS: I accept that. That says to me that people need to be aware that management feels personal initiative is an asset in this company.

B: I think that's evaluative and global. People may need to be told to come in early, take a short lunch, leave after six and work at least one Saturday per month. If that's what you're looking at.

PETERS: But it might not be. It might be other things.

B: Well, whatever it is.

PETERS: It's frustrating to have to tell people those things. If they don't do them on their own, they're not going to like doing it because they were told. Why should I have to tell people to be here by 9? I'm forcing them to do something they don't want.

The president was reexperiencing a dilemma that he (and other chief executives) had often experienced before—he wanted people to accept his norms for effectiveness, but he wanted them to do it because they wanted to. The dilemma led him to make contradictory statements—on one hand arguing that the president has the right to set norms, on the other, saying he should not have to tell people what the norms are because that would coerce them. The discussion helped him and the group to see that the dilemma is resolvable only when the president can create a relationship in which his norms are confrontable.

The third seminar provided additional evidence that significant learning for adults needs to be iterative and redundant. The group had "learned" the difference between espoused theory and theory-in-use, yet decided to generate cases that included only espoused theory. They had learned that an individual's theory-in-use tends to be stable over time, yet they did not use that knowledge to build a bridge between past and present behavior. Those and other learnings had to be experienced repeatedly before they could be integrated. The repetitiveness of the learning can be frustrating for participants, but is not surprising in a learning process that attempts to alter behavior programs that were learned over many years and countless iterations.

The third seminar did not significantly increase most executives' ability to generate Model II behavior in real time, but it did increase their ability to diagnose Model I and Model II behavior as the behavior was occurring. Such a diagnostic capability is a necessary precursor to the capacity to generate Model II behavior in real time.

KEY EXECUTIVE GROUP: FOURTH SEMINAR

The fourth seminar for the key executives consisted of a half-day meeting. The group had met in advance to develop an agenda that focused on several questions related to the effectiveness of Model II: (1) If we are open and confront one another, does that necessarily lead to better results? (2) How do we put the "whammy" in Model II, since Model II behavior often seems weak? (3) Can you use Model II with people whose competence is not very high? (George Peters made an assertion that Model II only worked well with people whose competence was high.) (4) Can you use deadlines in a Model II world?

Although the questions asked whether Model II was effective, they suggested that the deeper problem was people's understanding of the model. For example, there is no problem putting the "whammy" in Model II if one understands the model. Nor is there anything in Model II that suggests that deadlines should not be set, or that people have the right to ignore them once they are set. The fourth seminar was used to explore what the group really knew about Model II behavior. To do that, I generated two brief case situations that dealt with one of the questions the executives had raised: how do you deal with deadlines in a Model II world?

One case asked the executives to design a Model II conversation to deal with the following case situation:

> *You are a manager and have a task that you feel must be performed within two weeks. You would like X, one of your subordinates, to do the task. You are confident that X can do the task well, but your past experience with X leads you to have serious doubts that X will honor the deadline.*

There was considerable variation among the responses, ranging from interventions that showed no resemblance to Model II to interventions that were close approximations. The following is an example of the former:

MANAGER: As we have discussed before, we need to have accurate data on last year's sales-by-period. This should include items A, B, etc. Do you see any problem in having this data by two weeks from today?

SUBORDINATE: No, I see no problem. I'll get right on it.

MANAGER: Great! I'm putting it on my calendar for two weeks from today. Shall we make it at 10 a.m.?

The manager assumes a cooperative subordinate, says nothing about his concerns on the deadline issue, and does nothing to invite testing of his assumptions. Everyone in the group was clear that it was a Model I intervention, except the person who generated it.

B's intervention was more typical—it included elements of both Model I and Model II:

MANAGER: I have a project which I feel needs to be completed in two weeks. Before you get into it, I'd like to discuss it with you.

SUBORDINATE: OK.

MANAGER: (describes task) Is there any additional help or information you need?

SUBORDINATE: No, I'm OK.

MANAGER: Can we talk about the two-week deadline, because it's my experience that you've had problems before on deadlines. Do you feel you can meet it this time?

B's opening statement ("I have a task which I feel needs to be completed in two weeks") is a description of her reality and is consistent with Model II. But the second statement assumes that the subordinate is going to do the task. In the final intervention, the first sentence (". . . because it's my experience that you've had problems before on deadlines") is again consistent with Model II. But B undercut that by asking, "Do you feel you can meet it this time?", which encourages the subordinate to provide an espoused answer of "Yes."

C's intervention is an example of an intervention that more closely follows Model II governing variables in this situation:

MANAGER: X, I have a task that has to be completed in two weeks. (Describes task) I feel I'd like you to take it on. I'm confident you can do it, but past experience leads me to feel less certain that you'll meet the deadline. How do you feel about the task? Would you like to do it, and can you meet the deadline?

C's intervention shares the relevant information that he possessed, and opens the possibility of testing the assumptions that C can do the task, wants to do the task, and meet the deadline.

Most individuals fell short of Model II responses to the case, but the nature of the short-fall varied from person to person. Some avoided dealing with the deadline issue. Others raised the deadline issue, but then asked X simply for a promise to do better next time. Others failed to test whether the task or the deadline made sense to the subordinate.

In most cases, the gap between what people produced and what they aspired to produce did not occur because they did not understand the concepts intellectually. A person who did not provide the opportunity for the subordinate to test was well aware of the idea of testing assumptions. The nontesting occurred because the person did not know he was doing it until he received feedback. Each individual had an historic process for encoding intent into behavior. The learning process had produced more significant impact on people's intents than on their encoding processes, which still retained Model I dynamics.

Why has it taken so long for Model I encoding processes to be altered? An easy answer is that processes that took years to learn can be expected to require more than a few days to unlearn. But analysis of the seminar tapes suggests another possibility. The tapes show that seminar time was primarily devoted to discussion of theory and to giving feedback on individuals' behavior in case situations. But relatively little time was given to the invention process—how does one invent a Model II behavior in response to a given situation? Much of the feedback in the seminar focused on past behavior that had occurred outside the seminar. That suggests that a higher percentage of seminar activities needed to focus on the design process—generating Model II options, getting feedback on those options, testing the disparity between what was intended and what was produced, and repeating the cycle.

EXPANSION OF THE LEARNING PROCESS

A learning experience for the key executive group was conceived as the first step in an organizational learning process. For the process to have a significant impact on the culture of the company, it needed to expand to include larger numbers of people. At AA Stores the program has expanded both horizontally, to include Bill Hanson and managers reporting to him, and vertically, to include subordinates of the key executive group.

Operations Executives

Bill Hanson, the chairman of the board, was responsible for the operations division of AA Stores (basically, for the management of the company's retail stores). Hanson had initially adopted a hands-off policy with respect to the learning process. He advocated a contract with George Peters in which each could do his own thing—Peters could get involved in trying to change his behavior, while Hanson would continue to manage the way he always had. As Peters' learning continued, he became more and more convinced that Hanson's autocratic approach to management was a significant impediment to the organization's effectiveness.

Historically, Peters had avoided overt conflict with Hanson and had tended to use subtler and more manipulative approaches to influencing his partner. As Peters began to move toward greater openness and willingness to confront, he began to raise his concerns about Hanson's management style. The initial result was an increase in conflict and polarization between the two. Hanson concluded that part of the problem was that Peters was relying heavily on an external consultant, while he had no consultant of his own. (Hanson knew that, on a number of occasions, Peters had telephoned me long distance to get feedback on his approach before he went into an important meeting. Hanson saw that as a sign of Peters' dependence on me.) He suggested to Peters that he would like to meet with me, and it was agreed that I would spend a morning with Bill Hanson, and that the three of us would meet jointly the same afternoon. In the morning, Hanson indicated he was concerned that he and George Peters were on a collision course. As he saw it, he was willing to let Peters do anything he wanted in terms of changing his approach to management. What bothered Hanson was that Peters was no longer willing to reciprocate. (Hanson also felt that the conflict between the two of them was aggravated by mediocre business results.) Hanson described his theory of management as pure Model I:

HANSON: Now you probably won't like this, but my idea of developing people is to break them, strip them of their creativity, then teach them the right way to do things.

CONSULTANT: You were right—I don't like it.

We discussed many of the implications of Model II, particularly for a company in which there were two top executives. Hanson indicated that there were some parts of Model II he liked. He had always considered himself more open and less manipulative than George Peters, and liked those aspects of Model II which implied openness and confrontation of issues. He asked whether one had to embrace all of Model II, or could you "treat it like a cafeteria—take the parts that you like." I said that I would not want anyone to embrace all of Model II until they had the opportunity to explore its implications for their own behavior. As a learning strategy, it was certainly possible to explore parts of it at a time.

In the afternoon meeting, Peters and Hanson both agreed that there were two basic issues: (1) their mutual respect for one another (aggravated by the fact that each did things that caused the other person to feel disrespected) and (2) Peters' feeling that Hanson's management style was harmful to the next level of management and inhibited the development of capable, independent managers.

When the two men tried to discuss specifics, they had difficulty—there was a competitive dynamic that had a life of its own in their relationship. Each had a mental file of examples in which he felt the other's behavior was ineffective or defensive. At the same time, Hanson acknowledged the possibility that he could become more effective, and made a Model I offer to try to change to Model II:

HANSON: OK. George, suppose I agree to modify my behavior and change some parts of it to become more like Model II. Would you accept that?

PETERS: Well, I'm excited by that possibility. But I don't think I can say yes or no because I'm not sure what that will mean. How do you feel about that answer?

HANSON: Poor. I feel I'm making an offer and saying I'm willing to go halfway, but you're not willing to accept that. You're asking me to bend to your will.

PETERS: That's not what I'm saying. I'm willing to explore this on an equal basis, but I don't feel I can give you a definite answer until we do.

The message from Hanson was, "I'll go part way, and you go part way, and we can compromise." I suggested a different contract—an agreement that each of them would engage in a process of mutual inquiry and learning. That might or might not mean a change in either person's behavior. At the conclusion of the meeting, they agreed that each would reflect on what had happened and that they would meet in a week to discuss a set of guidelines for such a process.

In subsequent weeks, as the dialogue continued, Hanson reached the conclusion that it made sense to create some kind of learning experience that would involve him and his subordinates. He considered the possibility of using an alternative educational approach, and attended a Transactional Analysis workshop to test whether that might be appropriate. He finally decided he wanted to consider a seminar that I would lead for him and his key subordinates (except for those who were already in the original seminar group). I agreed to have an initial exploratory meeting with his group (during the same visit at which the key executive group was to have its third seminar).

Many of the operations managers were initially skeptical because, in their view, the only change in most of the key executives after two seminars was an increase in behavioral jargon, unalloyed with any improvement in behavior. A discussion of the difference between espoused theory and theory-in-use, and of the difficulty in changing the latter, helped them to understand how such a discrepancy might exist. Eventually, all members of that group chose to go ahead, and the group has since participated in two learning experiences that paralleled the design and learning outcomes in other groups. The group has reached the point of understanding more about Model I and about their own behavior, and an understanding of some of the concepts in Model II, but has not changed significantly in ability to behave consistently with Model II governing variables.

The fact that Bill Hanson was willing to participate in such a learning process with a group of his subordinates is one indication of the possibility that the organizational learning model can work. Hanson was perceived by many to be an antagonist to the learning process who was closed to learning. His behavior did not justify those pessimistic predictions. He has not become a zealous advocate of Model II and has serious doubts that he wants to continue to invest the enormous amount of time and energy that he sees as necessary to develop Model II behavioral skills. But he also feels that he has learned from the process and that his management philosophy has changed as a result. He is much more convinced that the evolution and growth of the company are rendering his historic management style obsolete, and that he needs to put much greater emphasis on developing subordinates who can be effective, independent decision makers. Hanson's response suggests that a model for organizational learning that emphasizes free, informed choice can be effective even when individuals are initially skeptical and when they are not coerced by a higher authority to participate.

Middle Management Group

A third learning group—for persons at the third level of management in the company—was formed in response to initiatives from three different sources: (1) middle managers who were intrigued by the process their superiors were experiencing, and wanted to have a similar opportunity, (2) members of the key executive group, who felt their own ability to apply what they were learning would be enhanced if their subordinates had a similar learning experience, and (3) the president, who was concerned that a number of people—some of whom were likely to hold key roles in the future management of the company—were not being exposed to the learning process.

As an experiment, a group of middle managers was invited to participate in a learning group whose leadership was to be provided by the president and two members of the key executives group. The president and his two colleagues openly acknowledged their limitations as educators, but felt the experiment was worth trying for two reasons: (1) it was a chance to test their capacity to develop effective learning environments without outside help, and (2) there were limitations on the availability of outside help that made it difficult to have the group on any other basis.

The experiment produced paradoxical results: the group members valued the learning experience and felt a strong commitment to keeping it alive. At the same time, they concluded that their learning was being inhibited by the leadership they were getting. They felt it was difficult to separate George Peters' role as president from his role as seminar leader, and they doubted the ability of the leaders to behave consistently with Model II. The group was able to raise those issues, and, at the time of this writing, plans are under way to arrange for a middle-management seminar led by an outside professional.

REVIEW OF AN ORGANIZATIONAL LEARNING PROCESS

Organizational learning was defined as the process by which an organization learns to manage its own theory-in-use to make it consistent with the organization's espoused purposes. It was hypothesized that such learning required the organization to move its own theory-in-use toward Model II. There is no known way to create a Model II organization through fiat or structural change. Model II norms are possible only if organizational participants can behave consistently with the governing variables of valid information, free and informed choice, and internal commitment. That led to the hypothesis that an organizational learning process needs to begin with the creation of learning experiences for key decision makers to help them move toward Model II, followed by the gradual expansion of the process to include an increasing number of organizational participants.

The sequence of events at AA Stores has now moved through the following stages:

1. The president began to participate in presidents' seminars, and made a personal commitment to alter his own management style.
2. The president's initial efforts were unsuccessful—he became less confident of his style, more inconsistent, and more confusing to his subordinates.
3. At that point, the key executives were invited to participate, and chose to do so. They also became personally committed to altering their own behavior.
4. The initial impact was to create lower confidence, more confusion, and greater inconsistency among the key executives.
5. The president's own learning progressed to the point where he was able to be much more open and confronting than he had been before.
6. The president reached a period of greater confidence and ability to confront earlier than many of his subordinates. When his behavior did not invite confrontation (and sometimes, even when it did), the subordinates often avoided challenging him.
7. At the same time, two additional learning groups were formed. In each case, members developed a commitment to the learning process, but also began to experience some of the initial confusion and inconsistency.

Until now, the learning process at AA Stores has involved the creation of a separate learning experience for each of several groups. That method creates several problems: (1) individuals who are in separate groups have little understanding of one another's learning experience, (2) constancy of group membership is difficult to maintain over long periods of time as people change jobs and enter or leave the company. The organization has now established a task force, with members from each of the existing learning groups, to coordinate the continuation of the learning process, and to explore new ways to form and reform groups, and new formats for learning.

What is the impact of such a learning process on the business success of the company? During the first year of George Peters' learning, he felt confused about Model II and dissatisfied with his effectiveness. His behavior became less confronting, less decisive, and more abdicating, as he tried to avoid controlling people. That period was also a period of relatively weak business results. The president believes that the business slowdown was related to his own ineffectiveness and his inability to confront key executives who were not performing well. Historically, he had surrounded himself with managers who were relatively passive and dependent, even while espousing a desire to move toward "professional management." As his learning deepened, he became aware of his fear of key executives whose competence and internal strength were high enough that they did not need him to make important decisions. As Peters' confidence in himself and his understanding of Model II increased, he was able to look at his own impact on his subordinates, to confront the norms of passivity and low initiative, to remove individuals who were not performing effectively, and to bring in new executives who were more aggressive, independent, and willing to confront. The result, in Peters' view, is a much stronger management group that has made it possible for the company to resume rapid growth, and has enabled Peters to devote more of his attention to the strategic issues that affect the long-range success of the company.

At the time of this writing, there is still an imbalance between the president's willingness to confront and his subordinates' capacity to challenge him in return. But if the subordinates' learning patterns parallel the president's, that imbalance should gradually decrease.

In each group, the transition process from Model I to Model II has required a long period of time (measured in years) and has produced an actual decrement in confidence and effectiveness in the early phases of the learning process. Whether it is possible to accelerate the learning process and eliminate the decrement requires further research and the development of new educational approaches.

The process at AA Stores is unfinished. There are still relatively few individuals who have reached the point where they can consistently generate Model II behavior under real time conditions, but there is widespread commitment to keep moving in that direction. The changes are noticeable. Where executives used to treat the biases and limitations of the two top managers as unconfrontable and largely unalterable, there is much greater freedom to confront and to offer feedback. Where the second level of management once felt dependent on the top, they feel increasing freedom and responsibility for the overall health of the organization. Where the president blamed his subordinates and they blamed him for problems in the relationship, both are much more willing to explore their own responsibility for those problems. The spirit of these changes was captured in a statement to me by a manager who recently came to work at AA Stores, as he tried to describe the climate of the organization:

> *You know, I've never worked any place like this before. The places I've worked, the boss tells you what to do, and you do it. Here they ask you to say what you want to do, then let's sit down and talk about it. Other places I've been, everybody's pushing and clawing to get their own numbers up. Here they talk about openness, confronting, mutual dialogue. It's harder this way, because I don't know the game as well, and it's confusing. But it's sure as hell exciting.*

The effort at AA Stores began with the question: Is a Model II organization possible? The question is still unanswered, but the company has moved as close to that goal as any organization I have seen. There is still much to do. The managers have not yet reached the point at which they can apply the governing variables of Model II to many of the really difficult problems of the business. They have only begun to address the problem of redesigning organizational structures and control systems. They have not yet had to face the question: Once we have created a Model II world inside our organization, is it then possible to redesign our external relationships with suppliers and customers? Is it possible, for example, for a business to survive that takes seriously the values of valid information and free, informed choice in relationships with customers? The theory-in-use of every existing organization implies that the answer is no. Yet the spreading decay in our institutions and our society suggest that, in the long run, a different answer has to be found.

CHAPTER

$$\boxed{13}$$

LEARNING DOUBLE-LOOP LEARNING

THE OBJECTIVES OF THE LEARNING ENVIRONMENT

The objective of the learning environments is to help individuals to develop and master Model II theories-in-use. This means that the individuals should be able to produce Model II behavior, governed by Model II variables, having Model II consequences on the environment, on learning, and on effectiveness. The criteria for learning therefore go beyond changes in values and behavior. The new values and behavior must be produced in ways that help to create Model II environments (minimal individual defensiveness, minimal group and organizational defensiveness, and learning-oriented norms such as trust and individuality) and Model II consequences for learning (disconfirmable processes, double-loop learning, and public testing of theories of action).

PROBLEMS OF HIGH COMPLEXITY AND LOW SPECIFICITY

The learning objectives are so complex that they have to be decomposed into more manageable subunits, dealt with sequentially, and eventually reintegrated. The problems of decomposition and recomposition have vexed all those interested in increasing learning effectiveness. What is the best way to break down the whole into parts such that the parts may be eventually reintegrated?

To make matters more difficult, the problems of decomposition are not only complex, but they are also of low specificity. For example, people may come to be aware of problems such as how to increase motivation and commitment for work, how to increase the production of valid information for crucial issues, how to decrease destructive intergroup rivalries, and how to increase problem-solving effectiveness in organizations. These are problems conceptualized at a highly abstract level. They lack the specificity required if useful invention and effective production are to occur.

SOLVING AND IMPLEMENTING COMPLEX
LOW-SPECIFICITY PROBLEMS

One of the underlying concerns of the inquiry is to discover-invent-produce-generalize about effective processes for (1) solving complex problems of low specificity in such a way that (2) the solutions are implemented and monitored effectively so that (3) the problems remain solved.

One way human beings can begin to cope with complex problems is to decompose them into manageable parts, deal with the parts separately and sequentially, reintegrate the solutions into a whole. The participants learned early that they could not decompose the problems by themselves. Indeed, they could not even define the problem with relative accuracy without the help of others. For example, in the cases brought to the learning environment by the participants, the problem as defined by the president tended to be redefined under inquiry. To recall one example, G said that he had a problem with T. T made promises to get things done that often he could not keep. T, according to G, often worked on the wrong problems. G therefore saw the problem as helping T to become better organized and to develop more valid priorities.

Next, G was queried by the group to give examples of his problem with T. When G produced the actual behavior, his colleagues concluded that (1) G overcontrolled T, (2) G tried to get T to see the world as he did, and (3) G withheld several important feelings about T (e.g., G wondered if T could learn, could change, would organize his work, etc.). The conclusion was that G could be causing T to behave the way that G found problematic; T as "the" problem now became G as a cause of T's problems.

Further questioning of G by the group as to why he had not leveled with T long ago produced the fact that G felt hesitant because he disliked the confrontation that would be involved. This hesitation, in turn, led G to wonder if he were "strong enough" to be president. These doubts created more tensions for G, who reacted to relieve these tensions in ways that could have given T mixed messages. Without realizing it, G could cause some of T's problems by G acting in ways that would suppress his doubts about his leadership capabilities. Thus G withheld his doubts about T until his inability to express his doubts angered G (with himself). This resulted in actions that overcontrolled and monitored T.

Thus valid decomposition of problems required the inputs of others. It led to iterative learning processes in which the problem was redefined as more information was generated. Valid decomposition also seemed to move toward discovering the actor's personal responsibility in the problem as well as the responsibilities of the others involved.

There were several reasons why these trends were productive of learning. First, all valid learning depends on generating valid information that is understandable and available when needed. Valid information will not be produced without the relevant actors examining their causal responsibilities in the problem. Second, if one individual seeks to minimize distortion and own up to his or her responsibilities, that increases the probabilities that the other(s) will follow suit.

Third, iterative learning requires internal commitment to inquiry so that "outsiders" are not required to keep the motivation for learning high. Again, commitment to inquiry increases with becoming aware of and owning up to one's personal responsibilities.

Along with an internal commitment to inquiry, a commitment was also necessary to find solutions that were satisfactory. The learners found it necessary to satisfice among any technical factors and humane factors that were involved. An overemphasis on either type of factor tended, at best, to lead to satisfactory solutions that were not able to be implemented.

We learned that commitment to iterative learning, to owning up to one's personal responsibilities, and to be willing to aspire toward satisfactory solutions was not adequate. Much depended on the kind of dynamics the individuals created for each other and for the group as congruent with Model I. Let us reflect on the second seminar. It was characterized by the participants espousing their desire to learn and to help others to learn. Their theories-in-use were primarily Model I. When someone attempted to discover, it resulted in the following sequence of action.

A participant (P) would ask for feedback about his case. He would usually summarize the main meanings of his case and then say, in effect, "Now let's hear from you. I want to learn, so tell me honestly; let's not hold back!"

P would receive two types of replies. One type of reply was positive (e.g., "That was an excellent way of handling it"); the other type was negative (e.g., "That was terrible," or "Hell, you messed that up"). Both replies were abstract evaluations and nontestable.

Such replies tended to make P feel attacked and misunderstood. P would not state these feelings because they would violate Model I governing values. He might reply, "You do not really understand the real situation," which would also be an abstract evaluative response and one that was not testable publicly. The response, in turn, was met with more Model I reactions. A circular set of processes resulted that tended to inhibit learning and effective communication among the members.

The same self-sealing, nontestable processes also occurred when members attempted to invent and to produce. P, for example, might say to the group that he had learned to be less controlling and more supportive. P then invented the solution of helping people to be more at ease with him. The group members' reactions (again, during the early phases) included saying such things as "Excellent," "Now you're cooking," etc. When D attempted to produce a new scenario to E's case, he was told that ". . . it was the best Model II response I ever heard." (Chapter   ).

In other words, in all the phases of the learning processes, there resulted what could best be described as abstract categories whose meanings were negative, positive, or attributive. Moreover, the categories were not testable publicly.

Such information could not become the basis for learning nor for altering theories-in-use. It is true that, during the early seminars, the participants reported that they were learning under these conditions. Yet our analysis indicated that they were either not aware of the ineffectiveness of the feedback that they were receiving or giving, or they were aware, but, in keeping with Model I governing variables, they tended to hide their views and express appreciation for the feedback. Since no changes followed the feedback, the others (who had heard the expression of appreciation) began to wonder if the individuals would ever learn. They began to feel a sense of hopelessness. If they expressed their disappointment, they were usually met with coldness and then anger. These reactions were interpreted as signs of "brittleness" in the individuals. Having made such attributions, the individuals were inclined to feed back positive information in order to prevent any further disruptions in the relationships.

These dynamics were altered so that toward the end of the fourth session and onward, Model II dynamics began to be used. Let us return to G and his problem with T. We saw that the group members advocated their positions openly and strongly, yet they combined them with inquiry. They asked G to present the case with directly observable data; they helped G to redefine his diagnosis so that it included his role in the problem; they helped G to redefine his diagnosis in a way that was publicly testable; they helped G to invent and produce ways to test his diagnosis with T; and they helped G to invent and produce conditions that would enhance trust, informed choice, and validatable information between T and himself.

How can we describe the processes that led to these changes? One possibility is to use the concept of the learning cycle that was described at the outset. The reader may recall that it was defined as beginning with discovery. Individuals discovered meanings that they intentionally or unintentionally created, the meanings that they wished they created, their espoused theories, and their theories-in-use. Discovery motivated the individuals to go to the next phase of invention, *if* they discovered inconsistencies within their espoused theories or their theories-in-use, or *if* they behaved incongruently between their espoused theories and theories-in-use.

Invention was the process by which people designed new meanings and new behavior to attempt to reduce inconsistency and incongruity as well as increase their ability to produce the consequences that they intended.

Next was the production phase. The individual produced the meanings that he had invented. Finally, there was the generalization phase in which the learning was generalized beyond the specific case. We noted that the learning cycle was an analytical concept. In real life learning could begin at any phase and feed back to the others, (see Fig. 1). For example, one could go from production back to discovery then to invention, and then to a new production, and finally to generalization (or to another invention or to another discovery).

We now know that one of the limitations of this concept of learning was that it did not inform us of the different requirements between Model I and Model II learning. Also, the model did not tell us much

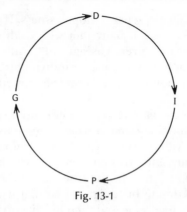

Fig. 13-1

about the transition from Model I to Model II, which was a complex double-loop learning process.

We also know now that the participants were unaware that they did not know how to discover-invent-produce-generalize consistently with Model II. Nor did they know that they did not know. Nor were they aware that they would tend to create interpersonal and group dynamics that would reinforce their blindness and inhibit double-loop learning. Under these conditions, it was unrealistic to expect the participants to begin their learning process by identifying the problems correctly and to decompose them effectively. The faculty had to come to the aid of the participants.

It follows from the above that the first step should be to help the participants become aware that they did not know that they did not know. But how may this be done? One strategy would be that the faculty tell them. But how would the participants be able to understand or believe the faculty's diagnosis when they were blind to the fact that they were blind? If they accepted the faculty's diagnosis, it would have to be on faith. But for the faculty to take this route would be to encourage dependence and nontestability. These would be Model I conditions. If the participants rejected the faculty's diagnosis, they would have no way to test its validity, and such rejection would have provided the basis for competitive win-lose conditions, and again Model I.

LEARNING DOUBLE-LOOP LEARNING

How may individuals be educated (1) when they do not know what or how to learn, (2) when they do not know that they do not know what or how to learn, and (3) when they live in a world that encourages double-loop learning at the espoused level but is full of individuals and institutions whose respective theories-in-use are not Model II.

One way out of the dilemma was to design instruments that would produce "naturally" the inconsistencies and incongruities that the faculty believed existed in the participants' theories-in-use. Doing this "naturally" meant that the instruments should be so designed that, whatever behavior was produced, the participants would own up to it genuinely as theirs, as they themselves being personally responsible for it (and not the instruments). If the inconsistencies and incongruities were surfaced in this way, it could be predicted that the participants would become motivated to reduce them, because inconsistencies and incongruities violated Model I governing variables. If it was true that they were blind to these factors, it could also be predicted that they would ask "how come?" If they took both of these steps, they would be on their way to double-loop learning.

The assumptions behind this strategy may be expressed as follows. Discovering complex double-loop problems required the efforts of all involved. Thus, when A wanted to learn how to deal with B, he needed B to help him define the problem. A and B therefore needed a relationship that was minimally distortive of information. One way for A to help create these conditions was to minimize the probability that he would behave in ways that would make B defensive and maximize the probability that B could confront A. In order to insure this condition, A would have to reduce the inconsistencies and incongruities that he created. Hence the instruments designed for discovery were used by the faculty to help A become more aware of these inconsistencies and incongruities.

But becoming more aware was not adequate. The reader may recall that, when the presidents began to invite further discoveries beyond those immediately generated by the cases, they were counterproductive; when they attempted to produce their own inventions to discover, they were frequently turned down by others; and when they attempted to generalize, they were frequently told their generalizations were incorrect. This meant that the members had to focus on new meanings to discover, to invent new ways to discover these meanings, to produce the new discoveries, and to generalize about their discoveries.

Similarly, when it came to inventions, we learned that the members had to discover that they did not know what to invent, they did not know how to invent, they did not know how to produce their inventions, and they did not know how to generalize about invention. The same conclusions held for the production and the generalization phases.

This meant that, in order to learn double-loop learning, individuals (who were programmed with Model I) would have to learn about each phase of the learning cycle. *Each phase of the learning cycle had a learning cycle of its own. The learner was faced with learning cycles within learning cycles.*

Learning cycles within learning cycles are illustrated in Figure 2. Each phase may now be said to have four phases of its own. In order to prevent confusion, we will call these steps. Thus every phase of the learning cycle has four learning steps.

This suggests a matrix. The verticle axis is the original learning cycle of discovery-invention-production-generalization. The horizontal axis is discovery-invention-production-generalization about each of the phases (see Table 1). Being competent in learning how to learn means that one can behave competently not only with the requirements in the verticle boxes A, B, C, D, but all twenty boxes.

Let us examine the processes of learning to learn more closely. They may be depicted, initially, in the form of a matrix. The vertical columns A, B, C, and D represent the learning cycle described above. The horizontal columns depict the learning steps required if each of the phases is to be achieved. Column 2 represents the discovery that one cannot do whatever is in the horizontal column (e.g., cannot discover, produce, in-

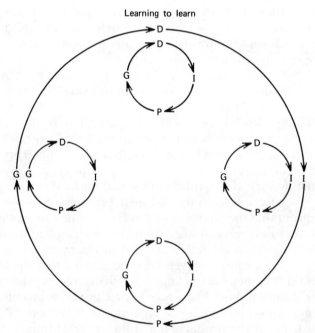

Fig. 13-2 Learning to learn.

Table 13.1

LEARNING HOW TO LEARN

Phases			Steps		
A: Discovery	1 Discover espoused theories theories-in-use, inconsistencies, incongruities.	2 Discover that they do not know how to discover what they want to discover.	3 Invent how to discover.	4 Produce behavior needed for discovery.	5 Generalize about effective discovery processes.
B: Invention	6 Invent new meanings.	7 Discover that they cannot invent what they want to invent.	8 Invent how to invent.	9 Produce the invention.	10 Generalize about effective invention processes.
C: Production	11 Produce the new meanings.	12 Discover that they cannot produce what they want to produce.	13 Invent how to produce.	14 Produce the production.	15 Generalize about effective production processes.
D: Generalization	16 Generalize the new meanings to similar and to different settings.	17 Discover that they cannot generalize what they want to generalize.	18 Invent how to generalize.	19 Produce the generalizations.	20 Generalize about effective generalization processes.

vent, and generalize.) Column 3 represents the inventing that is required in order to learn how to discover, how to invent, and how to generalize. Column 4 represents the behavior required to produce the discovery, the invention, the production, and the generalization. Finally, column 5 represents the generalizations relevant to the learning about each phase.

A. Discovery

A1:   The presidents, with the help of the case studies and tape recordings of their back-home behavior, as well as of the behavior in the learning environment, were able to discover that their theories-in-use approximated Model I. This discovery created new ones, because many of the executives espoused Model II behavior on the part of the superiors, including themselves. As they questioned themselves about the incongruities, they made other discoveries that were highly relevant. For example, some became aware of how much they enjoyed controlling others, how much they believed that without unilateral control the world would collapse, how that assertion could be self-sealing. They also discovered that they were highly influenced by the legacy of Model I, namely, (1) behavior that inhibits inquiry, (2) learning skills that are designed for single-loop learning, (3) a predisposition to blame external causes for their problems ("I have to control others, otherwise things would go to hell'), (4) a tendency toward self-sealing processes, and (5) an inability to decompose difficult problems into manageable subunits that can eventually be reintegrated into the more complete solution or action.

A2:   The data also suggest (and our theory would predict) that the presidents, with their Model I theories-in-use, did not know how to discover these insights by themselves. They were not skilled at self-reflection and double-loop learning. They did not test views publicly; indeed, they tended to state their views in ways that made them untestable.

Moreover, the presidents did not know that they did not know how to discover. Nor were the presidents aware that they were programmed with theories-in-use that would lead them to create learning environments in which double-loop learning was inhibited.

A3:   The presidents therefore had to invent ways to discover the inconsistencies, incongruities, and unintended consequences described above. But it is extremely difficult to invent ways to discover what one is not aware requires discovery. It can be accomplished with the help of individuals (e.g., the faculty) who do know how to learn how to learn and are aware of what requires discovery. The faculty designed instruments to generate such learning. The cases describing the difficult interventions were one such example; the tape recordings of back-home behavior another. The faculty, early in the history of the seminar, also identified episodes in the interactions, among the presidents, which they replayed to the members so that they could learn how they were behaving toward each other.

The participants soon learned that their effective inventions for discovery were based on directly observable data and tended to be dilemmas, inconsistencies, and incongruities inferrable from that behavior.

A4: Once the inventions were made, the individuals had to produce the behavior with as minimal distortion as possible. The presidents learned that holding back their behavior simply meant that they would learn very little. They also learned that it was important to produce behavior that reflected as genuinely as possible their skills and competences. Producing scenarios according to what they thought might be Model II behavior, when in fact their present theories-in-use were Model I, caused difficulties because it became painfully obvious that they could not behave congruently with Model II in the learning seminar.

A5: Generalization occurred when individuals took the lessons learned in A1 through A4 and applied them to other episodes and problems during the seminar and later, in the back-home setting.

B. Invention

B1: The next step was to invent new meanings based on the discoveries just made.

B2: Again, one of the first learnings was that the presidents could not invent the new meanings by themselves. They needed the feedback from others to learn, if the meanings they constructed were to be confirmed by others. The presidents also learned that they could not invent meanings based on the discovery that their present meanings were not those intended. There was a gap between discovery and invention. The reader may recall the many episodes in which, after discovering that their solution to solving a problem approximated Model I, the presidents tried to construct other possible scenarios. However, every scenario they invented tended to approximate Model I.

The inability to invent new and desired meanings frustrated and upset the participants. As adults, they rarely had difficulty in inventing (i.e., thinking effectively about) solutions generated from their discoveries. The frustration was magnified with these presidents, because they had prided themselves on their capacity to reason quickly, design effectively, and analyze practical problems effectively.

B3:   One of the most important lessons the participants had to learn was to invent in slow motion. This was especially difficult for the presidents, who were competitive and had viewed themselves as quick at their verbal triggers. The faculty had to take a dominant role to slow them down and to help them make explicit the reasoning that informed their actions. For example, E's statement that he wanted R to volunteer for a job became much more complex as he made his reason explicit. He wanted R to volunteer for a position, yet E also wanted to control the invitation for the position. Also, E did not want to tell R that he (E) did not trust R to speak openly with him. E feared that R would "salute" and take the job without expressing his doubts, although he said to R that he (E) was certain R would feel free to reject the invitation.

After surfacing this information, E, with the help of the others, invented a scenario that focused directly on the problem and the dilemmas as E saw them.

One of the lessons that took quite a while for the participants to learn was that they held much of the information that was needed to invent effective scenarios. Their big problem was that they had learned never to use the information to design their actual approach. The reader may recall the cases (in Chapter 6). The material on the left hand side of the pages was central to the invention of effective scenarios, yet the presidents kept it covert and private.

B4:   The next step was to produce the inventions in one's mind or as written scenarios. Another way to produce inventions would be to role play different subparts of the design until one had a design in mind that appeared satisfactory.

B5:   Finally, the persons learned to generalize about the difficulties in inventing and the requirements for effective intervention under different conditions.

C. Production

C1:   The next step was to produce the behavior in role playing. The individuals now strove to translate the meanings that they had invented into actual behavior.

C2:   Again, one of the early discoveries made by the presidents was that they could not produce what they had invented. The gap from invention to production was as large, if not larger, than the gap between discovery and invention.

The frustration was greater than in the previous cycle, for several reasons. It was compounded by the frustrations related to their inability to invent. In addition, the presidents were accustomed to producing whatever they wished to produce. Indeed, these presidents pictured themselves as especially effective producers of whatever they wished to produce.

C3: Next, the presidents had to learn to invent the productions. This meant that they had to be able to generate cognitive maps, in their heads, of the correct grammar to use to describe dilemmas, to ask for feedback, to invite confrontations, etc.

C4: Next, the presidents had to learn to produce the productions. For example, they had to strive to speak in directly observable categories, something they found initially to be awkward. They also found it difficult to speak in terms of dilemmas because, as the reader may recall, they considered such statements as signs of weakness. They also had difficulty in inviting feedback. As one president stated it, "I just can't get the words out. It is easy to think that I want feedback, it is quite another thing to ask for it."

C5: Finally was the generalizing about the learning regarding the difficulties of producing the behavior that they intended to produce.

D. Generalization

D1: This represented the task of generalizing about the total learning process in a given episode, to other episodes in the seminar, to back-home settings, and to new concepts of budgeting, of pay, and of organizational structure.

D2: One of the important discoveries to be made about generalization was how much time had to pass before generalization was possible. The presidents learned that they sometimes had to let completed episodes "simmer" in their minds for several days to weeks before they could generalize from them. It appeared that locomoting through all the stages was so involved that it was not possible to see the forest because of the trees. No one, including the faculty, came to understand the nature of the "simmering" process.

D4: Inventions were also needed to help develop generalizations. One helpful mechanism the presidents developed was to listen to tape recordings of their sessions, weeks after they had ended. Several would listen to them while driving alone or with their wives during the evening. The presence of another person helped them to develop generalizations about their behavior. Another mechanism was the memoranda that each of the presidents would send to each other. One of the most facile in writing such memoranda was E. Several edited memos are enclosed below to show the evolution of his own thinking. Finally, the presidents learned to develop generalizations as they attempted to describe what they were learning, primarily to their subordinates, and secondarily, to friends and peers.

From this description of the learning phases and their respective steps in sequential order, the reader may develop the mistaken impression that they occurred sequentially. The phases or their respective steps rarely occurred sequentially, especially during the early phases of learning. They did take on the prescribed rational sequential form as the participants increased their learning and their competence.

Moreover, learning in any one of the boxes could feed back as well as go forward to other boxes. Examples of the latter were the many times that the executives attempted to go from discovery to production without going through the steps in each phase. Examples of the former were the many times the discovery of something, the invention of something, or the production of some behavior led to further discoveries calling for new inventions and new productions.

Another factor that produced discontinuities was that individuals were rarely free to keep their attention on their own learning. For example, even when the presidents were able to slow down and move more deliberately through the discovery phase, they might be stopped because their invention generated a discovery for another who then wanted to explore his discovery. One of the major triumphs occurred when the members were able to delay and queue up for their learning. Still other discontinuities were created by the group dynamics, which, early in the seminars, inhibited learning. They had to be explored and corrected if progress was to be made.

There is a third set of factors that acted to prevent learning from being as rational and sequential as the matrix suggests. The reader may recall that the presidents were deeply troubled at several points during the seminar. They were frustrated and bewildered when they discovered that they did not know how to discover, when they could not invent what they wished to invent, and when they could not produce what they wished to produce. These frustrations led to anger toward the faculty as well as increasing feelings of helplessness and decreasing sense of self-confidence. Finally, there were the moments when the executives discovered that they experienced fears, that they wanted to hide the fears, that to inquire why they wanted to hide from their fears meant a curious process of inquiry because to inquire about their fears was a process that they feared.

During these moments, the individuals slipped into a learning cycle that may be described as defensive. If handled incorrectly, the participants would not step back into the learning to learn cycle. At worst they would remain in the defensive mode; at best they would "progress" to their Model I cycle. They would not, however, return to the painful learning to learn cycle. The faculty attempted to help the individuals feel free to slip into the defensive learning cycle and learn from it in such a way that they returned to learning how to learn. This is discussed in more detail in the next chapter.

To summarize: The less competent the individuals in learning how to learn, the greater the probability that they would be unaware of the twenty phases and steps as well as the amount of time needed for each phase and its steps; the greater the probability of a sense of frustration, anger, disillusionment, and lowering of self-confidence as the awareness of the requirements of double-loop learning; the greater the probability of slipping into a defensive learning cycle (which is a single-loop learning cycle) or leaving the environment.

The learning to learn cycle therefore has at least four phases, with five steps to each phase. The more competent the individuals, the more they can compress the steps and the phases so that it appears as if they are moving from discovery to production. Competent individuals also know their limitations (or are able to sense when they are behaving incompetently). Under these conditions, they are capable of moving from the learning cycle and then to move through it, giving themselves adequate time for each phase and each step, as well as for the many feedback loops that will be required.

A MORE COMPLETE MAP OF THE LEARNING PROCESSES

Although the model above is more complex than the original ones, it is still not adequate. There are several other learning cycles that should be included. They may be illustrated as follows:

To begin, we recall that all the presidents (P) were unaware that they were major causes of the problems that they had identified to exist in others. Moreover, they were unaware that everything they would try to invent-produce-generalize about their problems with the other (O) in terms of Model II would be counterproductive.

To compound the problem, the group members (GM) were unaware that they would become a major cause of defensiveness when they attempted to help others. Moreover, the group members were unaware that everything they would strive to discover-invent-produce-generalize about how any given P could be helped to solve his problem with O would also be counterproductive.

In short, at the outset of the seminar, we had members who were unaware that they were unaware leading any given member who was also unaware of his unawareness.

Helping the participants to learn how to learn double-loop learning during the seminars would have to be generated at several different levels. They were:

1. The problems P had with O.
2. The problems P had with the group while they were trying to help him.
3. The problems the group had with any given P while they were trying to help him.
4. The problems that any given P began to discover he had back home as he tried to help another P during the seminar.

Thus every participant may be said to be involved in three complete interdependent learning cycles: one with himself and O, another with the group (or several cycles if the group could be broken down into subgroups), and the new problems that were surfaced while trying to work on the first two.

There are more learning cycles within learning cycles than even those just described. Indeed, if we attempted to make explicit every learning cycle that we identified, it would result in a picture that would be so complex, it is doubtful that anyone could use it for purposes beyond explanation. Given the finite capacities of the human mind, the person who wished to use the map would have to decompose it. We would then be faced with a new problem, namely, how do the presidents decompose a map that depicts a world so complex that they never used it in the first place?

This tension between explanation and action is a key one, and we turn to it, in more detail, in the next chapter. At this point, we wish to point out that maps that inform theories of action will not be designed to be analytically complete. They will be maps that will be knowingly incomplete and knowingly less rigorous. What will make them more effective is, first of all, a conscious awareness of their inevitable incompleteness. The holders will know that in order to make these maps accurate they will have to generate an on-line iterative learning process. The maps provide a basis for learning; the learning is joint with the relevant others, and then the action follows. Although such action will make problem-solving and decision-making processes take more time, two provisos should be added. First, the extra time necessary will decrease as the competence of the individuals involved to behave according to Model II increases. As the competence of those involved increases, the norms about how to handle problem solving of difficult decisions will also change. Experience to date suggests that the time taken will decrease dramatically, because the private meetings, wheelings and dealings of the Model I world, in which meetings are held to "pour holy water over decisions already made," will decrease greatly (Argyris, 1962, 1965). Moreover, the internal commitment to monitoring the implementation of the decision will increase greatly.

CHAPTER

$\boxed{14}$

CONCLUSIONS

THREE TYPES OF RARE EVENTS WERE PRODUCED[1]

The first conclusion of this study is that it is was possible to reeducate people whose theories-in-use were Model I to move toward Model II theories-in-use. Moreoever, it was possible to go beyond the traditional goals of education, namely, those of discovery of problems and concepts to teach people to invent and produce solutions within the learning environment under actual and simulated stressful conditions.

The experiment also demonstrated that it was possible to educate presidents to continue their learning in the back home setting of their respective organizations. In order to continue to reeducate themselves, the presidents had to create learning environments in their organizations conducive, for everyone involved, to learn Model II. This meant that in order to continue to reeducate themselves, the presidents had to create two profound changes. They had to enlarge their role of president from being a manager of the status quo (i.e., Model I conditions) to the role of an educator and intervenor for double-loop learning. This meant that they had to help their subordinates explore their theories-in-use and identify their dysfunctional aspects on each other, on their rela-

[1] The conclusions described at the end of each chapter are not repeated in this section.

tionships with their respective president, and with their subordinates.

But their intervention and educational attempts could not become credible unless the nature of the living system within each of their firms was altered. Model II cannot become credible in a living system in which competitive, win-lose, low-risk-taking interactions are rewarded, and cooperative problem-solving, high-risk-taking interactions suppressed. Therefore, the presidents had to focus on helping to alter the living system.

DOUBLE-LOOP LEARNING CONTINUES

As this book goes to press, nearly four years after the beginning of the seminar, the presidents continue to learn and to experiment. Some of it occurs as they meet with each other during the seminars. Most of the learning, however, is occurring within their organizations and in interactions with their subordinates. In every company there is a new climate of inquiry and learning that the majority of the subordinates report had not existed before.

This does not mean that the presidents or their subordinates are not making mistakes, do not experience setbacks, or are not expressing bewilderment and concern about the probabilities of managing large complex systems with Model II theories-in-use. As we shall see, all of these are happening. But the difference between now and when the program began is that the issues are surfaced and discussed. For example, G is striving to help the vice-presidents to see the inconsistencies and inaccuracies in their diagnoses of the causes of their organizational problems. The task is a difficult one because the vice-presidents appear to resist learning. G has not attempted to overcome the apparent resistance by utilizing his power to persuade them on the faultiness of their diagnoses, nor to start a fad in the organization related to Model II. Rather, he has attempted to follow the transition model of surfacing inconsistencies and developing actions to reduce and correct them.

Below, excerpts are enclosed from the transcript of a meeting that was held to diagnose the problem-solving and decision-making effectiveness of the top management group. The case begins at a meeting of the top management group (TMG). G said:

G: I would like to pose today the question of how effective are we as a top management group. Do we act synergistically? Do we tend to be mutually supportive or is ours mostly an individual effort?
     How do we feel about the effectiveness of this group? of these meet-

ings? Do we prefer the present arrangements or different ones in the way these meetings are held?

The responses came back quickly, led by the newest member of the group. He reported that he had talked to many people in order to get acquainted with the company. "The overwhelming view at the middle and upper levels is that everyone is running on their own, and things are disorganized. The lower levels say that they do not get adequate or clear direction . . . In my experience, this is the loosest-run organization I have ever been in."

Two others agreed with the first, saying, in effect, that this was not a new diagnosis. A fourth member added, "We talk too much before we want to do things." A fifth said, "Or we talk too little to each other." "Yes, that's right," responded the previous speaker, "we talk too much or too little depending upon our interests."

The discussion turned quickly to solutions. They were: (1) the company needed strong leadership at the top and (2) strong financial control. Someone said that part of the problem was that he never had adequate information in order to give direction to the marketing program. Another added, "We are not a team. Everyone looks out only for self (and that is one reason why many of us do not have or give adequate information)."[2]

Let us pause for a moment to reflect on the events so far. The discussion began with a request for the group to reflect on its own theories-in-use. Problems were identified, and solutions were presented relatively quickly. It is interesting to note that the problems defined are the responsibility of individuals and the group dynamics of TMG. For example, looking out for one's self-interest, not providing adequate or clear policies, and talking too much or too little are behaviors that TMG members are responsible for and could change. Yet the solutions proposed so far are to impose strong leadership and strong financial controls. There is no evidence that strong leadership or strong financial controls can eliminate the causes identified above. The most that either of these solutions could do is (1) drive underground the causal factors, (2) blame or punish the guilty more quickly, and (3) add a quantum jump level of control on the group which, in turn, could (4) reduce their sense of responsibility for curing the problem.

The group continued with creating solutions. They included (1) a new organizational structure to make unambiguously clear who reports to whom (thereby eliminating the practice of different managers violating

---

[2] Words in parentheses are author's summaries.

lines of authority), (2) reduce segmented groups, (3) increase up-dating on who is doing what, and (4) develop more effective forecasts. Again, all these solutions are rational if it is assumed that the major causes of these problems are outside the behavior of the individuals and the dynamics of TMG.

Why, in a group of six people, is the reporting structure unambiguously clear? Evidence collected during previous sessions suggests the opposite. Everyone knows the reporting structure, but in a crisis (and management by crisis is the mode) everyone, led by the president, violates the structure. The lower levels, in turn, do the same. Hence the sense of disorganization and confusion. Moreover, there may be some value to keeping the organization flexible for genuine crisis. A strict reporting structure can become a rigid one. Each group wishes to protect its own turf. But such protection reinforces the segmented autonomous, noncooperative groups that the top wishes to reduce.

Similarly, what makes it difficult for six people to up-date each other? They are at the top, and can meet whenever they wish. The answer is, as one member described it, self-protection. Indeed, he gave an example in which he was thinking of selling some of his inventories to meet a capital requirement leveled by G. He knew that if he did this, he could meet the production goals but would be in difficulty if marketing sold more than they budgeted. The marketing man became angry and said he should have been told about this possibility because he was pushing the sales people to beat the budgeted targets.

G: What I am hearing is that we don't look at the whole problem. Each one of us worries about our own, and we say that we have nothing to do with it if it is not our decision.

The responses to these comments, which were supported by all, included:

Maybe we should have regular meetings.
Yes, and let us start with an analysis of the financial results.

Again, these appear to be valid solutions in the sense that they might begin to control the dysfunctions cited above. However, they do not attack the causes. They represent an aspirin cure for migraine headaches. Unless the causes are eliminated, the new sessions will become dominated by the same dynamics. These dynamics do not encourage accurate listening.

For example, G was describing a problem:

G: (During that meeting I realized that) we were being faced with the shut-
         ting down of a plant. I was trying to avoid hasty decisions. (In times of
         stress, it is too easy to close a plant down.)

VP$_1$: You didn't say that to me. (I didn't understand your comments that
         way—at all.)

VP$_2$: Each of you was looking at the problem differently.

VP$_3$: It was obvious, G, that you were not concerned with the working capital
         problem.

G: Wait a minute. What makes you feel that I was not concerned with the
         working capital problem?

VP$_3$: Well you said you were concerned with the plant shutting.

G: Yes, I was.

VP$_3$: Well that's not a capital problem to me.

G: (I can't agree but the more important issue is that) my reaction when you
         say that I am not worried about the capital problem is anger—anger—
         anger.

VP$_2$: (Somewhat embarrassed) Do we need a referee here?

He then stated that such problems could be eliminated with a sound information system.

G: (Maybe we need that but as president) what I am also hearing is that I
         have to weigh my words very, very carefully. I would like to have a group
         that I can express what I am feeling (without it upsetting people and with
         the probability that I will be confronted.)

VP$_1$: In the interests of objectivity (he turned the conversation to financial is-
         sues).

The transcripts are replete with examples in which the vice-presidents
were not hearing each other or G accurately. Yet, no one checked out
the interpretations that he was making, except G (as he did above). Here
we see an example in which a vice-president made inferences about G's
interest in the cash problem and never checked them out. G surfaced the
issue, but there was little learning. All realized that the vice-president
had misunderstood G. But no one explored how this misunderstanding
developed, and more importantly, what prevented people in this group
from testing publicly their private interpretations. The moment G began
to deal with the kind of group and the kind of climate that he needed, a
vice-president turned the group's attention to more objective matters.

This comment was followed by a long discussion on better marketing
and production programs as well as "better communications." G agreed
and said:

G: OK. I think we have identified that the role of this group is to raise *all* the relevant questions. (We need a group whose members will confront each other constructively.)

All nodded affirmatively, but no one commented on this summary. The discussion turned to the generation of more examples of misunderstanding, lack of teamwork, etc. It is a curious process. The examples just given are similar to the ones given at the beginning of the meeting *and* similar to the ones described in several meetings during the last two years. Why the repetition? Yet, if the presidents asked that question, I doubt that the group would respond, even though they had just agreed to deal with all relevant questions. It has become apparent that relevant questions are those that deal with rational, nonemotional, nonthreatening subjects (i.e., questions that do not violate Model I governing variables).

G, without intending it, created an opportunity to test this assertion. After listening to more discussion on technical issues he said:

G: (We have allocated most of our time to discussing those issues. What I would like to ask us to do during this period is) to examine our group problem-solving processes. Do we have a synergistic effect? I'd like to identify some of the barriers to effective problem solving in this group.

The response was immediate and in line with the analysis. The individuals began discussing organizational issues, apparently ignoring or not hearing the question. About half an hour later, the vice-president in charge of personnel attempted to summarize some of the problems identified during the session, about the "new" TMG meetings. He included that the group members had agreed (1) to be fully prepared, (2) not to go into detailed issues, but to stick to policy problems, and (3) to reduce snap judgements, personal biases, and tendencies to look out for number one. He also suggested a form that might be developed to diagnose the dynamics of the group. He ended up by reminding them of the previous agreement that there was a need for a new and strict reporting structure, as well as more frequent financial reporting and tighter financial control. So the meeting ended with everyone feeling that they had accomplished something important.

G, however, changed his mind when he read the transcription. He now felt that the discussion had never dealt with his point and indeed, that the idea dropped, "like a dead balloon."

This unawareness is an important phenomenon. It is similar to the unawareness that we described that was manifested by the presidents while moving from Model I toward Model II. The members were apparently oblivious to the number of times that they skirted G's question. Indeed, G was also unaware until he read the transcript. It is data such as these that raise a question about the value of evaluating group meetings by asking people to give their views or by filling out forms. Experiments might be tried in which such forms are filled out or comments elicited a second time, but only after the members have read a transcript of their meeting.

Another possibility is that the members were not at all oblivious to what they were doing. They knew that they were skirting the issues, and that was their goal. If so, then it confirms that the dynamics of the group do inhibit the honest expression of views. A reading of the transcript will show, I believe, that the president tried very hard not to impose the diagnosis as his program. One reason he did not confront people when he felt his questions were being ignored was that he did not wish to coerce the members. Again, we see the dilemmas of power, especially when one wishes to create a double-loop learning system.

One possibility would have been for the president to have surfaced the dilemma and ask for a discussion. However, without someone to help them overcome their individual and group defenses, it is doubtful that G could have succeeded. It appears that G is caught up in the same implicit assumption that the faculty made at the outset of the program. The reader may recall that we believed that if people could surface the inconsistencies and incongruities, and if they understood the relevant concepts involved in making such inquiry viable, then learning would proceed according to the model of surfacing inconsistencies/identifying new solutions/experimenting with the solutions and selecting a solution (Argyris and Schon, 1974).

We have seen that the model is simplistic, because people can fulfill all the criteria described above and, because of Model I theories-in-use, they will not be able to perceive the problems correctly. Even when they do, their help will tend to be counterproductive.

Let us now turn to another example of double-loop learning that continues to occur in the back-home situation. B, as we may recall from Chapter 12, has introduced the concepts of Model II theories-in-use with the help of Dr. Lee Bolman. The top management group went through a process of testing out the sincerity of B in introducing Model II. As they began to see by his actions that B meant what he said, progress began to occur. At the outset, many of B's subordinates expressed very positive attitudes toward Model II and worked diligently with B, each other, and Dr. Bolman to learn the concepts.

As progress continued and Model II theories-in-use began to become a reality, some subordinates developed second thoughts. They began to question the greater degree of overt cooperation required among the vice-presidents by Model II.

For example, B reported a meeting with a key executive, identified as N. N set his goals for the next year and met with B (and the planning director) to discuss them. During the meeting, N made it clear that his major concern was meeting his goals. He was not concerned about others' meeting their goals, nor about the impact that his request for financial support might have on others. The former was their problem; the latter was the president's problem.

B, on the other hand, was concerned that (1) N's goals might be too high, (2) such goals might lead N to behave in ways that were counterproductive in the long run, for him and for the company, and (3) that N should face up to his interdependency with others.

N was continuously expressing frustration and bewilderment. He would tell B that he was sure that he could achieve his objectives, yet, when B asked him to describe the basis for his certainty, N would respond, in effect, "OK, if you don't believe me, you give me a lower figure to make and I'll make it." When B would ask about the methods that might have to be used and the pressure that might have to be brought on others to achieve the goals, N would respond with a sense of bewilderment. As long as nothing illegal was being done, what difference did it make how he achieved the results?

When the director of planning reminded N of a recent experience in which N got in trouble with others in the company while he was singlemindedly trying to achieve certain goals, N said "That's the last time I'm going to tell you anything . . ."

B: I get the feeling that you are working on an approach of let's keep everything under the carpet. (That worries me because) we can talk openly about issues here.

N: (laughing) No, I was just teasing.

B: But I'm curious. Why is it that you feel that you couldn't openly discuss issues? Why is it that in jest you say to (director of planning) that's the last thing I'm going to tell you . . . Is there something about this process that leads you to feel you can't deal. . . . ?

N: No, it has nothing to do with this process.

AND LATER

B: I am concerned that you may be overreaching.

N: So then what am I supposed to do? How do I react to that? . . . All I can say is I have my plans; they make sense to me. If you don't agree, tell me.

B responded that he wanted to problem solve and reach a joint decision.

N: Alright, I'm having a lot of problems right now (laughter). I really am. It
    would be much easier for someone to say, this is what we want—go do it.
B: You like the Model I approach, right?
N: It's so much easier for me.
B: I believe you.
N: I mean, it's really true. It is so hard for me to understand. I mean, I under-
    stand what we're trying to do with this (Model II). I really dig it. It is just so
    damn hard for me.

And as the book went to the printer, that was one of the central
problems all the presidents were facing—namely, their subordinates
were finding the transition processes very difficult. Moreover, they, as
presidents, were having difficulty partially because they were not as competent as they wished they were, partly because compounding the
problems were the everyday pressures of achieving goals, and partly
because their subordinates did not understand.

It appears that B and D have had the most success in their back-home
settings. They attribute this success to the fact that one of the faculty
members (L) has helped them by working with their top management
groups. The faculty member was better able to explain the theories, to
respond to questions, and to help the subordinates examine their own
behavior. Although data do not exist to confirm the hypothesis, I believe
that L (or any other competent interventionist) would have an easier
time than the leader because there is less projection on him.

If the progress continues, some insight will be obtained because A, G,
and F have decided that they need third-party help. G and F will use E as
a third-party interventionist. A wishes to use L. E, on the other hand, will
attempt to spread the learning within the organization without the direct
intervention of a third party.

MODEL II THEORIES-IN-USE GENERATE IMPORTANT
PRACTICAL CONSEQUENCES

The character of the problem-solving processes in the presidents' organizations have begun to change. First, all the presidents report that these
processes are more open and candid than before. More importantly,
they report, the openness has been developed with an increased sense of
confidence and inner contentment on their part.

For example, D writes:

I am more content with myself and others, at work and at home. I express myself more freely and more accurately. I can be wrong without remorse, ineffective without anger. I can be right without victory, effective without pride. I know more clearly when I am angry, hurt, disappointed, and frustrated. I am learning to express these feelings in a nondefensive way.

Most of the subordinates report that they too feel more free with each other. Interestingly, the initial reaction to the presidents' attempts toward introducing Model II was less openness until the subordinates made certain that their presidents really meant it when they said they wanted Model II as their theory-in-use. Once they realized that the presidents were genuine, the subordinates opened up.

The result was that more information of vital concern to all was discussed publicly within each TMG, rather than in cliques. Also, subordinates expressed a greater degree of commitment to decisions made. The increased commitment led, in turn, to a more effective monitoring of the implementation processes, with quicker and more accurate correction of any errors. Moreover, most of the subordinates and all the presidents reported that "difficult topics" could now be raised with less fear that they would cause individuals to become defensive.

The increased effectiveness in problem solving and decision making has led to A's group cutting nearly $400,000 off their budget. Moreover, they were able to decide to stop the continuance of a nonprofitable division that had been regarded as A's pet project and not confrontable. They were able to accomplish these two objectives and simultaneously strengthen their group cohesiveness and problem-solving effectiveness. Before the program, such confrontation would have been rare or, if it did occur, would have pulled the group apart.

B reported that the organizational changes made and the giving of greater responsibility to the subordinates have been significant factors in the high profits made during the time when the economy was in a recession. Because it is not possible for me to present evidence that unambiguously relates the changes to the increased profits, I will refrain from giving the figures B sent to the group. However, I can report that most of his subordinates concur with his diagnoses. However, even if all of them are wrong, it can be stated that changes toward Model II did not appear to detract from the positive financial results.

F reported that, after relieving X of his command, several very key problems began to surface. X had "bet the company" on a new product. F, as a result of several candid meetings with his TMG reported, "Our situation was a little like the Edsel—everybody was doing a magnificent job until the marketplace proved that the Edsel didn't sell . . . When the bottom fell out (of our project), the group was astonished, and it was not any one vice-president's fault."

F's group has since gone on to correct its errors and to bring the company back on to a profitable course. All this was done, reported F, without his having to "take over" in the old Model I style. But, F reported, it was not clear sailing. "I believe (initially) the group accepted its participatory role as a means for the group to participate against me, or to protect itself from me."

F apparently did not become angry or defensive toward the group but entered into a series of long and difficult problem-solving meetings to help extricate the company from its difficult position. He wrote, ". . . as I became more open minded, I also became a better listener than I had previously been. I think this led to more questioning and interruptions on the part of all the participants . . . openness is contagious.

"My behavior is far from where I would like it to be. The speed with which we must sometimes move . . . is definitely debilitating to the Model II process. But this in itself speaks very strongly for trying to slow down a meeting and get all the feelings and thoughts on the table.

"(It appears) that we may have passed the crisis and be onto something very exceptional."

We could continue these examples of the usefulness of Model II theories-in-use. The message would be repetitive. The presidents believe that, when Model II theories-in-use are utilized effectively, they can produce positive practical consequences related to the *more difficult decisions within an organization* (e.g., drastic cost cutting, reorganizing, relieving a chief executive officer, recognizing an Edsel, and recognizing the ineffectiveness of divisions within the organization).

THE CONCEPTION OF LEARNING CHANGES

As we examine the changes that have and continue to occur, it is possible to see a change in the presidents' conceptions of what is important learning. First, the presidents have learned to differentiate between single-loop and double-loop learning. Although they see the necessity and usefulness of the former, it is the latter that captures their involvement and attention. I believe that the reason for this is that they now appreciate more clearly than ever before how organizations are designed and managed *not* to double-loop learn. They also realize the importance of double-loop learning if their organizations are to detect and correct important errors as well as become able to detect when they cannot detect and correct organizational errors.

Second, they express a greater tolerance for complexity and inter-dependence of factors involved in the important problems. They are less impressed by packages that promise to change their organizations within a year. They have developed a realistic, and hence a very long-term perspective about organizational reeducation.

In this connection, I notice now that they look for the dilemmas embedded in definitions of problems or proposed solutions. Whereas, four years ago, a dilemma was something to hide (or not even see), now the surfacing of a dilemma is a sign that the problem-solving process is working. Apparently, having learned to deal with dilemmas involved in learning Model II, they have become more open to exploring dilemmas in all aspects of organizational life, including the dilemmas built into the present concepts of ownership and formal leadership.

Third, the presidents are able to differentiate between learning for discovery, learning for invention, and learning for production. They see more clearly the importance of the latter if individuals and organizations are to become more efficient and effective. They also realize more clearly the importance of directly observable data connected to appropriate concepts for effective learning. Before, they used to condemn abstractions, yet speak in abstractions. They also prided themselves in being concrete, yet their stories were primarily understandable only by themselves.

Finally, the presidents are beginning to see learning less as process that leads to outcomes and more as processes that lead to outcomes which in turn generate *developmental phases*. It is these developmental phases that map important learning, not only because they point to where they have been and to where they are now, but also because they project a thrust into where they might be going in the future. Two such maps are presented below to illustrate the points being made. Note that both think of their learning experience in developmental terms, that neither paints a rosy picture of linear learning, that both diagnose the strengths and weaknesses of the experience to date, that both look toward the future, but each one somewhat differently. B focuses more on structural and systemic changes that he wishes could be made. E focuses on personal and interpersonal changes, especially as they relate to problem solving and decision making.

E: After Session 3

Now, I began to learn about manipulation in practice, and as a result of these somewhat painful revelations, I developed a limited agenda for change. It included (1) the unconflicted use of authoritarian behavior, without guilt, when appropriate, (2) the sharing and mutual development of the information base, (3) sharing the creation of tasks and objectives, (4) becoming more open with, and toward, others, and (5) testing everything.

These objectives seemed modest and reasonable, but this didn't prove to be true.

E: Between Session 3 and 5

This was not a period of behavioral change for me. I do think there is sufficient data to measure these specific, although limited, areas of progress:

1. I did gradually become unconflicted in the use of authority. I also came to believe that the use of authority was not necessarily Model I.

2. I had a great deal of difficulty in sharing with others during the information-gathering and processing period.

3. I became pretty good at revealing my position, being open, after my processing period was over, and I remained open to changing that position. However, I found that, if you stake out a carefully thought-out position, you inhibit others, and so it doesn't always help to be open at this stage. It is too late.

4. I think my performance was satisfactory, most of the time, in a mutual assignment and description of tasks.

5. It was easy for me to become a tester. This was natural for me. I have been, and continue to be, very skeptical of myself as well as of others. In fact, the theory of testing gives me a rationalization for my persistent skepticism.

6. I developed a good level of skill at seeing behavior in others that was destructive to the group process. I had little or no skill, however, in recognizing the same destructive behavior on my own part.

E: Session 5

Here, you (refers to the group) really caused me to fully understand the coercive part of my style. I had begun to understand coercion through persuasion, and you added to that understanding, but you also helped me to understand coercion through moral position. It is important for me to say here that what I came to understand was the implication of coercion at the behavioral level rather than the intellectual or theoretical level. When I began to feel the coercion, actually feel it happening, then I began to think that I could cope with it.

As I try to reduce my control of others, I am less willing to continue to be controlled. Somehow, I was willing to lose (be controlled) when I often won (controlled others). But, my pleasure at winning and my tolerance for losing have declined.

My current objectives are:

1. Listen more closely to myself—try to pick up and modify coercive behavior early, while it is happening. This is possible. I hope to demonstrate it by my behavior this summer.

2. Continue to try to share more during the information-gathering and processing period. Working in this direction, I am trying a slightly different technique. I am taking earlier, more speculative positions, positions of higher risk, but I delay reaching even tentative conclusions that might inhibit others. Another way that I describe this, for my own benefit, is that I attempt to hold longer in an open-to-all-options stance. This is sympathetic to, and helpful in, the execution of my nondecision theory.

3. Listen more closely to others and extend testing more deeply into all assumptions. This means, to me, that I must be more sensitive to the subtleties and nuances of what others say. I describe it as listening more deeply than to just the spoken word.

4. Be alert to the ways others control me and resist that control.

B: Phase 1

I recognized involvement with "the group" as an excellent tool to professionalize the management of our company. On exposure to Model I and II, I decided on the following resolutions:

1. I must change my behavior within the company as well as my management style.

2. Corporate executives must make more decisions, and I must avoid invading the turf for which they hold responsibilities.

3. In order to achieve this, I must be less involved in details, which circles back to Item 1.

In summary, I was "in love" with what Model II represents. However, I did not take a pragmatic approach to the issue and failed to recognize that:

1. My entrepreneurship was the management STRUCTURE of the company.

2. Whereas, the executives concurred it would be great for me to change my behavior (i.e., leave them alone), many lacked the skill and often the ability to fill the ensuring void.

3. The as yet incomplete knowledge of Model II behavior, plus my normal tendency to become overenthused with a new idea and ACT at all cost led into trouble as I suppressed my leadership.

Effect on the company—lost of conceptual dialogues, very little constructive action.

B: Phase 2

I was frustrated and saw Model II was not working, but did not understand what was wrong. Consequently, my self-confidence as a manager went down, and I was more and more uncomfortable, disillusioned, depressed, and distressed. The meetings of our group had resulted in my leaving them feeling inadequate and less clear why Model II was not working for me and envious why my intellect and ability to change seemed to leave me behind (the group's) achievements.

Effect on the company—sales were flat, earnings were off, the company was going nowhere. This continued to be the state of affairs for the first half of 1974. In an effort to search for a way out of this frustration, I started feuding with my partner, who blamed the poor corporate performance on me and my love affair with behavioral science . . .

B: Phase 3

This started somewhere last summer. My desire was to undertake self-appraisal and search out what was wrong. In this process, I finally saw certain realities that I was unable to recognize in the past. They included:

1. The company lacked real STRUCTURE. (There was no SYSTEM where people could act in place of my entrepreneurship.)

2. Many of our executives were NOT the quality or the kind of decisive managers I deluded myself to think they were.

3. I had changed some of my behavior (leadership and management

style), and as a result, the company was operating in a vacuum and worse off than before (pre-Model II).

Having come to see this, I decided the time had come to take positive and decisive action to face the above, and started working on this last fall.

Effect on the company—I returned to active management and have been working longer and harder the past nine months than ever before. I am trying to act as a leader instead of a dictator. I am committed to a PROCESS that involves executives in resolving problems. So far, the visible results for the company have been substantial (cites detailed figures).

B: What Now?

As a result of my involvement with you—the group—and my consequent experimenting with my behavior and management style, I have come to see blind spots within me. I have also learned weaknesses of my management style, exemplified by the fact one cannot substitute changes of behavior for sound management style.

Another result of the suppression of my entrepreneurship was that I was able to see clearly the realities and abilities of the people I had surrounded myself with.

Here are my present concerns:

1.   I have brought several new people into the company, all of them experienced in their field. What happens if we do not agree on standards? What time frame is reasonable to measure their effectiveness?

2.   Those managers I consider "borderline" in adequacy are made up of two kinds, namely,

a.   Those we have overpromoted—being blind to the reality of their expertise and stimulated by what I perceived Model II required.

b.   Limited-experience college graduates promoted into responsible jobs for which they had little previous training, and often reporting to managers (see a.).

I am very concerned how to agree to set "reasonable" standards and time frames, and evaluate which ones "make it."

Imbued with the present dynamics of the company, I want to continue the growth rate, but recognize this requires motivated, capable, effective executives. My tendency is to set high standards for myself. I am an eternal optimist. At the same time, I may also set standards for subordinates

that are neither realistic nor reasonable (repetition of the lack of pragmatic approach, see phase 1). I recognize that borderline managers
make it easy to rationalize that I should control them. I also see the di-
chotomy of having people (see a and b) and expecting high results from
them.

This is the PROCESS I feel it is my greatest challenge to work
through.

RECOMMENDATIONS FOR THE DESIGN OF PROFESSIONAL, LEADERSHIP EDUCATION

Every profession may be conceived of as having two interdependent
theories of action. One is technical, and the other interpersonal. Each of
these, in turn, have espoused theories and theories-in-use.

In every encounter, the professional has to learn the proportion of
each that is necessary in order to provide high-quality service. For some
problems, the interpersonal aspects are crucial, while for others, the
technical aspects are more crucial.

This relationship may be depicted as follows (see Figure 1). The horizontal axis may represent the degree to which interpersonal competences are required (ranging from 0 to 9). The vertical axis represents
the degree to which technical competences are required. Problems may
be plotted at any point along both axes. Thus there may be problems
that require few technical or interpersonal competences (1-1) as well as
those that require high amounts of both (9-9). There may be problems
that require high technical, but minimal interpersonal, competence (9-0)
and vice versa (0-9).

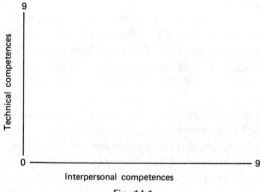

Fig. 14-1

The professional, in every encounter, has to discover how much of each of these competences is required. Discovery about either dimension is interdependent with the other. For example, the way a manager, lawyer, or doctor asks questions (interpersonal) may influence the information received, from which inferences can be made about the technical requirements.

To use our models, the professional has to manage simultaneously two learning cycles: the technical and the interpersonal. To date, it has been presumed that, if the professionals were well educated, they would have been taught to discover the technical problem, to invent and to produce solutions, and to generalize to other clients. This presumption may be unfounded but, for the moment, let us consider it as valid.

If the findings in this and the previous studies (Argyris and Schon, 1974) are not disconfirmed, the typical professionals are able to use the learning cycle for technical aspects, but are not able to use the learning cycle for the interpersonal aspects, because they tend to be programmed with Model I theories-in-use. Moreover, the probability is very high that they are not aware that they do not know how to learn how to learn, and that their clients or peers will not help them to overcome their blindness. Finally, if for some reason they learned about their inabilities to learn, their clients or peers would not be able to help them.

The Need in Professional Education

All professionals, if they are to behave competently, be a source of reform, and create conditions for their continual development must be helped:

1. To become aware of their interpersonal and technical espoused theories and theories-in-use, as well as any inconsistencies within each, and incongruity between each.

2. To become competent in learning how to learn at the interpersonal and technical levels.

3. To be able to operate effectively on the technical level while simultaneously learning how to learn on the interpersonal level, or vice versa.

The faculty should be competent in the same areas so that they can produce courses in which the students are learning the above, and simultaneously the faculty are researching and learning more about effective professional education, as well as effective institutional reform.

A PROPOSAL [3]

In every professional school courses should be offered that help the students (1) to become aware of their espoused theories and theories-in-use as well as the inconsistencies within them and the incongruities between them, (2) to learn how to learn to move from Model I toward Model II, and (3) to become skillful at producing Model II behavior under conditions of zero to moderate stress.

One design that could be used would be a modification of this course.

For beginning full-time students, a one-week course might be offered just before the fall term begins. This could be followed up with a three to four-hour seminar course during the fall and spring semesters. The course could be designed to be flexible in the utilization of the hours. The time in the seminar could be spent in three to four-hour periods per week, or, some weeks could be omitted so that several long week end sessions during each semester could be possible.

For practitioners, the course structure could be more flexible. It could begin with a one-week full-time seminar and then move to a schedule of two to three days every two to three months. On the basis of the experience so far, at least a two-month period between sessions is necessary. People need the time to reflect and digest their learning; they need time to plan and design their back-home experimentation; they need the time to identify the appropriate time and place for their experiment; and finally, they need time to write up and reflect on their experimentation.

At the moment, it appears that seminars for full-time students and practitioners will require about one faculty member to every six students. This is especially important for the seminars with the practitioners. We have found that practitioners come to every learning setting overloaded with cases and problems, and that they work extremely hard because the learning has immediate application for important problems facing them. We have found these seminars exhilarating and exhausting, and sessions going from 8 a.m. till 12 a.m. (with discussions during meals) are not uncommon. Moreover, once the practitioners begin to utilize their learning, it is possible that they may wish to introduce other practitioners into the learning process. This places an immediate demand for more seminars.

The seminars with the practitioners have enormous potential for raising the quality of professional service. If designed and administered well, they can help place the school at the forefront of manageable and do-able double-loop reform of practice. One way to spread and magnify

[3] The proposal focuses on the interpersonal theories-in-use. However, a complete theory and education for reform must eventually include the technical theories-in-use.

the impact of the seminars is to populate them with professionals who hold top positions in their fields (i.e., top administrators in education, health, business, law, architecture, planning, etc.).

As these people learn, they can produce new possibilities for the people below. For example, the presidents began to work with their vice-presidents and also began to offer learning opportunities to people at the lower levels. Moreover, they encouraged double-loop activity in the design of new structures, information systems, and reward systems. Since the encouragement came from the top and was *active* and *continually reinforced* by the behavior of the top people, the institutional barriers toward change were more easily overcome.

Also, if one begins at the top, there is a higher probability of the change programs being of a much higher quality and having a more realistic level of apsiration. For example, these presidents questioned consultants or personnel people who told them that a two-to-three-year program could be designed to change their organizations. As they said, they knew that after three years, they had just begun to learn; why should it be easier at the lower levels?

The longer time perspective also makes it possible for the faculty to do sound diagnostic research and for them to develop themselves and to contribute knowledge. It also makes it more possible to involve advanced graduate students. They could use the organizations as settings to conduct doctoral level research and/or as opportunities for internship. Similarly, the seminars will open important opportunities for faculty research. One of the biggest frustrations these presidents expressed with the two faculty members was their lack of availability. Many were willing to have competent faculty work with them in the back-home setting. The reader should keep in mind that one group of ten top individuals can produce from one to ten more seminars in the back-home setting.

PART

$$3$$

METHODOLOGICAL NOTES

CHAPTER

15

METHODOLOGICAL
NOTES

THE VALIDITY OF THE INFERENCES MADE ABOUT
THE LEARNING AND THE RESULTS

The most frequently used data in this book are taken from tape recordings and presented in the form of episodes. The length of the episodes varied from a few minutes (e.g., when one president misunderstood another) to several hours (helping A deal with his problems with Z) to several days and across several sessions (helping F deal with the president of one of his companies). Two questions that may be asked about these episodes are (1) How do we know that the participants experienced the episodes as described by the writer? and (2) How do we know that episodes were not excluded that could have provided the basis for a different picture? [1]

There is no doubt that great selectivity was exercised because only twenty percent of the tapes were transcribed. Moreover, the final selection included only a small fraction of the transcribed material.

[1] Some comments on the definition of a size of an episode are included later in the discussion.

One reason that many pages could be eliminated without distorting the picture is that human communication is highly redundant and repetitious. People seem to say the same message in many different ways. They do so because sometimes they are thinking out loud; other times they are making up their cases as they go along; still other times they do not wish to relinquish speaking in order to persuade others or to prevent others from speaking, but most of the time, because they want to feel that they communicated their messages in ways that reduce the probability that they have not been heard (see, for example, the Nixon tapes).

A second reason why many pages could be eliminated is that there were many examples of a particular episode. For example, almost all the presidents had cases of difficult vice-presidents. Only a sample of these is presented to reduce the possible redundancy and repetitiveness in the book.

A third reason why material was excluded is that the participants did not experience it as relevant. The danger with this type of exclusion is that the reason no one experienced it as relevant could have been that they were blind. The blindness could have been caused by the defensiveness of people or defense-producing factors in the environment. If everyone was influenced by such defensiveness, the omission would have gone unrecognized. If only some people were influenced, the attempt to exclude an episode became a cause of inquiry. The faculty and the participants knew that lack of clarity about episodes or censorship of them could be a sign of defensiveness; hence, such episodes were discussed thoroughly before being discarded.

Another cause of blindness could have been the theoretical perspective presented by the faculty. The advantage of a theory, namely, that it organizes complexity, is also its Achilles heel, because all theories exclude some phenomena. The faculty, and eventually the participants, might have become systematically blind to episodes that, if identified, could have led to a different picture of the learning processes and the results.

One way to deal with these last two types of potential error is to repeat the experiment with different subjects, under different conditions, and with different faculty. Still another possibility is to have observers who are not familiar with the theory observe simultaneously and/or reexamine the existing raw data. I hope the appearance of this book will stimulate such research.

Another way to deal with these types of potential errors is to observe the presidents as they attempt to repeat the experiment when they begin to introduce Model II in their organizations.

Before we examine this possibility, let us return to the seminars that the presidents attended. Is there anything in these seminars that could be used to check the validity of our inferences? The answer is, quite a lot, because in our type of demonstration–experiment, the participants were personally and centrally involved in making certain that error and distortion were kept to a minimum. They worked hard to test any possible source of error and distortion because, on the basis of the evidence that was generated during the seminars, they were going to choose to continue to go through a difficult learning process *and* to attempt to introduce Model II into their organizations. As one president put it, "When you realize what is involved (in moving from I to II, and then managing an organization with Model II), only a damn fool would not question every assertion and every recommendation." Thus learning and checking for validity became the central concern of everyone in the seminars.

Let us reexamine the history of this experiment more systematically with the hope of shedding light on these questions of validity. First, there are several levels of inference made by the faculty that require checking.

1. How do we know that the inferences made by the faculty about the meaning episodes had for the participants were valid? For example, when we inferred that the interpersonal relationships were characterized by competitiveness and win-lose, how do we know that the participants experienced them in a similar manner?

In an experiment tied with learning, this question is a central one for the faculty and the students. The faculty selected episodes in order to enhance learning. The first step was to see if the participants agreed with their diagnosis. The reader may recall that, especially in the early stages, there were significant disagreements. For example, the faculty asserted that seminar 2 was full of competitive dynamics that produced little learning. The presidents believed that seminar 2 produced much learning. Both went to the tapes to listen to portions of the seminar in order to deal with the discrepancies. The writer cannot recollect identifying an episode as worthwhile for learning that the presidents did not discuss before they accepted the episode or did not question the choice after they had discussed it for a while. Moreover, as the learning progressed, the presidents began to select episodes for learning, and their learning value was confronted by their peers.

2. How do we know that the assertion by the faculty (during the early stages of the program) that almost all behavior was Model I was valid? Is it not possible that the concepts of Model I and II are inadequate to capture the variance that exists in "real" life?

Again, these questions were asked continually by the presidents. The last thing they expected to learn was that almost all their behavior was Model I, especially when some of them espoused aspects of Model II. The reader may recall that the presidents confronted the faculty when they asserted that all the cases (in session 3) represented Model I. Several presidents insisted that E's case was a fine example of Model II. A lengthy discussion ensued in which many views and arguments were explored. The presidents finally arrived at the conclusion that E's case did represent Model I. The reader may also recall that the presidents were in disagreement about their own diagnoses of each others' cases. We frequently read of a president asserting that he had an episode of Model II behavior only to have that assertion successfully questioned by the others.

Perhaps the most powerful test was that the faculty were able to produce scenarios that were significantly different from those created by the presidents. In other words, if all the presidents' attempts were asserted to be Model I, and if the presidents disagreed with this assertion, and if the faculty could then produce a scenario that the presidents agreed was significantly different from theirs, this suggests that the categories of Models I and II are valid, and the problem was that the participants were not able to produce Model II theories-in-use.

Once the presidents began to internalize the Model II theories-in-use, another test appeared. The test surfaced when the presidents began to differentiate between gimmicks and genuine changes toward Model II. In making explicit the gimmicks, they provided further data about the pervasiveness of Model I theories-in-use. A gimmick was behavior that was consistent with one or more categories of Model II, but not with all the categories. For example, an individual might be able (by mimicking) to advocate and inquire without having altered his governing values (variables). Whenever this happened, the discrepancy became apparent as soon as the person ran out of skills that he had acquired by observing and mimicking. Once the individual ran out of stored (but not internalized) skills, he reverted to the governing variables to produce new skills, which meant that he returned to Model I behavior.

3. How do we know that inferences such as that the presidents were unaware that they could not discover-invent-produce-generalize double-loop learning were valid?

Again, because of the nature of the demonstration–experiment, this question was at the forefront of attention of all the presidents. As we have seen, the presidents were not ready to accept that they were unaware that they could not double-loop learn. What convinced them that this inference was valid was the great number of times it was illustrated by their own behavior during the seminars. For example, A, G, D, and F changed significantly their diagnoses of their problems with "difficult" subordinates as a result of the discussions within the seminars. As they looked back on what they discovered, they realized that the first lesson was that they did not know how to discover effectively the causal factors involved in their difficult cases. Then they found that the solutions they invented and felt certain were congruent with Model II were not. Similarly, they learned that their peers questioned their production of the solutions. Thus, the inferences the faculty made were made public and were confronted continuously by the presidents.

Some readers may wonder if there could not have been a process of brainwashing going on during the seminars that made it difficult for people to see certain issues and to confront them openly. The reason that I do not believe brainwashing processes were involved was that central to the entire project was the encouragement by the faculty of confrontation of them and of the participants. Indeed, if the faculty erred in the eyes of some of the participants, it was in that they showed too much patience with those who confronted them.

A second reason that brainwashing would be difficult to establish was that the confrontation did not remain only at the cognitive and affective levels. Recall that the learning included inventing and producing solutions. Moreover, the solutions were about problems that were related to people who were not present; they were eventually to be carried out in different settings with people who had no knowledge of Model I and Model II; and the execution of which was to be evaluated by the vice-presidents, the presidents, and the faculty by referring to tape recordings, as well as observations.

The back-home experiment is a key validation process, because it represents an attempt at replication with a new population and under significantly different conditions. For example, we saw that the vice-presidents raised the same kinds of questions about the credibility of Model II; they developed similar frustrations and angers; they manifested similar inabilities to be aware that they could not discover-invent-produce-generalize double-loop learning; they confronted their faculty (the presidents and Dr. Bolman) with the same issues and with similar intensity as did the presidents with their faculty in this experiment. Moreover, learning progressed in those companies in which people generated and faced directly observable data, in which they surfaced and examined inconsistencies, in which dilemmas were valued as bases for learning, in which they focused on the counterproductiveness of their group dynamics, and in which they examined the dilemmas of power and cures that made the illness worse.

The back-home experiment also helped to provide a particular kind of validation of the processes and phases that we have suggested the presidents went through in order to learn double-loop learning.

It should be made clear that we are not asserting that the phases we have developed represent *the* sequence of phases. Such generalizations must await much more research. But, more importantly, it is not clear that a theory of action perspective requires that one phase be identified. There may be several ways to move effectively from Model I toward Model II. The key issue is to define these ways and to specify the costs and benefits of each.

Thus all that is being asserted is that the model presented represents *a* sequence of phases *and* that this sequence was not incongruent with what was known about Model I and Model II (e.g., people programmed with Model I (1) should be able to single-loop learn and have great difficulty in double-loop learning and (2) should inhibit each others' learning and be unaware of this fact, etc.).

ON DEMONSTRATION EXPERIMENTS

There are several different ways to attempt to understand phenomena. One of the most powerful is to create them. When researchers are able to create cancer, they will have gone a long way in understanding and predicting it. One technology available to create events is the experiment. The experiment is designed to give the user the most unambiguous, precise information about what caused what. It is unambiguous because a good experiment controls the relevant variables systematically, varies others systematically, and, because of the random nature of assignment of subjects supported by the use of control groups enables one to make relatively accurate statements about causal relationships among variables. The statements increase in precision as they are stated in quantitative terms. Thus to be able to say that there is a curvilinear relationship between X and Y is to specify the functions of X and Y in a relatively precise manner.

There are costs attached to the use of traditional experimental methods that are especially relevant when one is interested in the applicability of knowledge—especially knowledge that deviates from a Model I world. First, in order to achieve control over the dependent and independent variables, the researchers must create an artificial world from which they can exclude those variables that should be excluded. The researchers must also define the tasks, the performance levels to be required of them, as well as the time perspective of their involvement. Finally, the researchers must select the subjects and assign them to conditions that are usually kept secret and are unchangeable.

All these conditions are consonant with Model I theories-in-use. Hence the theory of action embedded in rigorous experimental research is contradictory to the education being designed to learn Model II theories-in-use.

Interestingly, the traditional complaint about rigorous experimental technology is that it creates a world so different from reality that, at best, the results are not generalizable to the noncontrived world. This complaint requires modification because, as we have found, people do strive to obtain all the power that they can in order to make their experiments come true.

The big danger with experimentally produced knowledge is the theory of action implicit in the technology that produced the knowledge. Such technology produces knowledge that requires a Model I world, which therefore reinforces the status quo, which therefore makes experimentally produced knowledge usable only if the interested users are able to generate as much power over their subjects as the experimenters had over theirs. Hence, even if the typical arguments against experimentation (e.g., their simplicity) were overcome, the result would be knowledge produced by Model I theories-in-use leading to conclusions supporting Model I theories-in-use (Argyris, 1975).

The task is to learn how to obtain knowledge that is as unambiguous and rigorous as possible and that is applicable to a Model II world. Little is known about this technology.

We must find research methods that do not reject unambiguity, public verifiability, preciseness, and repeatability, but do so in ways that are congruent with Model II theories of action.

The book represents a very primitive attempt in this direction. The intent was to study how to make specific events come about (i.e., the presidents choosing to move and their moving toward Model II through internal commitment), to produce evidence that the events were created, and to produce generalizations about how others could make these events come about.

The structure of the experiment varied significantly from typical experiments. We could not design the experiment ahead of time and require the subjects to follow the design. We could not decide a priori and without the cooperation of the subjects which variables to focus on, which should be the independent and dependent, which should be varied, and how they should be varied. We could not refuse to stop, discuss, and alter the experimental conditions. In short, we could not manifest the degree of control suggested by the theories of action of experimental research (Campbell and Stanley, 1967).

This does not mean, however, that the question of the internal validity of the experiment should not be faced. This demonstration–experiment should be subject to questions about the potential for unrecognized distortion, especially since the research is intended to be applied. Internal validity is concerned with the question of whether, in fact, the experimental treatments make a difference in this specific experimental instance (Campbell and Stanley, 1963, p. 5). In order to answer the question accurately, eight different classes of extraneous variables have to be examined. They are history, maturation, testing, instrumentation, statistical regression, selection, experimental mortality, and selection-maturation and interaction. Although our demonstration–experiment is not a true experiment in the traditional sense, it is instructive in exploring each of these issues.

The experimental treatment in this study was not a one-shot affair that was administered uniformly to each participant. For example, the faculty designed experiences for the individuals to learn, but these lessons were learned at different times and with different intensity by the participants. The experimental treatment was repeated, in several different forms, sometimes by the faculty, and later, mostly by the subjects. This meant that, for some participants, the experimental treatment was redundant and/or more reinforcing than for others. Another characteristic was that the experimental treatment was never kept secret from the subjects. Indeed, one sign of the success of the experiment was that the participants could reproduce the experimental treatment whenever they needed to do so. But, did not knowing the experimental treatment bias the behavior? The answer is negative because, as we have seen, knowing Model II did not guarantee the ability to produce on-line Model II behavior. The participants had to experience many hours of painful learning and develop new theories-in-use in order for the experimental treatment to be effective.

Turning to the possibility of history confounding the results, we know that the data were collected at many different points, by using tape recordings and written cases. For example, data were collected over a period of fifteen months that indicated that all of the participants used Model I theories-in-use. Then data were presented that the presidents were beginning to learn Model II. Yet data were also presented that, after they had begun to learn Model II, they continued to use Model I theories-in-use.

The same data also suggest that maturation processes (growing older, more tired, etc.) probably did not have an appreciable effect. The executives did not begin to alter their behavior until the end of the third session, which was nearly fifteen months after the beginning of the experiment. Once they began to alter their behavior, they switched from

Model I to Model II and vice versa for the next two years. More importantly, in order to alter their behavior, we know that they had to go through the learning to learn cycle. The reader may recall that some chose to enter the learning to learn cycle earlier than others. If learning to learn was not necessary, F might have been able to solve his problem with the group and with X during the latter part of the third or the early part of the fourth seminar. Only after F showed that he was willing to learn from the confrontation (i.e., go into the learning to learn cycle), did he begin to alter his behavior. Also, G began to alter his behavior at a later date than others because he had resisted surfacing and experimenting with his theories-in-use. Finally, there was the gap between producing the appropriate behavior within the seminar and then reproducing it in the back-home setting.

These data also suggest that testing or instrumentation could not be confounding variables. The participants took many tests related to their theories-in-use during the first three seminars and were still unable to produce different theories-in-use. Even when they had a map of what they were being tested on, they could not produce behavior. As to changes in the calibration and/or observers, our experience was that the calibrations and observers changed (during the phases in which behavioral changes were said to occur), yet there was a high degree of agreement on the direction and speed of the change. For example, when A role played how he would deal with the vice-president, the group stayed with the problem for four hours one day and nearly two hours the next day until everyone was satisfied that A could produce a Model II intervention. Next, A tape recorded the behavior during the actual intervention. The tapes showed that he was able to reproduce the intervention, and, when he was not, he was able to own up to the fact. The tapes also showed that the vice-presidents who were not taking the course could identify changes and/or incongruities on the part of A.

In the cases of B and G, their vice presidents' comments on tapes or to L (during interviews), and to B and G during learning sessions, confirmed the original diagnosis of Model I behavior and helped to confirm or disconfirm the changes as they began to appear within the organization.

One cannot say much about statistical regression, the bias due to selecting individuals based on extreme scores, because of the small number of participants and because so little normative data are available to inform us about extreme scores. Future research will have to focus much more closely and systematically on individual differences in learning.

Selection bias also presented an interesting problem. The participants were self-selected after some experience with the seminar. They were not randomly selected. Thus the results may not be said to apply to all individuals. The most that can be said is that they apply to individuals who choose to learn. Given our Model II values, we are not interested in research that attempts to get people to learn who do not choose to enter the learning environment. We are therefore placing a limit on knowledge—a limit based on the assumption that social science technology should not violate individuals' free choice.

Free choice, however, does not necessarily mean high motivation to learn. The presidents exhibited a wide range of motivation when they entered. Moreover, the strength of their desire to remain in the learning environment varied with different conditions. When they were frustrated and angry, their motivation tended to be low. When they were succeeding, their motivation tended to be high. But, whatever the case, they had the choice of quitting (as two did after the second seminar).

There is also the issue of comparison groups. At this early stage of knowledge, it is doubtful that comparison groups are possible or required. How can one design comparison groups if it is true that most people's theories-in-use approximate Model I—hence they do not know that they do not know how to discover-invent-produce the behavior that they may espouse? Once large populations become competent in Model II theories-in-use and research is done to compare different learning designs in order to see which is more efficient, comparison groups would be relevant. To put this another way, all research on learning has used as subjects people who are presumed capable of producing the desired behavior. We are at the stage where many who come espouse Model II, but are not capable of behaving according to its requirements.

ON DEFINING UNITS OF BEHAVIOR

We have suggested that the units are so complex and so rare that identification of entities is more relevant to understanding and predicting than is measurement. We have stated also that theories-in-use cannot be altered without directly observable data. What the participants had to learn to invent and produce, as well as to identify "in" others, were complex entities composed of directly observable data.

For example, we may recall that it took A nearly six hours to discover-invent-produce a scenario that he intended to utilize to confront his vice-president, who was reputed to be considering leaving the organization.

The product of these many hours was a unit of Model II behavior that was composed of nearly two pages of directly observable data. (A's confrontation of the vice-president.) A also produced, through the confrontation of the others, several other possible scenarios, each depending on a particular response by the vice-president. Producing these other scenarios in an on-line manner "proved" to his fellow presidents and to himself that A could produce a Model II iterative learning cycle.

These are complex and molar units composed of directly observable data. A might have told the others that he was going to go back and "confront constructively" the vice-president. He could have defined his actions as including that he (A) would own up to his feelings, be open, take risks, and help the vice-president to do the same. All of these would have been viewed as units of espoused behavior. The units of Model II behavior had to be produced at the level of theory-in-use. It was that requirement that took the six hours.

Moreover, if A had sent a letter stating that he had dealt with the vice-president "constructively" and that he had owned up to his errors, was open, took risks, and helped the vice-president to do the same, we would have told him that such data was uninformative.

But most social science observational category schemes are constructed at this level of generality. Indeed, I have constructed such a scheme and have shown that it has power to explain and to predict (Argyris, 1965, 1970, 1974). The focus of this learning and research is to create social science knowledge that goes beyond explanation and prediction to bringing something about. The focus is on creating effective action.

I can recall vividly how I would present to a group of executives the analysis of their problem-solving processes based on quantitative patterns generated by the scheme of categories. In almost all the cases, they found the analysis convincing and compelling. However, they could not use it to design new behavior or even to understand how they produced the patterns in the report. Whenever we focused on bringing about learning and change, we always left the categories and went to the tape recordings. We had to examine relatively directly observable data; we required concepts that focused on patterns of behavior that were produceable by human beings.

There are two implications of this analysis for the definition of units. The first is that the units are too complex and spread out in time to be considered as units that can be described by typical measurement procedures. The focus of assessment should therefore be on recognizing and counting the entities as they are produced. As cognitive psychologists suggest, our "units" of measures are complex entities. *Entitation* becomes more important than quantification.

Second, the reasons that the Model II units take time to produce are (1) their creators may not be skilled, and (2) their production is not under the complete control of their creators. The effective production of a unit of Model II behavior depends on the feedback given by the relevant others in the setting. Consequently, the process of producing Model II behavior is usually iterative. It is not only necessary to produce the Model II behavior, but to show that the production was responsive to the feedback given by the individual with whom the actor was communicating.

Much research is needed to understand how to identify rigorously entities as they occur. The observation of entities will require individuals who can monitor the complex processes that produce the complex patterns. Contrary to the usual definition of units, these will not be defined so simply and microscopically that any observer can produce them reliably. The observation of these entities will require highly skilled observers and methodologies that help them to track the generation of these entities. The concept of rigor will have to be altered, as well as the concept of precision. The processes of entity identification will require the capability of observing reliably few, but highly complex, units. Rigorous definition of a unit will probably be related to the strict adherence to the operational rule that a unit must manifest all the necessary characteristics of Model II action (i.e., congruent with Model II governing variables or values, behavior, consequences on the environment, learning, and effectiveness).

The participants in the learning environment also face at least the same challenges. They too have to be able to create and monitor iterative processes that help them to produce Model II entities. Thus the task of the researcher-observer is included in the task of the actor. Hence, whatever technology is learned about entitation identification can be helpful to the actor. Also, whatever the actor learns to create and monitor, his actions can be useful to the researcher-observer. They will be subject to as much inquiry as the substantive issues being communicated.

There is a very practical implication of these consequences. They permit us to differentiate between genuine Model II behavior and "gimmicks." Gimmick behavior is any behavior that does not approximate all the criteria of Model II but that the actor considers adequate. For example, the reader may recall that F returned to his back-home setting vowing to be less unilaterally controlling. The data show that he did indeed reduce his participation (he withdrew). However, the data also show that, as soon as he was induced back into the conversation (partially by subordinates who were bewildered by the change in behavior), his governing variables had not changed, nor had his behavior that influenced learning (e.g., he still was win-lose oriented and suppressing feelings; he still defined his views in ways that were not publicly testable).

This implication, in turn, produces insights into the age-old issue of behavioral change. It should be clear by now that the focus on behavior is a key foundation of this perspective. Behavior is used to infer discoveries, to invent solutions, and to test productions. One of the signs of progress was when the participants spontaneously asked for or gave directly observable data to illustrate their inferred categories or concepts.

But behavior change is *not* enough. As pointed out above, behavioral change is a gimmick when it is not informed by a theory. But to produce a theory-in-use, we need, as we have seen, behavior from which to infer it. But to produce new behavior, we need theories to guide it. These circular processes require research, for, if they can be made explicit, we will know more clearly the conditions under which practice guided by theory leads to new behavior, and when new behavior, publicly tested and found effective, leads to reflection that builds a theory-in-use.

There is another reason why the end objective of education should be the production of theories-in-use, and not simply new behavior. It is not possible for any learning experience to teach all the behavior individuals will need in the future. Indeed, it would be highly inefficient to do so, because one would need to know in detail the events that a person is to experience and the reactions of the people in them to the specified behavior of the actor. Consequently, what needs to be taught is a theory-in-use to guide the individuals in their on-line actions as well as how to monitor the effectiveness of the theory-in-use. In addition, there is the need to teach how to produce new theories-in-use from experience. It is learning at this level that will reduce the probability of gimmickry, while increasing the probability of effective double-loop, on-line learning.

THEORIES OF ACTION AND OTHER COGNITIVE PERSPECTIVES

Some readers may wonder about the relationship of a theory-of-action perspective to other cognitive perspectives. In *Theory in Practice,* Donald Schon and I related our perspective to the work of several cognitive theorists. They included Angyal (1941), Bateson (1972), Polanyi (1958), and Simon (1969). Along with Simon, we proposed that, when people designed behavioral strategies and acted according to those designs, they produced behavioral artifacts. Whereas Simon considered behavioral artifacts to be separate from the environment, we asserted that the environment was not independent of the behavioral artifacts. From our point of view, the behavioral strategies (artifacts) in interaction with the governing variables produced the behavioral environment. Polanyi's concept of tacit knowledge was helpful to us in understanding how learning about complex actions may have to remain tacit and the probable role of rules or heuristics in transforming the learning into action. Bateson's ordering types of learning into levels similar to Russell's theory of types made it possible for him to differentiate levels of learning. For example, second-order learning was learning that examined the first-order learning processes. Second-order learning was deutero-learning. In our view, deutero-learning occurred when individuals reflected on their theories-in-use. However, we differentiated double-loop learning from deutero-learning. Double-loop learning was deutero-learning with the purpose of questioning and altering the governing variables and the behavioral strategies of one's theory-in-use.

We also acknowledge our agreement with Watzlawick, Beavin, and Jackson (1967) regarding the importance of understanding the meanings that arise in communication (a debt all of us owe to Reusch and Bateson, 1951), as well as the importance of trying to understand the heuristics or rules people use to govern their communications.

However, we began to have difficulty with some of the clinical interventions as described in a recent book (Watzlawick, Weakland, Fisch, 1974). They tended to be informed by Model I theories-in-use and, at times, impressed us as gimmicks. By gimmicks we mean that the change made was usually at the behavioral level without focusing on the governing variables, on the consequences of the behavioral world, and on the consequences for learning and problem-solving effectiveness. For example, the individual who is plagued with insomnia is advised to try to stay awake; the individual who trembles involuntarily is told to practice creating trembling. If we understand their logic correctly, it is to change the meaning of the situation, not through insight, but through trying to shift the insomnia and the trembling from the involuntary to the voluntary domain. The strategies are Model I because they require complete compliance, they are unilateral and, in some cases, they may require deception.

Because they are Model I theories-in-use does not make them wrong. It may be that, for the population they are dealing with, such strategies are necessary. The presidents' seminar was begun with a Model I theory-in-use. However, it was stated openly, and confrontation was invited. But such a strategy may work because the presidents are able to confront. How can a person who trembles or is unable to sleep rationally confront the effectiveness of a therapeutic strategy if the person is unaware of the causes of the problem in the first place? The best the person can do is to evaluate the strategy in terms of the outcomes. But this implies a dependence on the therapist's assertion that the strategy will help. This suggests the need for research on the ethics and rules of transition as well as of relating theories of action to the unconscious.

So much for an overview of some cognitive perspectives with which we share common intellectual roots and to which we have expressed indebtedness. Now let us turn to another group of cognitive-personality theorists with whom we share the same assumptions about the human personality and its potential. However, we differ in our views of how individuals attempt to actualize their potential, how they go about choosing alternative courses of action, and how they make organized sense out of the complicated activities of giving meaning to their lives.

Deci (1975) has recently written a thoughtful analytical review of the work of many of these scholars. In his book, he explores in detail the underlying assumptions of these cognitive approaches to understanding human motivation. Embedded in these assumptions is an implicit model of the nature of human personality and its potential. We should like to make this model explicit as a basis for comparing our perspective with those scholars included in the review. The assumptions about human motivation and behavior are:

1. A cognitive approach assumes that people decide what to do on the basis of their evaluations of the likely outcomes of their behavioral alternatives. Then they behave in accordance with their decisions (Deci, 1975, p. 15).

2. Most behavior is considered to be under the person's voluntary control (Deci, 1975, p. 15). There is a basic assumption that human beings are proactive; they are concerned about being "origins" of their behavior and not "pawns" (de Charms, 1968).

3. An underlying motive is the need for competence (Angyal, 1941; White, 1959). People with such a motivational base will seek situations that provide (1) optimal or realistic challenges and/or (2) opportunities to conquer challenging situations. In the case of the former, human beings seek out incongruity, uncertainty, and dissonance. In the case of the latter, they attempt to reduce incongruity, uncertainty, and dissonance (Deci, 1975, pp. 57 and 161).

4. People make choices about what to do by processing information they receive from the environment or from their memory. In making choices, people work with cognitive representations of the environment (Deci, 1975, p. 93). These cognitive representations are meanings constructed by human beings. The construction of meaning is a fundamental question in the psychology of motivation (Maddi, 1970, pp. 137–186; Wexler and Rice, 1974). Indeed, understanding people's personal constructs is a valid basis for understanding human behavior (Kelley, 1955).

We agree with all these assumptions. They describe a point of view about motivation, human choice for action, and constructing meaning that is congruent with the theory-of-action perspective.

Important differences arise, however, in regard to how individuals behave in order to choose, to be proactive, to be origins, and to experience a sense of competence. Let us focus on the motivational models of Atkinson (1964), Deci (1975), and Vroom (1964). All three models of human motivation use decision analysis as the theory of behavior, in both the explanatory and normative senses.

For example, Vroom's model suggests that the force toward some action (F_i) is determined by the valence of each of these outcomes (V_j) and the expectancy that the action will lead to each of the outcomes (E_{ij}). The force toward the ith action is a function of the algebraic sum of the valence of each outcome (V_j) multiplied by the expectancy that action i will lead to outcome j:

$$F_i = f\left[\sum_{j=1}^{n} E_{ij}\, XV_j\right]$$

Vroom's model argues that the motivation of an action may be understood by identifying all its consequences, assigning each a valence it has for the individual, and multiplying that valence times the probability of the consequence. The model is attributed to actors as an actual theory of their behavior. Apparently Vroom claims that actors usually go through such analysis (Deci, 1975, pp. 111–113).

To those working to develop theories-in-use, such modeling presents several questions. First, and perhaps least important, is the request for evidence that people go through such analysis. It appears to us that going through the decision analytic processes would take so much time that action would rarely be possible in the real world. Not so, may be the response. People, as a result of learning, can retrieve from their memory appropriate information that permits them to make these calculations with extreme rapidity. But, on the other hand, we know that the human mind is finite in its information-processing capacity (Miller, 1956) and is much slower than computers (Simon, 1969). If this information is retrieved and used with such millisecond speed, it must have been organized and packaged (in the form of a map) ready for use. But, if it is organized, it must have some pattern or form that informs human action. Such a map would be, in our terms, a micro-theory-in-use. But, so far, theories-in-use are not the concern of these scholars.

One reason that theories-in-use are not of concern to these scholars may be related to the purposes of the models they invent. Models may be created to focus on how to calculate the outcomes. Models may also be created to represent the processes that lead to the outcomes. The models of these three scholars focus on the processes of calculating the outcomes. The processes involved in these models are those which describe how people calculate outcomes, but not how they create or generate the meaning of the factors that are used to calculate the outcomes. The latter processes are those in which the theories-in-use are embedded.

In order to illustrate the point, let us take the concept of valence in the Vroom model.[2] "Valences" of outcomes, or "costs and benefits of actions" (to use the welfare economist's language), can be ascertained only within the context of value-laden *theories* built for the situation. Valences depend on theories. "Getting a job" has the "valence" that it has because of the meaning constructed for "getting a job" within a certain situation, which flows in turn from the normative/descriptive theory constructed for the situation. Atomic events in isolation are neither "positive" nor "negative."

There is no way to calculate costs and benefits except within the context of such a theory. But the assumption that events carry "valences" or "costs and benefits" on their face *appears* to exempt us from the need to formulate such a theory. What it actually does is to allow the theory to remain tacit. Hence, theory building and meaning creation, rather than mere calculation, are at issue in decisions to act.

How is it plausible to the decision analysts such as Vroom (and to the welfare economists who use similar models) that actions or consequences, considered as behavioral atoms, carry their "valences" or their "costs and benefits" as inherent properties?

The metaphors of physics and economics provide larger frameworks that appear to make this possible. In physics, "valence" is a property of each atom determined by the number of electrons in the outer ring. Valences can be quantitatively compared, and attractions and repulsions among atoms precisely described. Chemistry consists in the formulation of the rules governing combination of atoms, by precise quantitative ratio, on the basis of valence. Hence, within physics or chemistry, if you know that x is an atom, you can also know what its valence is.

Within economics, every decision is considered as an investment (an allocation of a resource) whose consequences have costs and benefits determined by the utility functions of the actor (or whatever body is taken as the subject of costs and benefits). The economist does not care much about the process by which costs and benefits are assigned to actions as long as they are generated in a way that is reliable and precise within the

[2] The material on pages 267–268 represents a joint formulation developed by Donald Schon and myself.

requirements of the calculation. It is possible to compare consequences and to calculate them because values are reduced to a common currency—cost and benefit in, for example, dollars.

But in actual decision situations, actions and consequences are valued contextually in terms of the meanings created for them within some theory projected onto the situation. "Consequence" does not have a "valence" independent of its meaning within such a theory-laden context, nor is its value within that context necessarily subject to arithmetic calculation. Nor does a "consequence" have "costs and benefits" independent of these things. The (in this case) combined metaphors of physics and economics may be the sources of this strange belief in the inherent values of atomic consequences.

The result is, in the case of Vroom, the ignoring of the processes by which meanings are created and valences developed. But these are the processes that are informed by theories-in-use. We argue therefore that these processes cannot be relegated to the status of black boxes. We have no objections to relegating the processes of calculating outcomes to black boxes. Indeed, the suggestions of some scholars have the effect of relegating these processes to the status of black boxes.

These scholars argue that people do not use the decision models with the degree of completeness required by such models (Simon, 1969). People, they suggest, decompose their problems; they attempt to solve the sub-problems; they use heuristics or rules for action that cut across much of the calculations required by decision analysis. But again, the questions arise: What knowledge is used to define a problem? What meanings are created that inform decomposition? How are heuristics or rules organized, stored, and retrieved? If these functions are accomplished by creating constructs interrelated into theories-in-use, then what are these theories?

IMPLICATIONS FOR DESIGNING LEARNING ENVIRONMENTS

There are several important implications of using decision analytic models for designing learning environments. If the models do not provide information about theories-in-use (or their equivalent), they are not likely to become the basis for people learning to change their behavior. For example, if the presidents learned how to calculate outcomes, it would still leave them with the task of understanding how they generate their own meanings and how they create a world that limits them importantly in the knowledge they will obtain of the meanings held by other actors. Without such information, they could not calculate accurately their own or others' valences or expected outcomes. Also, education that focuses on helping them to learn to calculate valences and outcomes would miss the fact that the presidents were unaware that they could not discover-invent-produce about problems that they considered important. Without this kind of information, the presidents would have little insight into their on-line learning processes.

Without the kind of information just described, it appears unlikely that learning environments can be designed to help the presidents learn how to unfreeze their theories-in-use or how to help them improve their capacities for on-line learning.

Vroom and Yetton (1973) would respond that learning environments can be developed by using their decision analytic model. In order to engage the argument, we must first describe something about the kind of world that a decision-theoretic approach tends to create.

The world the decision analysis approach implies may be obtained by conceiving of people as interacting in order to achieve a particular purpose. The model assumes that calculations of the decision-analytic sort are done privately by each actor—even when such analyses require references to the thoughts, feelings, and behavior of other actors. The model does not allow for joint inquiry into the meanings, consequences, and values of actions—and hence does not need to address the problem of creating conditions for effective joint inquiry.

The model, instead, treats actors as insulated calculators who can interact only in contests or games wherein each guesses at the calculations being performed by the other. How then is interaction dealt with? One way is to assume that actors are engaged in contests or games and bargaining in which the rules can be specified. If the notion of a game is accepted, it is possible for the individual calculators to guess what calculations the other is performing. From this follows the Schelling, game-theoretic approach to interpersonal interactions. Interactions are games or contests that can be resolved only by Model I win-lose behavior or by bargaining.

There may be other situations in which the insulated calculator role may be interpreted as a sign of mistrust or rejection. For example, let us consider the presidents in the learning environment designed to help them become more effective. President A turns to B and asks him to assist him in some role playing, or to visit his company and interview some of the officers. If B decides to try to make that decision by identifying the possible outcomes, by assigning them valences, etc., and if he were to do all these calculations privately, it is understandable that A may feel annoyed, frustrated, and possibly rejected. But could not B make that decision quickly, on the basis of his experience with A? Yes, he could, if A's request was not, in B's view, counterproductive. And this is a very important problem in many human relationships. A and B believe that they have an open relationship. One day A asks B to do something that B believes would harm A, but he does not know how to say so. This is especially true if A begins his request by saying "Because you are a very close friend, I wish to ask you . . ." Joint, open, on-line inquiry is needed in order to work through the problem.

But joint, open inquiry focusing first on discovering the meanings people hold and second on altering these meanings is not a part of the decision analytic model. It is at the core of Model II.

Now we may return to examining how the insulated calculator metaphor influences the learning environments designed specifically to help people become more effective. Vroom and Yetton (1973) have developed a learning environment in which executives focus on diagnosing their espoused theories (the instruments used do not help the executives diagnose their theories-in-use). After the executives diagnose how they say they behave under different conditions, they may then compare their choices to the choices made by a sample of successful executives that Vroom and Yetton have studied. In other words, the executive's attention is turned to the choices other successful executives have said they have made. The difficulty, from a theory-of-action perspective, with this strategy is that it provides the learner with no insight into the meanings that the successful executives created and used to make their decisions. Moreover, it limits the criteria for success to the limits of present practice. But if present practice, at the theory-in-use level, is primarily Model I, the probability of the executives being exposed to Model II alternatives is very low.[3]

There are therefore differences in the learning environments people are exposed to that depend on the model that underlies the education. According to Model II, the executive is taught to focus first on understanding his and others' meanings. Second, the definition of outcomes and their probabilities becomes a process of joint inquiry. Third, it is important to ask double-loop questions about existing criteria of effectiveness. Advocacy is combined with inquiry, and calculations of outcomes are done as much as possible in interaction with others.

RESEARCH NEEDED

The study has raised many questions that require further inquiry. Some of these questions are presented below.

[3] I believe that Vroom goes beyond the limits of the diagnostic instruments when he works with executives. It would be helpful if Vroom included his theory-in-use in the published material of his learning environments.

The Development of Espoused Theories and Theories-in-Use

How are espoused theories and theories-in-use developed and internalized? Under what conditions are espoused theories learned first, and theories-in-use developed and internalized? Under what conditions are espoused theories learned first, and theories-in-use learned second? Under what conditions does the opposite developmental sequence occur?

How do individuals develop blindnesses to the inconsistencies within their theories of action (espoused and theories-in-use), and incongruities between their espoused theories and their theories-in-use? How is the blindness maintained under conditions in which it is dysfunctional to effectiveness? Under Models I and II, how is the role of ignorance related to inconsistencies and incongruities?

How do the parts of the theories-in-use develop their apparent differential potency? For example, under what conditions does the potency of the governing variables vary? The same may be asked for the behavioral strategies, the environmental factors, and the learning factors. What is the relationship between any two sets of factors or among more than two sets of factors within the espoused theories and the theories-in-use? When one (or more than one) is varied, what happens to the other variables?

Is it possible that different espoused theories, theories-in-use, and different degrees of inconsistency and incongruity lead to different readinesses to learn, different defensive learning cycles, and therefore may require different learning environments?

Explication of the Discovery, Invention, Production, and Generalization Activities

How can the learning of each of these activities be enhanced? What knowledge do individuals need to monitor their learning for every phase of the cycle? Especially absent to date is research on the processes of generalization. What is effective generalization? Does its effectiveness vary with different conditions?

How does the context influence what is considered appropriate discovery-invention-production-generalization?

What are the mechanisms that lead to and maintain the phenomenon of unawareness?

To what extent do people recognize the wheels-within-wheels phenomenon of learning cycles? How do they integrate these multilevel learning cycles in order to learn and in order to act? Is this information used differently when the individuals are learning to learn and when they are learning to act?

Are different learning processes used when people analyze their behavior to develop cognitive maps such as their theories-in-use from the learning processes used when people are designing and carrying out their actions?

Learning as a Cognitive Process of Pattern Recognition or Entitation

One key process is the on-line capacity to create meanings by creating entities or patterns. How do individuals come to organize reality the way they do? Also, by what processes do people invent the next action steps they must take? How do they produce new theories-in-use? What are the dialectical processes between espoused theory and theory-in-use, between theory-in-use and feedback from the environment, and between theory-in-use and inferences about others' theories-in-use?

How do individuals monitor their processes of creating entities and patterns when such creations take long periods of time and/or when the creative processes are periodically suspended and begun whenever the conditions appear appropriate?

How Do People Deal With On-Line Complexity?

The learning cycle has four phases. The learning to learn cycle has twenty phases and steps. The professional encounter can include technical and interpersonal aspects, which means that the professional may be faced with a complexity of forty phases and steps. Clearly this information is much too complex to be admitted into the on-line arena of action.

How do individuals choose to simplify? By what processes do the individuals decompose the problems into manageable units? Are there more effective decomposition processes for different conditions and different problems?

The Processes of Moving From Model I Toward Model II as Experienced by the Individual Members

Research is needed that focuses on the nature of the processes that each individual participant experiences. The fragmentary evidence collected suggests that there is variance in these processes as experienced and as conceptualized by the individuals. Could the way they reflect and conceptualize their respective experiences influence what they learn and the pace of learning?

B, for example, notes that he went through several phases. During phase 1, he was "in love" with Model II. He was committed to changing his behavior and to leaving his subordinates alone so that they could have greater freedom. However, the withdrawal created a vacuum that the subordinates were not ready to fill. The results included many conceptual dialogues but little constructive action.

During phase 2, B was frustrated because Model II was not "working." His self-confidence as a manager went down, and he was more uncomfortable, disillusioned, depressed, and distressed.

Phase 3 began with the realization that his withdrawal was not an effective strategy (the opposite to Model I was not Model II). Second, he also realized that many of the executives were not the quality of managers ". . . that I deluded myself to think they were."

Phase 4 marked his reentry into active leadership. He was now advocating more, but instead of unilaterally controlling others, he was striving to encourage inquiry and confrontation about what he was advocating.

E also conceptualized his learning as going through several phases. However, his conceptualization was different from B's. For example, during phase 1, he became aware of how manipulative he was as a leader. His first "limited agenda for change" included (1) the unconflicted use of authoritarian behavior when appropriate, (2) the sharing and mutual development of the information base, (3) sharing the creation of tasks and objectives, (4) becoming more open with others, and (5) publicly testing everything.

The next phase was one of consolidation and reexamination of learnings. He learned to become somewhat less unconflicted, but experienced a great deal of difficulty in sharing with others during the information-gathering period. He became more candid about his position, yet, in making it more explicit, he tended to inhibit others from being more candid about theirs.

The Process of Moving From Model I Toward Model II, as Experienced by the Faculty

As mentioned at the outset, the faculty were competent to behave according to Model II under zero to moderate stress, and they had extensive experiences in dealing with the ambiguity, emotionality, frustration, and tension that were predictable before the experiment began. The skills required under these conditions have been described elsewhere (Argyris and Schon, 1974).

Research is needed to focus on the faculty's experience of the transition process that complements the research suggested above to describe the experiences of the individual members. Do faculty go through phases in their learning? How do they experience being educators as the activities become known and predictable? How can they continue their own double-loop learning if their world becomes increasingly prescribed and focused on others gaining learning that they have already gained? What are the relationships among faculty members during the entire history of the experience?

Error making is also an important issue. How do the faculty deal with their own errors and the errors of their colleagues? What is the impact of error on the learning processes of the participants?

How Do We Design More Effective Learning Environments?

Knowledge about the processes of decomposition, about the different impacts of different espoused theories and theories-in-use, and about entitation and pattern recognition will be extremely valuable in helping us to design more effective learning environments. However, knowledge is needed about the number and patterning of the learning sessions, the sequencing of the sessions (should the seminars begin with short appreciation seminars and be followed by a seminar of one week or several days?) and how much time should go between seminars —should the time lapse vary with the stage of learning and the rate of learning of the participants?

Research is also needed to identify the valid and viable processes that may be available to move from Model I toward Model II. Such learning processes may vary, for example, according to profession, to age, to the amount of time the students have available, and to the degree to which the students are wedded to Model I theories-in-use.

Another related issue is the identification of the costs and benefits of the different learning processes. For example, it may be that process A helps students learn the most, while process B is slightly less effective but significantly less costly.

In examining costs and benefits, the problem of transfer of learning must also be included. How can the learning be designed to maximize the probability for learning and change in the back-home setting:

The Relationship Between Learning and Skill Practice

One of the most important gaps that surfaced during these seminars was our lack of understanding of the role of skill practice. There were many times when it appeared that a set of skill practice exercises were needed. If Model II has a technology, it should be possible to develop practice experiences in order to learn the skills required.

The experience with this and other groups suggests that skill practice sessions should be informed by the governing variables. The faculty and students should be asking themselves constantly: the development of skills for what purpose?

What is the relationship between the development of confidence in the new skills and the development of new governing variables? Sometimes it appeared as if the individuals would not internalize the new governing variables until they felt confident they had mastered the skills related to the governing variables. For example, the individuals would not internalize free choice until they could behave the skills required to bring free choice about. However, it also appeared that they could learn the skills of free choice more quickly if they had internalized the values related to them.

New Technology for Data Gathering That Enhance Learning and Research

Research is needed to develop technology that may speed up the learning processes, as well as enhance their effectiveness. At the moment we have tape recordings, long scenario cases, and short scenario cases as the prime technology for gathering data from the students. Are there other ways to gather data? For example, would it be more effective if we observed the students in their back-home settings? What value would interviews with subordinates, peers, and superiors have?

Are there new kinds of cases that can be designed? For example, what would be the value of designing cases in which respondents give information about more macro-level problems of intervention? Could one develop role playing, panel groups, or other technologies to generate more data as well as to enhance learning?

Another way to explore the data-gathering process is to inquire about the selection of students and subjects. For example, would it be more effective to begin the education with the total back-home group, with a part of the back-home group, or with individual members from different back-home settings.

Turning to subjects, would it be more effective to integrate these learning environments with those that teach policy making, planning, managing, financial controls, etc.? If so, how should these subjects be integrated (serially, overlapping and simultaneously, parallel, etc.)?

What Is the Relationship Between Learning of the Kind Illustrated Here and Therapy?

Research is needed to illuminate the connection between different kinds of individual and group therapy, and the reeducation processes described in this book. Such research will help to make explicit the similarities and dissimilarities. This knowledge, in turn, can help specify how these different reeducative processes can help each other to become more effective.

The research should also help to specify the strengths and limits of each process. This is especially important for the learning environments implicit in this research, because it is not designed for the use of traditional forms of professional therapy.

Such research should explore early on the relationship so often cited in the literature between emotional learning and cognitive learning. Indeed, it may first wish to question this distinction. In the work so far, emotional experiences have greatly affected the discovery activities and, somewhat less so, the invention processes. However, the effectiveness of the production, generalization, and the invention processes may be largely determined by cognitive variables and maps. Research is needed to specify the role and the potency of emotional and intellectual activities in reeducation. For the readers who may be aware of the author's work in T groups, I should like to say that I am deeply impressed, as a result of my research, by the importance and usefulness of the cognitive factors. I am also impressed, as was pointed out in this book, with how potent an emotional experience it can be to ask people to become cognitively clear about their theories-in-use.

What are the more effective ways by which the learners can become carriers of the new theories-in-use in the back-home setting? How can "hosts" to the new concepts be identified and supported in the back-home setting?

How can learning environments be designed in the back-home setting that will maximize the control the back-home members have over the choice of, and learning about, their own theories-in-use and the requirements of moving toward Model II theories-in-use?

The Need for Model II Methodology

The design and execution of research is typically based on an espoused theory of action called the scientific method. Most research activity is informed by theories-in-use that approximate the scientific method with varying degrees of rigor. The theory-in-use embedded in the established concepts of rigorous research is congruent with Model I (Argyris, 1967, 1975). As pointed out (Argyris and Schon, 1974), the theories-in-use produce environments and knowledge that are congruent with their governing variables and behavioral strategies. Research designed by a Model I theory-in-use therefore will *not* tend to produce Model II knowledge.

An interesting illustration of this suggestion may be obtained by reading a group of books written by leading experimental psychologists. Their objectives in writing these books included showing that social science knowledge is applicable and that it could be used as a basis for a better life (Argyris, 1975). However, a careful examination of the generalizations that emanated from the research (all of which was based on Model I methodologies) showed that the world that would be produced was consonant with Model I. This conclusion was derived by examining research results that the scholars had considered "neutral" to Model I or Model II.

To be more specific, let us take the basic research on attitude change. These studies showed that, if a speaker was attempting to influence the attitudes of an audience that was "smart," it was important to present all sides of the issue. If the audience was not very smart, the results show that the speaker should present only one side of the issue. The conditions under which these data were obtained included keeping the experimental treatments secret (Argyris, 1975). Thus a more complete statement of the two generalizations above would mean that, in both cases, they should be prefixed with the statement that, "When the speaker keeps secret his knowledge that the audience is 'smart' or 'dumb', and when he keeps secret that he has a strategy based on the knowledge of whether they are 'smart' or 'dumb,' then, if he presents both sides to the 'smart' audience or one side to the 'dumb' audience he will tend to be effective (Argyris, 1975)."

The objective of this research is to produce generalizations that conform to Model II criteria and therefore help to generate a Model II world. Advising individuals to withhold the conditions above from the audience is to use a Model I theory-in-use and to create a manipulative world (which was the world created by the experimenters when they designed their experimental setting) (Argyris, 1975).

Another reason why research on theories of action will require different methodologies is related to the fact that the test of theories of action lies in their effectiveness. This means that the discovery of a particular bit of validated information, which is the objective of typical science, is not adequate. Information is required that informs the user not only if the knowledge is valid but if it is effective. It is perfectly possible (indeed, some have argued that it is typical) that knowledge produced by research can be highly valid but benign or uninformative of practice.

Construing the task of research to produce valid knowledge about effective actions alters significantly the research tactics and the criteria for acceptable theory. For example, dissonance theory has been one of the major theories in social psychology. To my knowledge, there has been little interest shown in what is effective or ineffective dissonance. Given such interest, the criteria for a successful experiment would also change from those presently used to conduct research in dissonance phenomena. For example, it is perfectly possible to conduct research on dissonance theory and show that the findings are significant at, let us say, the five percent or one percent level of confidence. Given that the problem studied was interesting and given sound methodology, the research would not be rejected because it did not reach, let us say, the 0.0001 level of confidence.

But what if we assumed that research results that did not produce such high levels of confidence had a low probability of enhancing human effectiveness? This assumption would not be severe, since life is full of complexity, and it would take powerful variables to overcome the existing complexity in the noncontrived world. It was these kinds of powerful variables that the presidents needed to overcome the resistances from individuals, groups, and policies and practices to begin to create a Model II world. Under these assumptions, the research whose results were satisfactory at the 0.05 or 0.01 levels of confidence would now be considered unsatisfactory *not* on criteria of truth but on criteria of effectiveness.

Granting effectiveness equal status with truth would require that the conditions under which the research was conducted would mirror, as much as possible, the conditions under which human beings learn and behave in real life. One result of this emphasis would be that the decomposition of problems would vary significantly from present practice. If one focuses only on the production of truth, it is possible to decompose complex problems into relatively autonomous subparts that may ignore their relationship with the larger problem from which they were derived. This is what happened with the research on group dynamics that was decomposed to study more rigorously the impact of various leadership styles on human behavior and performance. They lost their connection with the original problem. This disconnection did not matter because each research study accomplished its objective of adding to truth (even though they said little about effectiveness in the noncontrived world).

In research that attempts to inform us about effectiveness, the meaning of the parts depends on the "whole" problem from which the parts were derived. For example, let us consider research that was designed to learn more about increasing the effectiveness of the learning cycle (discovery—invention—production—generalization). Let us imagine further that the problem was decomposed into a series of studies about the first phase, namely, discovery. The relationships of discovery to invention, to production, to generalization were suspended (ignored) temporarily, in order to study discovery as rigorously as possible.

The data that one would obtain from subjects who knew that they were discovering without the intent to invent and to produce what they were discovering would be different from the knowledge obtained if the same subjects were asked to discover with the objective in mind to invent, produce, and generalize about the discoveries. We had many episodes in the learning environment in which people discovered but gave little thought to invention or production. The individuals soon realized that what they had discovered was not particularly relevant to invention and production.

Adults, in everyday life, may have to decompose complex problems, but they may not use the decomposition strategy appropriate for present-day conventions of rigorous research that would be to define the parts rigorously and autonomously from each other and the whole. Human beings may deal with complexity by decomposing a problem into relatively poorly defined parts and, at the same time, keeping one eye on the whole. Accuracy would then be produced by repeating the experiment or action until the information needed was obtained. Accuracy may also be produced through redundancy and overdeterminedness in behavior. These two factors, in turn, may be altered as experience dictates; again iterative processes are the key in on-line learning.

The plea being made is to take the decomposition processes of everyday life and design research based on these processes. One mechanism to accomplish this objective is to create experimental conditions that do not violate too harshly noncontrived reality. An excellent vehicle that meets these criteria is the creation of learning environments designed to help individuals become more effective (such as the ones described in this book). This will tend to assure that the reality from which individuals are asked to learn will be such that the learnings will be transferable to new environments and/or that it becomes an integral part of the learning to study and solve the problem of transferability into the noncontrived world.

The advantage of learning environments as the module for experimentation are (1) the motivation of the individuals to learn will be high, (2) the probability of iterative learning conditions will be high, and, (3) the probability of generating valid information and taking a very hard-nosed view of the results will be high.

These conditions, I believe, were illustrated in this project. The members of the learning seminar showed very high commitment to learning. They generated among themselves and brought in from their respective back-home settings many critical problems to be resolved. They invented and produced solutions in the learning environment and did the same in the back-home environment. Finally, the presidents took a very hard look at any claims of progress. For example, they confronted F with his claims of a Model II relationship with X that helped F see X's performance so differently that X was removed from his position. They confronted E, the individual they felt began the seminar closest to behaving according to Model II, with his relatively low degree of experimenting. They developed a level of aspiration that pictured moving toward Model II as a life-long process. They became increasingly persistent in collecting directly observable data about their performance and spending hours reviewing their own tapes.

BIBLIOGRAPHY

Angyal, A., *Foundations for a Science of Personality,* New York Commonwealth Fund, 1941.

Argyris, Chris, and Donald Schon, *Theory in Practice,* Jossey-Bass, 1974.

Argyris, Chris, "Some dangers in applying results from experimental social psychology," *Am. Psychol.,* Vol. 30, No. 4, 1975, pp. 469–485.

Argyris, Chris, "Some unintended consequences of rigorous research," *Psychol. Bull.,* Vol. 70, No. 3, 1968, pp. 185–197.

Argyris, Chris, "The CEO's behavior: Key to organizational development," *Harv. Bus. Rev.,* Vol. 51, No. 2, 1973, pp. 55–64.

Argyris, Chris, *Interpersonal Competence and Organizational Effectiveness,* The Dorsey Press, 1962.

Argyris, Chris, *Behind the Front Page,* Jossey-Bass, 1974.

Argyris, Chris, *Intervention Theory and Method,* Addison-Wesley, 1970.

Argyris, Chris, *Integrating the Individual and the Organization,* Wiley, 1964.

Atkinson, J. W., *An Introduction to Motivation,* van Nostrand, 1964.

Bateson, Gregory, *Steps to an Ecology of Mind,* Ballantine, 1972.

De Charms, R., *Personal Causation: The Internal Affective Determinants of Behavior,* Academic, 1968.

Deci, Edward L., *Intrinsic Motivation,* Plenum, 1975.

Kelly, George A., *The Psychology of Personal Constructs,* Norton, 1955.

Maddi, S. R., "The search for meaning," Nebraska Symposium on Motivation, Vol. 18, 1970, pp. 137–186.

Miller, G. A., "The magical number seven, plus or minus two: Some limits on our capacity for processing information," *Psychol. Rev.,* Vol. 63, 1956, pp. 81–97.

Polanyi, M., *Personal Knowledge,* University of Chicago Press, 1958.

Ruesch, Jurgen, and Gregory Bateson, *Communication: The Social Matrix of Psychiatry,* Norton, 1951.

Simon, Herbert A., *The Sciences of the Artificial,* Massachusetts Institute of Technology, 1969.

Vroom, Victor H., *Work and Motivation,* Wiley, 1964.

Vroom, Victor H., and Philip W. Yetton, *Leadership and Decision-Making,* University of Pittsburgh Press, 1973.

Watzlawick, Paul, Janet H. Beavin, and Don D. Jackson, *Pragmatics of Human Communication,* Norton, 1967.

Watzlawick, Paul, John Weakland, and Richard Fisch, *Change,* Norton, 1974.

Wexler, David A., and Laura N. Rice, *Innovations in Client-Centered Therapy,* Wiley, 1974.

INDEX

AA Stores, Inc., 186
Accuracy, 279
Action, 11, 143, 226
   approach, 182, 194
   theories of, 3, 4, 5, 6, 15, 73, 211, 244, 263, 270
Advocacy, 89, 103, 114, 134, 150, 270
Appreciation seminar, 33–37
Angyal, A., 263, 265
Argyris, C., 3, 4, 17, 20, 23, 25, 31, 35, 36, 72, 76, 150, 227, 234, 245, 257, 261, 274, 277
Artifacts, 263
Artificial, theories of the, 11
Assumptions, 5, 6
Atkinson, J., 266
Attributions, 52, 78, 159
Attributive categories, 214
Autonomy, 150

Back-home settings, 43, 97, 103–108, 115–136, 151–171, 220, 228, 234, 255, 276
Bateson, G., 263, 264
Beavin, J., 264
Behavior, 3, 5, 8, 9, 11–12, 18, 21, 41, 73, 125, 159, 183, 199, 260, 263, 265
   strategies, 17, 19, 22, 97, 108, 263
Benefits, 274
Blindness, 54, 73, 252, 271
Bolman, L., 27, 50, 151, 183, 234, 255
Brainwashing, 255

Calculator role, 269
Categories, 261
Change, 183, 185, 261, 263
   agent of, 186
   learning, 238
   programs, 247
Chief executive, 186

Choice, 22, 207, 208, 210
Cognitive approach, 263, 265, 272
Cognitive variables, 276
Commitment, 22, 37, 208, 213
Communication, 252
Comparison groups, 260
Competence, 265
Competitiveness, 91, 92, 93, 97, 109, 137, 159, 205, 229, 253
Complexity, 212, 239
Confrontation, 43, 153, 155
Congruence, 14
Consequence, 268
Consistency, 12–13
Constancy, 10–11, 13
Control, 52, 134, 220; theory of, 4–5, 15
Costs, 274
Credibility, 127

Data, 44, 112, 255, 258, 260–261, 275, 279
Deadlines, 201
De Charms, R., 265
Deci, E., 265, 266
Decisions, 238; analysis, 266, 269, 270; models, 268
Decomposition, 212, 213, 220, 268, 272, 274, 278, 279
Defenses, 174, 181, 182
Defensiveness, 22, 77–78, 184, 211, 225, 252
Demonstration experiments, 256
Dependence, 55, 57, 58, 198
Design, 203
Deutero-learning, 264
Developmental phases, 239
Dilemmas, 239, 255
Discovery, 25, 55, 96, 136, 151, 152, 212, 215, 216, 217, 218, 219, 220, 224, 226, 239, 254, 255, 269, 271, 279
Dissonance theory, 278
Double binds, 29, 77

283

Double-loop learning, 15, 20–23, 41, 73, 76, 96, 125, 184, 211–227, 228, 229, 234, 238, 254, 255, 264

Economics, 267
Education, 245, 265
Effectiveness, 212
Efficiency, 184
Effectiveness, 14, 18, 21, 22, 97
Entitation, 261, 262, 272, 274
Entity identification, 262
Error making, 274
Espoused theories, 4, 6, 14, 35, 73, 95, 184, 193, 201, 206, 215, 219, 245, 246, 271, 272, 274, 277
Essentiality, 22
Evidence, behavioral, 199
Existence, 8
Experimentation, 112
Experiments, 256–260
Explanation, 226
Explanatory theory, 4, 5

Faculty, role of, 27–32, 77, 79, 224, 273
Fears, 132, 135, 224
Feedback, 35, 52, 197, 203, 214, 223, 272
Feelings, 26, 34, 124–125, 131–132, 137, 143
First-order learning, 264
Fisch, R., 264

Games, 269
Generalization, 25, 136, 152, 212, 215, 216, 217, 218, 219, 220, 223, 225, 226, 254, 255, 271, 279
Gimmicks, 262, 264
Goal achievement, 183
Governing variables, 9–10, 12–13, 14, 17, 18, 20, 21, 95, 97, 185, 208, 254, 258, 275
Group dynamics, 24, 73, 216, 230, 234, 255
Guideposts, 26

Hanson, B., 187
Heuristics, 26, 268
History, 258

Incompatibility, 12
Incongruities, 219, 220
Inconsistencies, 219, 220, 255
Inference, 8

Information, 184, 208, 210, 213, 222
Inquiry, 89, 114, 136, 150, 213, 224, 270
Instrumentation, 258, 259
Instruments, 54, 221
Intelligence, 94
Interaction, 258
Interpersonal theories, 244, 272
Intervention, 115
Invention, 25, 76, 95, 96, 97, 115, 136, 143, 151, 152, 203, 212, 215, 216, 217, 218, 219, 220, 221, 223, 224, 225, 226, 239, 254, 255, 269, 271, 279
Interative learning, 213, 261, 262

Jackson, D., 264

Kelly, G., 265
Knowledge, 6, 256; tacit, 8, 264

Leadership, 103, 114, 125, 130, 159
Learning, 8, 15, 18, 19, 21, 22, 24–25, 42, 55, 95, 103, 136–150, 174, 211–227, 228, 229, 239, 251, 255, 259, 261, 264, 266, 272, 275, 276
    adult, 4
    changes, 238
    cycles, 218, 226
    effectiveness, 212
    environments, 30, 31, 207, 211, 268, 274, 276, 279, 280
    iterative, 213, 261, 262
    organizational, 183–210
    see also Double- and Single-loop learning
Lombardi, V., 112

Maddi, S., 265
Management, middle, 207
Maps, 54, 97, 125, 223, 226, 239, 266, 276
Maturation, 258
Meanings, 219, 221
Memoranda, 223
Memory, 216
Meno, 8
Microtheory, 7
Middle management, 207
Miller, G., 266
Mistrust, 78–79
Model I, 17–20, 23–32, 35, 37, 42, 52, 53, 56, 57, 58, 66–67, 73–74, 75–79, 87, 96, 97, 125, 131, 134, 135, 150, 153, 155, 157, 181, 184, 185, 186, 187, 191, 192, 194,

195, 196, 197, 199, 201, 205, 206, 209, 214, 215, 216, 218, 220, 221, 225, 227, 228, 234, 245, 246, 253, 254, 255, 256, 257, 258, 259, 260, 264, 269, 270, 271, 272, 273, 277
Model II, 20–32, 42, 53, 56, 57, 58, 66–67, 73–74, 75–79, 87, 88–91, 95, 96, 97–98, 102, 103, 108–109, 113–114, 115, 125, 126–135, 138, 147, 150, 151, 152, 155, 163, 164, 171, 172–173, 184, 185, 186, 187, 191, 192, 193, 197, 200, 201, 202, 203, 205, 206, 207, 208, 209, 210, 211, 215, 216, 217, 220, 221, 225, 227, 228, 229, 234, 236–238, 239, 246, 253, 254, 255, 256, 257, 258, 259, 260, 261, 262, 270, 271, 272, 273, 276, 277, 280
Models, 266, 268, 269
Mortality, 258
Motivation, 260, 266

Negative categories, 214
Negative feelings, 26, 34
Norms, 15, 16, 200, 211

On-line complexity, 272
On-line questioning, 30
Organizational learning, 183–210
Overdeterminedness, 279

Participation, 162
Passivity, 198
Pattern recognition, 274
Peters, G., 186
Physics, 267
Plato, 8
Polanyi, M., 9, 263, 264
Positive categories, 214
Positive feelings, 26
Power, 22, 42, 134, 135, 150, 185
Practice, 24, 26
Predictive theory, 4, 5
Presidents, 34, 86, 228
Problem solving, 19, 165, 212, 225–227, 236
Production, 25, 76, 95, 96, 97, 115, 136, 143, 151, 152, 212, 215, 216, 217, 218, 219, 220, 222, 224, 225, 226, 239, 254, 255, 269, 271, 279
Professionals, 244–245
Projection, 174, 176, 181

Quantification, 261

Recomposition, 212
Redundancy, 279
Regression, 258, 259
Reporting structure, 231
Research, 270, 274, 275, 276, 277, 278, 279
Rice, L., 265
Rigor, 262, 277
Risk-taking, 229
Role-playing, 30, 222
Ruesch, J., 264
Rules, 268

Satisfaction, 184
Schon, D., 3, 4, 17, 20, 23, 25, 31, 35, 72, 150, 234, 245, 263, 267, 274, 277
Scientific method, 277
Second-order learning, 264
Selection, 258, 259, 275
Self-perception, 183
Self-protection, 183
Self-sealing, 16–17, 29, 52, 125, 177, 214, 220
Seminars, 246
Simon, H., 263, 266, 268
Single-loop learning, 15, 19, 24, 36, 73, 220, 238
Skills, 26, 124, 275
Specificity, 212
Standards, 200
Statistical regression, 258, 259
Strategies, 17, 18, 19, 20, 21, 22, 97, 108, 194, 263

TA, 206
Tacit knowledge, 8, 264
Tape recording, 30, 43, 223, 261
Technical theories, 244, 272
Technology, 27, 30, 256, 257, 275
Testability, 15
Testing, 15, 203, 258, 259
T groups, 276
Theories of action, 3, 4, 5, 6, 15, 73
  articial, 11
  control, 4–5, 15
  espoused, 4, 6, 14, 35, 73, 95, 184, 193, 201, 206, 215, 219, 245, 246, 271, 272, 274, 277
  explanatory, 4, 5
  micro, 7
  predictive, 4
  theories-in-use, 4, 6–20, 23, 30, 35, 41–42,

73, 75, 89, 95, 97–101, 108–109, 112, 125, 126–127, 135, 136, 151, 152, 159, 160, 181, 186, 201, 206, 207, 210, 211, 214, 215, 219, 228, 229, 234, 236, 238, 244, 245, 246, 254, 257, 260, 263, 264, 266, 268, 270, 271, 272, 274, 276, 277
Theory in Practice, 263
Therapy, 276
Time perspective, 95
Transactional Analysis, 206
Transition, 190
   Model I-Model II, 23–32, 91

Uncertainty, 132
Unconscious factors, 172–182
Unilateral control, 220
Unit of behavior, 260–263

Valences, 267
Values, 15, 16, 183

Variables, 256
   cognitive, 276
   confounding, 259
   governing, 9–10, 12–13, 14, 17, 18, 20, 21, 95, 97, 185, 208, 254, 258, 275
Video tapes, 44
Vroom, V., 266, 267, 268, 269, 270

Watzlawick, P., 264
Weakland, J., 264
Weakness, 160
Wexler, D., 265
Win-lose dynamics, 18, 52, 157, 229, 253
Withdrawal, 113, 114

Yetton, P., 269, 270
Young Presidents Organization (YPO), 34